"When I was a girl, books were my tea[...]
They gave me hope, dreams, direction[...] [act]ually
power—power to become who I wanted t[...] [b]e. This guidebook, compiled by a knowledgeable, story-spirited woman,
will allow adults to help girls find the great books that
nourish the spirit. I recommend it for all those who want
girls to grow up strong, free, bold, and kind."

—MARY PIPHER, author of *Reviving Ophelia*

Great Books for Girls

More Than 600 Books to Inspire Today's Girls and Tomorrow's Women

---

Kathleen Odean

Ballantine Books
New York

Copyright © 1997 by Kathleen Odean

All rights reserved under International
and Pan-American Copyright Conventions. Published
in the United States by Ballantine Books, a division of Random
House, Inc., New York, and simultaneously in Canada
by Random House of Canada Limited, Toronto.

http://www.randomhouse.com

LIBRARY OF CONGRESS CATALOGING-IN-PUBLICATION DATA
Odean, Kathleen.
    Great books for girls: More than 600 books to inspire
today's girls and tomorrow's women/Kathleen Odean.
        p.   cm.
    Includes index.
    ISBN 0-345-40484-X
    1. Girls—Books and reading.   I. Title.
Z1037.025   1997
028.1'6242—dc21   96-44392

Text design by Holly Johnson

Cover design by Barbara Leff

Manufactured in the United States of America

First Edition: January 1997

10   9   8   7   6

Dedicated with love to Isabel, Rosalie, Graham, Andrew,
Naomi, Shayla, Tyler, Noah, and Dana,
and to my students past and present at Moses Brown School

Contents

CONTENTS

Acknowledgments

I want to give my warm thanks to the following people who helped make this book possible: my fellow children's librarians, for their suggestions and their dedication to children and books; my colleagues at Moses Brown School, for their excitement about books, which makes my job such a pleasure; the staff at the Barrington Public Library, for cheerfully helping me obtain so many books; my editor Andrea Schulz, for her help and encouragement; my agent Lisa Ross, for her valuable support throughout the project; my friends Martha Wellbaum and Elizabeth Overmyer, for sharing their ideas and their love of children's books; and, finally, my husband, Ross Cheit, for his enthusiasm and love.

Introduction

"There are no heroines following the shining paths of romantic adventure, as do the heroes of boys' books. . . . Of course girls have been reading so-called 'boys' books' ever since there were such. But consider what it means to do so. Instead of closing the covers with shining eyes and the happy thought, 'That might happen to me someday!' the girl, turning the final page, can only sigh regretfully, 'Oh, dear, that can never happen to me—because I'm not a boy!'"

Amelia Earhart wrote these words in the mid-1930s, after her own adventure flying solo over the shining path of the Atlantic. Looking at the books available, she was "struck with the fact that girls are evidently not expected to join in the fun."

Today over four thousand children's books are published each year, far more than in the 1930s, but girls still get left out of much of the fun. Only a small percentage of the books offer the kind of brave, strong females that Amelia Earhart longed to read about. Yet more than ever, girls need such heroines to offset the barrage of negative images society presents about females. In this guide, I have brought together six hundred books about girls who defy the stereotypes about females in our culture. In these books, girls are the ones slaying dragons— sometimes literally, more often figuratively. They face challenges and overcome them, just as parents hope their daughters will do.

If you are a parent, you want to be sure that your daughter has a fair start in life. You want her to be free to make choices, to be active, to pursue a range of interests, and to speak her mind. But these crucial goals are undermined by what psychologist Mary Pipher calls our "girl-poisoning culture." Movies, television, magazines, and popular music give short shrift to strong, active women and instead place enormous emphasis on women's looks and sexuality. Few females can reach the standards of beauty set by advertisements and the fashion industry, leaving teenage girls with a constant sense of failure. They are increasingly prone to depression and eating disorders, and are pressured to use drugs and alcohol.

Sexism starts young. Research shows that even pre-schoolers harbor negative views of females and positive views of males. In one troubling academic study, three- and five-year-olds viewed a videotape of two infants playing side by side. Half of the children were told that the infant on the left was female and the one on the right, male; the other half were told the opposite. The children proceeded to describe the infant they thought was female as "small, scared, slow, weak, quiet, dumb, and soft." They described the one identified as male as "big, mad, fast, strong, loud, smart, and hard." The *same* infant was rated in negative terms when the children believed it was a female, in positive terms when they believed it to be male.

Myra and David Sadker, authors of *Failing at Fairness: How America's Schools Cheat Girls*, found that even as they got older, boys continued to hold a low opinion of what it means to be a girl. Of eleven hundred Michigan children who wrote essays on what life would be like if they were a member of the opposite sex, 95 percent of the boys saw no advantages and many disadvantages, which they described in disparaging terms. Forty-two percent of the girls articulated the advantages of being male: "They would feel more secure and less worried about what other people thought, they would be treated with more respect, they looked forward to earning more money at better jobs."

Children are constantly having the idea reinforced that males are important, females unimportant and sometimes almost invisible. The award-winning "Sesame Street" features far more males than females, in more active roles. Look at the popular toy Legos, a fine tool for creative play: Almost all the human figures are male. Video games were created relatively recently, but their packages show thirteen times more males than females, and many of the females in the games are victims of violence.

Unfortunately, schools, rather than countering this message, often intensify the problems facing girls. Research has revealed that most schools sustain gender stereotypes, to the detriment of female students. Teachers give more attention to boys and give them more constructive criticism. According to the Sadkers, boys are twelve times more likely to talk in class than girls, and teachers reprimand girls who call out or interrupt more often than they scold boys who do the same thing.

When students are asked to name twenty famous American women, most come up with fewer than five—not surprising, since schoolchildren read six times more biographies of men than women.

One unintentional but insidious practice of many educators is to perform tasks for girls instead of expecting girls to do it themselves, a mistake parents also make. In contrast, expectations for boys' performances are higher. The Sadkers give an example from a kindergarten in which a male aide showed boys who wanted to play a VCR tape how to insert it, a task the boys quickly learned to do themselves. But when girls wanted to play a tape, the aide simply put it in for them—throughout the entire school year. Presumably the boys got the message that they are competent and able to try new technological tasks, while girls learned to be dependent.

With the onset of adolescence, boys dominate math and science classes and girls become less actively involved in classes altogether. Meanwhile, girls' test scores take a nosedive. Although elementary school girls outperform boys on national assessment tests, girls' scores begin to slip in middle school. By high school, senior boys outperform girls on almost every standardized achievement test.

What can you do to help your daughters thrive in this adverse environment? Many factors are out of your control: Schools change slowly even under pressure from concerned parents, and the media shows little sign of changing. But you *can* take one important step toward safeguarding girls' sense of self by reading your daughters (and sons) books about strong females, and helping them find similar books for their own reading and school research. This guide will lead you to such books.

I was inspired to seek out these books by my work as a school librarian. Every day I read to groups of children ages three to eleven, help them find books to check out, and advise teachers and parents about books for children. I make it a priority to promote books that feature strong girls, but even for someone knowledgeable about children's literature, it's a challenge to find a wide range. Far too many books present boys as leaders and girls as followers. Boys go exploring, girls stick close to home. Boys take things apart, girls watch. Men are praised for accomplishments, women for being supportive.

Picture-story books, the mainstay of the preschool and lower elementary crowd, most often have main characters—human or animal—who are male. Even when gender makes no difference to the plot, the "default setting" is male. Many of the best picture-story books, such as *Dr. DeSoto*, the Frog and Toad series, and *Harry the Dirty Dog*, deserve their popularity, but unfortunately they have only supporting females or none at all. The only female in the ever-popular *Winnie the Pooh* is Kanga, the overly protective mother. I like to read these books to children, but I also owe it to both sexes to find equally appealing books about adventurous females.

Older children want "chapter books," as they call them, meaning longer fiction and informational books. Fiction books are more likely to have female protagonists than picture-story books are, but even so, those girls are not always strong characters. Most often they are caught up in problems with relationships or are focusing on friendships, family problems, or everyday life in school. Girls are far less likely than boys to be setting off on a quest or pursuing a goal outside of relationships.

Nonfiction is even more problematic, since it includes history and biography, areas traditionally dominated by books about men. Most sports books are geared to boys; technology books feature many more males than females. The list goes on.

What About Boys?

Of course, boys as well as girls need to read about strong women. In order to treat girls as equals, boys must grow up believing females are as important as males—a message that is not getting through, as the documentation about teenage boys sexually harassing their female schoolmates clearly indicates. Boys are not going to learn to treat girls and women with respect by watching MTV or sitcoms. But parents can give their sons books in which young and old females play dynamic roles and are honored for them.

Currently businesses owned by women employ one out of every four American workers. As women gain power in the workforce, even more men will work for women, yet very few children's books show a man working for a woman. A handful of valuable books show boys who look up to the daring girls who are their friends or sisters. In a few novels, boys who initially scoff at the idea of girls' being courageous change their minds by the book's end. I have included as many books like these as I could find.

A widespread belief that boys do not want to read books in which the main character is a girl, whereas girls are willing to read about boys, needs to be reexamined. In my experience, if a book sounds appealing enough, a boy will be interested. For example, I know a middle school boy—a dedicated ice hockey player—whose favorite book is *The True Adventures of Charlotte Doyle* by Avi, a novel in which a girl on a ship gets involved in a mutiny. Almost all the third-grade boys at my school love the Ramona series by Beverly Cleary after reading the first one in class. I find with younger children that one reading of *The Adventures of Isabel* by Ogden Nash, with hilarious pictures by James Marshall, has the boys as well as the girls eager to check out the book. Present the right book in the right way and most children will want to read it.

Brave Girls, Strong Women:
The Criteria

"Let her swim, climb mountain peaks, pilot airplanes, battle against the elements, take risks, go out for adventure, and she will not feel before the world . . . timidity."

—SIMONE DE BEAUVOIR

In selecting these books, I looked for girls and women who faced the world without timidity, either from the first or after overcoming their fears. I found female characters who are creative, capable, articulate, and intelligent. They solve problems, face challenges, resolve conflicts, and go on journeys. These girls are not waiting to be rescued; they are doing the rescuing. Nor are they waiting for a male to provide a happy ending: They are fashioning their own stories.

I sought out characters who have attributes too seldom associated with girls, such as bravery, athleticism, and independence. These girls take risks and treat setbacks as ways to learn. They differ from other girls in fiction by liking machines, insects, snakes, rocks and dirt, and large dogs. Some of them enjoy fixing things, some are good with numbers, and a few even get into fistfights (as do so many boys in books).

In picture-story books, the adventures might seem mundane—a trip to the pond or a bicycle ride—and the acts of independence small—digging a hole under a wall or refusing to leave a mud puddle. The problems the girls solve may seem commonplace. But it is the very act of a girl having an adventure, asserting her independence, or puzzling out her own solution that sets her apart from more traditional fictional girls. For in books, as in real life, adults tend to do things for girls, while they challenge boys to do things on their own. These seemingly mild books compare favorably indeed to the many books about girls learning to please their parents and friends. Girls don't need any more lessons in being nice; they need lessons in making decisions for themselves.

I was pleased when I found stories about girls working well together and cooperating to reach a goal, solve a problem, or defeat an enemy. Too many books about girls deal with jealousy between friends, and too few show the sort of easy companionship found in books about boys.

I looked for fictional mothers who encouraged strong traits in their daughters and even modeled them. It is all too easy to find portraits of mothers who protect their daughters to the point of holding them back from exciting opportunities. Frequently, spirited girls must disobey their mothers to pursue activities that their brothers are free to try.

The stories with adults as the main characters, mostly found in the picture-story books and folktales, center around women who are happy living alone and traveling alone. Breaking grandmotherly stereotypes, these older women travel far and wide, ride motorcycles, pilot airplanes, and prove fearless in the face of adversity. Women in these books work at a variety of jobs, sometimes running their own businesses.

Since folktales often perpetuate the passive role of females, it was exciting to discover dozens that break the mold. These tales tend to end in marriage, but only after the heroine has accomplished difficult deeds to win the husband, rather than the other way around.

In both folktales and fiction, the female protagonists most often confront danger in order to help family or friends. While boys set out on their quests to seek fame and fortune for themselves, girls set out to save someone. For instance, in *The Diving Bell* by Todd Strasser, the girl Culca invents a diving device, confronts a powerful ruler, and risks death underwater, all to save her brother from dying. It would be refreshing to see more stories about girls seeking challenge for its own sake, but for the time being, any girl-centered adventure, regardless of motivation, is a change from the norm.

Inevitably some of the "villains" in the books are female, although I avoided those who embodied the worst traits most often associated with women. On the other hand, some female antagonists are complex, interesting characters who make worthy opponents.

Inevitably and unfortunately, many of the main female characters are pretty or beautiful. Authors apparently feel obliged to supply their female heroes, especially in novels, with good looks—sometimes unconventional beauty, but beauty nonetheless. It is unusual to find a protagonist with a weight or complexion problem. Even when an author has broken free of clichés and described an ordinary girl, the book jacket is likely to show a pretty one.

In most of the books in this guide, the main character is a female. Occasionally a book will have a male protagonist and feature an exceptionally strong female in an important role. In *Just for Kicks*, a novel by Paul Baczewski, the male narrator is a teenage boy named Brandon whose sister has joined a boys' high school football team as the kicker. She plays a top-notch game of football and invariably speaks her mind. Brandon falls for a girl who also turns out to be assertive and athletic. The combination of two intrepid female athletes puts this novel on the list.

Historical fiction and fantasy figure heavily in the fiction sections for several reasons. One of the best fictional devices to send girls on adventures is to have them disguise themselves as boys. Many of the historical novels turn on such a disguise, which gives the girls a taste of the freedom available only to males of the time. Frontier settings, where men and women work side by side, also provide more opportunities for girls to be daring or heroic than modern life does.

Fantasy writers can create new times and places, including cultures where females and males are more equal. In some fantasy stories women have magical abilities that give them power equal to that of men. Sometimes science fiction writers hypothesize about future societies where sex differences matter less than they do now.

Modern fictional girls have fewer chances in their everyday lives to test themselves than girls in historical fiction or fantasy do. Being stranded in the wilderness, of course, is a good plot device for pushing a character to her limits. Sports are another good arena for testing character. In several books with contemporary settings, the girls get involved with civil rights or other, sometimes dangerous, political causes. In a few cases, the protagonist pushes herself to excel in music. I chose certain books about modern girls because the main character has a strong, often funny voice and a nonconformist view of the world.

Very few of the books are about a girl with serious emotional or family problems, even though such problems may build character. Some readers would consider *The Great Gilly Hopkins* by Katherine Paterson to be about a strong girl. Yet Gilly's tough exterior is the result of the pain she feels about being a foster child whose mother deserted her. She is smart but ends up hurting herself with her clever ideas. This outstanding novel, which isn't included, seems to me to be more about sadness than strength.

The informational books in this guide show women in active roles. Fortunately, more biographies than ever are being published about important women. Books on history have begun to emphasize girls and women, and more and more sports nonfiction books feature female athletes and the history of women in sports.

Making the Choices

I read or reread every book on the list as well as a few hundred that I chose not to include. I read most of the picture-story books and folktales aloud to groups of children, and asked older children to read and react to the novels.

To find the books, I drew on my fifteen years of experience as a children's librarian and also elicited ideas from other librarians, teachers, friends, and children. I searched through reference books, publishers' catalogs, and lists from libraries, wrote to organizations concerned with girls, and browsed through bookstores and library collections. Still, I have undoubtedly missed some good books about resourceful females and would welcome suggestions for future editions, to be sent care of Ballantine Books.

In general, the books listed are well written, with illustrations of high quality. However, a limited number are strong enough in their theme and content that I included them despite their obvious flaws. For example, a few books that focus on women in the workplace are pedestrian in text and design, but admirably serve their purpose of showing many women at many jobs. Biographies tend to vary greatly in quality; I could not avoid including some mediocre biographies that were the only ones available about important women. The annotations indicate such a weakness in a book.

I have included only books that were in print either in hardcover or paperback as I was doing my research, which leaves a host of out-of-print books available in libraries but not for purchase. An appendix lists some of these out-of-print books.

Many excellent books do not appear in this guide simply

because they center around boys or around traditional girls. Some types of books presented hard decisions, such as books about girls who make difficult sacrifices for other people, giving up something important to themselves. Such acts take a great deal of moral courage, but I believe that girls have plenty of examples of women giving of themselves for others. Females are taught to please and help others, to put themselves and their desires aside. Far more difficult for girls is finding the moral courage to face conflict to pursue their own paths and dreams, a plot element I did look for.

I found that at first glance certain books seemed to fit the criteria, but proved disappointing upon a closer reading. For example, many people suggested that I include *Madeline* by Ludwig Bemelmans. However, although she is *described* as fearless, Madeline does not actually *do* anything in the first book about her. Worse, her fellow students spend an awful lot of time crying. In *Madeline's Rescue*, however, which I did include, a female dog displays courage and Madeline shows admirable persistence.

Some readers will be surprised not to find their favorite childhood novels about girls. For example, *Anne of Green Gables* by L. M. Montgomery, which is not included, is a novel about an energetic and intelligent girl who initially seems to defy some of the restrictions put on girls. Yet at the end of the book, she consciously sacrifices her education to help her beloved relative. Even before she makes this decision, Anne has become dreamier and less given to speaking her mind than when she was young. It's a heartwarming book, but the lesson it ultimately offers girls is a very traditional one.

Caddie Woodlawn by Carol Ryrie Brink has similar problems, yet its strengths outweigh its weaknesses. Caddie herself is far bolder than most girls in children's books and promises to become a strong-minded woman. True, her parents are out to make her less wild and she seems to acquiesce. But as soon as she takes up the womanly art of quilting, she gets her brothers involved, too. Near the end, Caddie's sedate mother chooses the American frontier over a genteel life in England, a vote for adventure that gives a strong signal to her daughter.

For some reason, certain types of books about girls rarely get published. I was disappointed in my attempts to find much sports fiction or nonfiction about girls' sports teams, even though more than two million girls play high school sports. I was struck that the copy I read of *In These Girls, Hope Is a Muscle* by Madeleine Blais, nonfiction about high school girls' basketball, was donated to a school library and autographed by all the members of the varsity girls' basketball team, a tribute to what it meant to them. Books like this one, which was in fact published for adults, are far too scarce.

Despite the popularity of mysteries, not enough mystery novels have strong girl detectives like Drew Stevenson's Sarah Capshaw, who actually solve the problem rather than have the solution fall into their laps. Another weak area is animal fantasies of novel length, most of which have male central characters. A fantasy with a host of female animals along the lines of *Wind in the Willows* does not seem to exist. Almost no books tell stories about mothers and daughters having adventures together, or stories about several girls going on quests or journeys together.

How to Use This Guide

The guide is divided into six main chapters: "Picture-Story Books"; "Folktales"; "Books for Beginning Readers"; "Books for Middle Readers"; "Books for Older Readers"; and "Resources for Parents." Each book entry contains the author, the title, the illustrator, the publishing information, an age range, and a description. The publishing information includes the original year of publication; the hardcover publisher, with "o.p." if the hardcover edition is no longer available; and the paperback publisher. (Since hardcover and paperback status change rapidly, check with a bookstore for updated information if you want to buy a book.) If the book has sequels or related books featuring strong females, I have listed those last.

If a book won a Newbery Award or Caldecott Medal, I have mentioned it in the annotation. These are annual awards given to the most distinguished children's books of the year by the American Library Association. The Newbery Award is for writing, and the Caldecott Medal is for illustration. Several other outstanding books of the year are named Newbery or Caldecott Honor Books. I have served on both committees, and know the great care put into the selections.

The books listed in "Picture-Story Books" typically consist of thirty-two pages with pictures on every page. Most but not all have a short text. At many libraries these are labeled "E," which technically stands for "easy." But often a sign is posted that reads "E Is for Everyone" because the appeal of these books spans such a wide age range. Many of them have surprisingly sophisticated vocabulary—don't be deceived by the pictures. Preschoolers and early readers will enjoy listening to picture-story books read aloud, and as they become stronger readers, they will enjoy these books on their own.

Some of the books in "Folktales" are collections with just a few illustrations, but most are single tales with pictures on every page. They also appeal to a wide age range and are good for reading aloud.

The "Books for Beginning Readers" chapter is for children who are learning to read and those who are ready for short chapter books, typically children aged six to eight, although the age of beginning readers varies a great deal. The books may also suit older children, particularly those reluctant readers who find long books intimidating. This section includes Easy Readers, Short Novels, and Biographies, most of which have many illustrations. Easy Readers are specifically aimed at children who are at an early stage of reading, sounding out words and relying on pictures to supply clues about the story. Short Novels are for children who have a wider sight vocabulary and greater fluency. The Biographies range from heavily illustrated thirty-two-page books to sixty pages with much more text.

The chapter on books for middle readers gives ideas for children aged roughly nine to eleven, while the chapter on books for older readers covers roughly ages twelve to fourteen. Again, there is a lot of variation in the age ranges within each chapter; I've specified an age range for each book. Entries in "Books for Older Readers" generally have more challenging writing in terms of style or content or both than the entries for middle readers. *Lyddie* by Katherine Paterson is a good example of a book for older readers. Most books in "Books for Middle Readers" have congenial main characters, but Lyddie is a young woman whose poverty and hardship harden her in some ways. The reader needs to make a leap of understanding to sympathize with Lyddie and her choices. The unusually dense, carefully crafted writing is challenging, while the theme of employer sexual harassment requires emotional maturity from the reader. Not all books in this section are this sophisticated. Some are simply longer, have more demanding vocabulary, or concern older characters. Some include romance, and a few deal in part with sexual issues. Within these two chapters, the lists are divided into fiction (subdivided into genres) and biographies.

Most parents will want to browse through the appropriate sections, read book descriptions, and decide what sounds good. Do not be limited by the age ranges, which are loose guidelines, and don't confine yourself to only one chapter. Early elementary children who are strong readers and reluctant older readers present real challenges for parents. Look at the sections before and after your child's age for ideas. The annotations can also guide you to books for independent readers older than your child that you might want to read aloud.

Older children may want to browse through the guide themselves, reading the annotations and choosing books that sound appealing. Voracious readers are always looking for new ideas, and less enthusiastic readers may have a strong sense of topics that interest them.

Keep in mind that older children still benefit from listening to books read aloud. Often parents will conclude that once a child can read to herself, reading aloud serves no purpose. Not true. Even most older children understand far more words when hearing them spoken than they can recognize on the page. Think of the conversations full of long words you have with a young child. Books tend to use vocabulary that is even more complex, so reading aloud introduces a multitude of new words in context. Later, when your child runs across such a word on the page in her own reading, she will have heard the word before and will have a sense of what it means. Even if reading aloud did not enhance vocabulary and knowledge of grammar, it would be worth continuing past the early grades because it is such pleasurable time spent with a child. In a busy world, reading aloud offers a quiet, cozy interlude and a way to wind down at the end of the day. It also offers the perfect chance to discuss values and opinions about issues raised in the books.

Many of the novels in this guide are so wonderful that you should consider reading them on your own. Just three examples of beautifully written books, one from each fiction section, are *Sarah, Plain and Tall* by Patricia MacLachlan, *Tuck Everlasting* by Natalie Babbitt, and *Toning the Sweep* by Angela Johnson. The annotations highlight outstanding books. It's easier to recommend a book to a child if you have read it yourself and can describe it enticingly. Equally important, the sight of parents reading is one of the strongest incentives for children to read.

If you find at some point in your daughter's life that she quits heeding your advice about books, you might buy or borrow some of these books and leave them lying around. Or enlist the help of a favorite teacher or librarian to promote books about strong females. I recently read about a book group consisting of mothers and adolescent daughters who were reading young adult books and discussing them—a terrific idea if you can swing it.

The last chapter in this guide suggests other book-related activities, listing possible tie-ins to specific books, such as craft projects or field trips. It also gives tips on reading aloud, as well as information about locating books through bookstores and libraries and keeping up with children's book publishing. I have included an annotated list of other books and resources of interest to parents concerned about their daughters, a list of children's books on sex and growing up, and some ideas for parents who want to encourage their daughters' strength and independence.

My Hopes

Psychologists use the metaphor of girls losing their voices as they grow up surrounded by sexism and stereotypes. All too soon, the research shows, girls start doubting what they have to say and hence quit saying it. We need to give them books about girls and women who have found their voices or kept them strong and clear all along.

"You tell a story because a statement would be inadequate," Flannery O'Connor once wrote. Conveying a message through a book can be more effective than giving direct advice. You can tell your child to be brave or strong, but she is more likely to know what that means through immersing herself in a novel about a courageous girl. You can tell her that she should set her professional goals high, but it's helpful to back up that advice with concrete examples of successful women and how they accomplished their goals. These books will help girls internalize the message that they can be the heroes in their own stories, overcoming obstacles—slaying dragons—and making their dreams come true *themselves*.

As I read through hundreds of books about strong girls and women, I regretted that I had had so few of them available to me growing up in the late fifties and the sixties, when most books I read showed boys as leaders and girls as accommodating followers. Yet even now, I love reading these books and find them exciting and inspiring. I also have a great time sharing them with the children in my life.

"Writing and reading decrease our sense of isolation,"

wrote Anne Lamott in *Bird by Bird.* "They deepen and widen and expand our sense of life: they feed the soul." I hope that these books expand the dreams of young girls, decrease the isolation of adolescents, and widen the sense of life for all who read them.

1

Picture-Story Books

Picture-story books really are for everyone, but they find their greatest audience among preschoolers and early elementary grade children. These thirty-two-page gems can be read in one sitting, making them perfect for reading at bedtime or for entertaining a group of children. Most of the books in the following list are geared toward children three to seven. (Note that the age ranges in this section indicate ages for listening, not independent reading.) But do not be strictly limited by the age-range suggestions. A two-year-old book lover would probably enjoy many of the books marked "3–6," while eight- and nine-year-olds may independently read books marked for four- to seven-year-olds.

The best thing about reading these books with children is sharing their enjoyment of the story and pictures. You'll laugh together and bask in the warmth of happy endings. You'll probably find that favorite books become part of your family conversations and folklore. Along with the fun come the educational benefits of reading picture-story books with your children. Children absorb new vocabulary, hearing it in context and storing it away for the day when, as readers, they see it in print. They begin to understand the structure of stories and hear the beauty of well-written prose. Beginning writers can use these books as models for tightly crafted short stories. For adults as well as children, the illustrations are a special treat. Poring over the superb artwork in many of these books is like having an art museum at home.

When choosing books, be sure to check other sections of the guide for more suggestions, even for young children. Most of the folktales in the next section are also thirty-two pages long and filled with pictures. The collections at the end of the Folklore section also include some stories suitable for reading aloud to children four and older. The Easy Readers in "Books for Beginning Readers" are short illustrated books that can be read in one sitting; they appeal to preschoolers as well as beginning readers. "Books for Beginning Readers" also offers possible read-alouds in the list of novels and in the biography section.

Picture-Story Books

Adams, Jeanie. *Going for Oysters*. 1994. Hard: Albert Whitman. Ages 4–7.

Set in Australia, this book tells of a native family's weekend fishing trip. The narrator's family and her cousin's family take two dinghies and motor to Love River. After the two girls catch bait with a net, they go with the narrator's father to chop mangrove roots covered with oysters. The girls and their male cousins frolic together in the water, then eat and dance all evening. The next morning the narrator gets up early and catches the largest salmon she has ever seen, which she decides to gut and bring to her grandparents. The light-filled illustrations, which resemble batik, have a rough quality that suits the story's emphasis on the outdoors.

Alderson, Sue Ann. *Ida and the Wool Smugglers*. Illustrated by Ann Blades. 1988. Hard: McElderry. Ages 2–5.

Young Ida's family lives on a farm on an island in Canada, where one of their yearly chores is to round up their sheep for shearing. Ida is too young for the sheep run, much as she longs to help. She *is* old enough to carry bread to a woman on a neighboring farm who has just had a baby, though her mother warns her to watch out for sheep smugglers. When Ida does hear smugglers, she proves herself very responsible by guiding three of her family's sheep to the neighbors, conducting her own little sheep run. "You're a clever, brave girl," says the neighbor, and so she is. A simple story illustrated with pretty watercolors, this will appeal to young children who, like Ida, long to be older.

Alexander, Sally Hobart. *Maggie's Whopper*. Illustrated by Deborah Kogan Ray. 1992. Hard: Macmillan. Ages 4–7.

Seven-year-old Maggie likes to visit her great-uncle at his cabin, where they fish and play dominoes together. She hopes to catch a whopper, a fish as big as those her eleven-year-old brother catches. Fishing off the dock one evening, she does, and a wonderful picture shows Maggie reeling in the large fish. But a bear suddenly appears, heading toward the minnows next to her sleeping uncle. Maggie overcomes her fear of the huge animal and tosses him the fish, thus saving Uncle Ezra from a possible attack. Attractive water-color and pencil pictures convey the beauty of the woods and lake, and the warm relationship between the girl and the old man.

Alexander, Sue. *Nadia the Willful*. Illustrated by Lloyd Bloom. 1983. Hard: Pantheon, o.p. Pbk: Knopf. Ages 4–7.

Soft black-and-white pencil pictures provide the desert setting for this story about a bedouin girl. The daughter of a sheik, Nadia is known for her temper and willfulness. Only her older brother Hamed can calm her down. When Hamed fails to return from a trip and is believed dead, Nadia vents her grief uncontrollably. Her father, equally grief-stricken, forbids anyone to mention Hamed's name again. This rule drives Nadia into greater rages until no one wants to be near her. But one day she defies her father and begins to talk about Hamed, which eases her pain. When her angry father confronts Nadia, he realizes that his daughter has something to teach him, and he changes her name from Nadia the Willful to Nadia the Wise. Beautifully illustrated, this is a powerful book about grief and a strong girl who refuses to be silenced.

Alexander, Sue. *World Famous Muriel and the Magic Mystery*. Illustrated by Marla Frazee. 1990. Hard: Crowell. Ages 3–7.

Muriel is a smart girl known for her problem-solving abilities and her skill on the tightrope. One day Professor Ballyhoo invites her to watch a magician perform, but in the middle of the act, the Great Hokus Pokus disappears. Muriel and the professor discover clues to his disappearance, one of which scares the professor but not Muriel. After giving it some thought, fueled by peanut butter cookies, Muriel solves the mystery. Comic illustrations capture the fun of the chase and the energetic personality of the young sleuth. Muriel first tackles a mystery in *World Famous Muriel*, now out of print.

Andrews, Jan. *Very Last First Time*. Illustrated by Ian Wallace. 1986. Hard: McElderry. Ages 4–7.

An Inuit girl named Eva has gone down to the bottom of the sea to gather mussels before, but this is the first time she has gone down alone. She crawls through the ice to a frozen cavern, lights her candle, and gathers a pan of mussels. But then she goes exploring and loses track of time, until she is almost caught by the tide. After some scary moments when her candle goes out, the girl manages to light a new candle and rescues herself. It feels so good to have survived the danger that Eva dances in the moonlight while she waits for her mother, and later enjoys the mussels she harvested herself. The adventure, with details added in the colorful illustrations, feels like a rite of passage for a girl on her own in a dangerous place for the first time.

Asch, Frank. *Just Like Daddy*. 1980. Hard: Simon & Schuster. Pbk: Aladdin. Ages 2–5.

A bear child, dressed like its father but not identified as a boy or a girl, imitates all the father's actions as the family prepares to go fishing. "Just like Daddy," goes the refrain. But in the twist at the end of this simple story, the little bear catches a large fish, "Just like Mommy," while Daddy catches a tiny one. Most children are caught by surprise the first time they hear the end, and see the picture of the mother and child with big fish and the father with a tiny one.

Bang, Molly. *Delphine*. 1988. Hard: Morrow. Ages 3–5.

Delphine is a very large child who lives high on a hillside with a wolf, a lion, and a guinea pig. She careens down a hill, crosses a narrow vine bridge, and braves rapids and lightning on her way to the post office to pick up a present. All the while she claims to be afraid of the present she suspects she is getting, but as children will notice, the pictures show she is fearless. They may also guess from the clues that the present is a bicycle, which Delphine masters after some falls. The brief text is accompanied by colorful, exuberant paintings in which Delphine is depicted as much larger than life.

Barton, Byron. *I Want to Be an Astronaut*. 1988. Hard: Crowell. Pbk: Harper Trophy. Ages 2–5.

Simple in text and pictures, this book portrays a female proclaiming that she wants to be an astronaut. She appears in many of the book's pictures, at a control panel, putting on a space suit, and sleeping in zero gravity. Her fellow crew members have short hair and are not distinguishably male or female. Not an outstanding book, but a nice inclusion of women that could lead to a discussion of Sally Ride and other female astronauts.

Barton, Byron. *Machines at Work*. 1987. Hard: Crowell. Ages 2–5.

Using bold colors and thick black lines, Barton depicts

construction machinery: bulldozers, cranes, forklifts, cement trucks, and more. In work clothes and hard hats, women and men—referred to as "you guys"—demolish a building, dig up a road, stop for a meal from their lunch boxes, then begin to build a new structure and road. The women, indicated by their longer hair, drive trucks and swing pickaxes along with the men. Children will be more interested in the machines than the people, but meanwhile they may absorb the message that women can work at construction, too.

Bate, Lucy. *How Georgina Drove the Car Very Carefully from Boston to New York.* **Illustrated by Tamar Taylor. 1989. Hard: Crown, o.p. Pbk: Crown. Ages 2–6.**

Droll pencil and watercolor illustrations accompany the story young Georgina tells about driving her family to New York. With her parents in the back, her younger sister Madeline in the passenger seat, and cats everywhere, Georgina concentrates on her driving. Madeline has the leisure to greet some cows and horses, but Georgina is too busy being careful. She does pull over at a restaurant, though, and buys the family a fantasy lunch, mostly of desserts. She buys everyone presents with the change. The road from Boston to New York is unusually bucolic; Georgina even has to stop once for a pig. When they reach their grandparents in New York, Madeline announces that she wants to drive next, and generously Georgina agrees. A playful fantasy about two girl drivers, certain to appeal to children who want to drive or run their own lives—a wide audience.

Bauer, Caroline Feller. *My Mom Travels a Lot.* **Illustrated by Nancy Winslow Parker. 1981. Hard: F. Warne, o.p. Pbk: Puffin. Ages 2–6.**

A daughter contrasts the good and bad aspects of her

mother's traveling, using simple sentences beginning "The good thing about it is . . ." and "The bad thing . . ." The best thing is that the mother always returns. A useful book with attractive pictures, this captures a child's perspective and ends on a reassuring note.

Bauer, Marion Dane. *When I Go Camping with Grandma.* **Illustrated by Allen Garns. 1995. Hard: BridgeWater. Pbk: Troll. Ages 3–6.**

Written in spare, lyrical prose, this is a welcome variation on the more common books about grandfathers teaching grandchildren about nature. Beautifully textured illustrations show a young girl and her grandmother camping together, roasting marshmallows over the fire the grandmother has made, and climbing into their sleeping bags. The grandmother paddles the canoe to take them fishing, but having caught a fish, they choose to throw it back in and have pancakes for breakfast instead. They admire the gorgeous evening sky together and start the day with a hug. Soon, the girl predicts, she will be the one to start the fire, paddle the canoe, and throw the fish back into the water. A quiet gem of a book that may inspire children to invite their grandmothers on a camping trip.

Bellows, Cathy. *The Grizzly Sisters.* **1991. Hard: Macmillan. Ages 3–6.**

The Grizzly sisters, two naughty cubs, know how to enjoy themselves. When their mother sends them out to play and warns them not to disturb the beavers, they can't resist disobeying her. They find their powers thrilling and jump for joy at how bad they are. The next day, they disobey again and scare the Wolf brothers. When they encounter tourists, the humans quickly recover from their fear and haul out their cameras, to the confusion of the Grizzly sisters. Luckily they are rescued by that "all-powerful grizzly," their mother. The disobedient sisters may have learned a lesson, but the final picture shows them venturing forth again, this time with no warnings from their mother. Cozy watercolors depict the antics of the overgrown cubs, who do not wear the bows and frills so often found on female bears in books. Great fun.

Bemelmans, Ludwig. *Madeline's Rescue*. 1953. Hard: Viking. Pbk: Puffin. Ages 3–7.

Madeline is certainly one of the best-known personalities in children's books. Many children know that "To the tiger in the zoo / Madeline just said, 'Pooh pooh!' " In the original book named after her, Madeline's main adventure is a case of appendicitis. In this sequel, she creates excitement when she walks along a bridge railing and plunges into the water below. When a female dog jumps in and rescues her, Madeline and her classmates take the dog back to their boarding school and name her Genevieve. The school board makes the dog leave, but she comes back and provides a puppy for each of the girls. Madeline's popularity has endured a long time along with her reputation as an unusually brave and feisty girl. The delightful pictures were honored with the Caldecott Medal.

Best, Cari. *Red Light, Green Light, Mama and Me*. Illustrated by Niki Daly. 1995. Hard: Orchard. Ages 3–7.

Jaunty watercolors show an African-American mother and daughter taking the subway and striding through a city one morning. Preschooler Lizzie is spending the day at work with her mother, a children's librarian in a big downtown library. Lizzie helps her mother by imitating the big bad wolf at storytime, then helps clean up the room after the children have left. Through Lizzie's eyes, her mother's job appears to be a bit more wonderful than most jobs actually are. But the visit does convey the message that Lizzie, like most other girls, can expect to have a career herself someday. Surprisingly few books show a daughter going to her mother's place of work. Although the job is a traditional one for women, it is also one children encounter and can appreciate. The appealing pictures, full of light and movement, show a close relationship between the smiling mother and her enthusiastic daughter.

Bingham, Mindy. *Minou*. Illustrated by Itoko Maeno. 1987. Hard: Advocacy Press. Ages 4–8.

Written to inspire girls to be self-reliant, this story concerns a pampered female cat named Minou who suddenly finds herself alone when her owner dies. After trying unsuccessfully to find a new owner, the crying Minou is befriended by a streetwise cat named Celeste. "Come with me, and I will show you how to rely on yourself," says her new friend, who teaches her to find food, bathe herself, and cross streets safely. Finally Celeste finds her a job chasing mice at Notre Dame, where Minou takes charge of her own life. The large, pleasant watercolors illustrate famous sights in Paris. More didactic than compelling, the plot feels forced, but the intention is admirable. Final notes offer discussion questions and tips on helping girls become more resourceful.

Blegvad, Lenore. *Anna Banana and Me*. Illustrated by Erik Blegvad. 1985. Hard: McElderry. Pbk: Aladdin. Ages 3–6.

A boy narrates the adventures he has when he follows the lead of his spirited friend Anna Banana. She leads him into dark places, tells him goblin stories, and inspires him with her example of boldness. Overcoming his fear at the end, he proclaims, "I'm just as brave as Anna Banana!" In the appealing illustrations, Anna appears as a messy-haired girl in blue jeans, who incidentally wears glasses. She leaps down stairs, dances, swings, and runs—full of life. One of the welcome but rare stories in which a boy emulates a girl.

Blos, Joan W. *Lottie's Circus*. **Illustrated by Irene Trivas. 1989. Hard: Morrow. Ages 2–5.**

Reading a book about circuses to her cat and stuffed animals, Lottie imagines a circus in which she plays all the roles. She builds, paints, pops popcorn, blows up balloons, performs magic tricks, rides an elephant, does a trapeze act, takes a lion through its paces, and much more. She is equally at home in roles typically played by men, such as ringmaster, as in those played by women. And next time, she declares, she will have an even bigger circus. Lottie has a big imagination and no doubt of her unlimited ability, an appealing combination.

Brett, Jan. *Annie and the Wild Animals*. **1985. Hard: Houghton. Pbk: Houghton. Ages 3–7.**

Young Annie seems to live by herself in a cozy little house near the woods, with only her cat Taffy for company. When Taffy disappears, Annie tries to get a new pet by putting corn cakes at the edge of the woods. She is not alarmed when a moose, wildcat, bear, stag, and wolf respond, but she's disappointed because none of them is soft and friendly. Luckily, Taffy does return, with three new offspring. Many readers will enjoy Brett's elaborate illustrations and borders, which have a Scandinavian feel to them and provide a lot to look at again and again.

Brett, Jan. *Trouble with Trolls*. **1992. Hard: Putnam. Ages 3–7.**

A hardy Scandinavian girl named Teva decides to visit her cousins on the other side of a mountain. She puts her skis on her back and starts to hike up to the top, but soon she and her dog, Tuffi, are accosted by trolls, who want to take Tuffi. Teva tricks the first troll into taking her mittens instead. She encounters several more trolls, including two females, and ends up giving away her hat, sweater, and boots. But she manages to get them back at the top of the mountain, claiming she needs them to fly with her skis. A double-page spread shows Teva holding her dog and swooping happily down the mountain on her skis, having escaped the angry trolls. The pictures alone develop a subplot in the trolls' underground home, where they are lovingly preparing a bed for a dog. Detailed pictures with a needlepoint border show the young heroine completely at home on the mountainside and on skis.

Brinckloe, Julie. *Playing Marbles.* **1988. Hard: Morrow. Ages 3–6.**

In sun-dappled colored-pencil drawings, a girl draws a circle in the dirt, an invitation to play marbles. Two skeptical boys agree to play one game with her when she won't go away. The three realistically scruffy children settle down in the dirt, pouring their marbles out of pouches from their belt loops and choosing three marbles each. By the end of an evenly matched game, she has won their respect and they agree to meet again the next day. A simple, effective story, marred by the repeated use of the phrase "little girl" to describe a child who appears to be just as old as the boys. Nevertheless, it is a pleasure to see a girl challenging boys and holding her own in a domain the boys think belongs to them.

Brown, Marc. *D.W. Flips!* **1987. Hard: Little, Brown. Pbk: Little, Brown. Ages 2–5.**

D.W., younger sister of the better-known Arthur, is a self-confident, impetuous aardvark, in contrast to her more cautious brother. In this first book about her, D.W. thinks she's too old for her "baby" gymnastics class, but finds the first lesson more of a challenge than she expected. Determined to do well, she practices her forward roll incessantly all week, disrupting her family no end. During the next class, she impresses everyone with her prowess, to her great pleasure. This brief book presents a model example of a young girl succeeding in a physical feat through practice—an excellent lesson that doesn't read at all like one.

Brown, Marc. *D.W. Rides Again!* 1993. Hard: Little, Brown. Pbk: Little, Brown. Ages 2–5.

D.W. is back, and in a hurry to master riding a bike. She's willing to practice a lot when necessary, and to her delight, her persistence pays off. There's nothing shy or shrinking about the irrepressible D.W., who keeps readers laughing with her sharp (but not too disrespectful) remarks. For example, when her overly worried father concentrates on D.W. instead of where he's going, he winds up in the creek. So D.W. offers him her training wheels, which he has just agreed she no longer needs.

Browne, Eileen. *No Problem.* Illustrated by David Parkins. 1993. Hard: Candlewick. Pbk: Candlewick. Ages 3–6.

All five animal characters in this amusing tale are female, an unusual feature. One day Mouse receives a huge package from Rat, with a note that tells her to put the enclosed parts together and then come visit. The package contains a huge assortment of mechanical bits and pieces. Forgetting to read the instructions, Mouse constructs an unwieldy contraption she dubs the Biker-Riker. It does move, but tends to pop wheelies at unexpected moments. Wonderfully frenzied pictures show her bouncing along to Badger's house. Badger, who thinks she can repair the wobbliness, "No problem," takes it apart and rearranges it. The two set off in the "Jaloppy-Doppy" to see Otter, who rebuilds it into a boat. Luckily the three meet Shrew, who completely dismantles the whole thing and then reads the directions. Efficient as can be, she builds an airplane that flies them smoothly to Rat's house. Clever illustrations portray four intriguing machines made from the same parts, three of them moving in wild disarray. Although three of the females are more confident than mechanically inclined, they do learn that reading the directions makes mechanical projects manageable! A wonderful portrait of five female friends sharing a project and enjoying each other's company.

Brusca, María Cristina. *My Mama's Little Ranch on the Pampas*. 1994. Hard: Holt. Ages 3–7.

This second memoir based on Brusca's childhood describes the small ranch that her mother bought in Argentina. María and her brother spend their vacations working and reveling in ranch life. They go with their mother to an auction to buy cows, help her brand them, and check the fences. María loves to gallop around on her horse, Pampero, and learns from her mother how to drive the sulky, a cart hitched to a mare. She usually appears in a T-shirt, pants, boots, and her new gaucho belt, a girl who enjoys the outdoor life. Her mother serves as a good role model in that she runs a ranch and supervises cowboys. Lively watercolors create a sense of place, while the unusual endpapers supply extra details about ranch life.

Brusca, María Cristina. *On the Pampas*. 1991. Hard: Holt. Pbk: Holt. Ages 4–8.

Told in first person, this short memoir recalls a girl's summer on her grandparents' ranch in Argentina. She spends most days with her younger cousin Susanita, who knows all about horses, cows, and the other ranch animals. Susanita, an accomplished rider, teaches the narrator how to groom horses and persuades her to swim in the creek with their horses, a scary exploit. The gaucho Salguero teaches the girls to use a lasso, and they persist despite setbacks. The girls run carefree on the pampas, as the plains are called, having adventures and enjoying their friendship. Just before the narrator has to return to the city, she brings in the horses by herself and herds them to the corral. There her grandmother is waiting to give her a gaucho belt decorated with silver coins, recognition of the girl's new ranching skills. The action-filled watercolors combine with the details of ranch life to convey a magical time in a girl's childhood. Outstanding.

Burningham, John. *Cannonball Simp*. 1966. Hard: Candlewick. Pbk: Candlewick. Ages 3–6.

Fat little Simp is a dog who manages to survive on her own when her owner abandons her. Trying to escape from a cat, she is grabbed by the dogcatcher. But advised by the other dogs that this means trouble, she escapes over a wall when they reach the pound, and makes her way eventually to a circus. There a clown befriends her, and she returns the favor by coming up with a way to save his failing career. With careful planning, she succeeds by taking the place of the cannonball in the cannon he shoots. She and the clown live happily ever after, thanks to Simp's ingenuity. Burningham's characteristically wonderful drawings convey Simp's adventures and capture the fine spirit in her stumpy little dog's body.

Bursik, Rose. *Amelia's Fantastic Flight*. 1992. Hard: Holt. Pbk: Holt. Ages 4–7.

Amelia, who loves to fly, builds herself a compact red

airplane and takes off to see the world. On each page she and her plane are in a different country, and one short alliterative line describes her time there. "She was charmed by China, and Japan was just a joy." Striking bright pictures show a landmark or person from the country and Amelia happily at the controls of her plane. In Mexico, it malfunctions, but the clearly competent girl makes a few repairs. She arrives at home in time for dinner and a bedtime book, which has a rocket on the cover. Each page has an inset map showing the country she is in and her flight line from the previous place. At the end is a map of the world with a line following her whole journey.

Burton, Virginia Lee. *Katy and the Big Snow*. 1943. Hard: Houghton. Pbk: Houghton. Ages 3–7.

Katy, a bright red tractor, was "very big and very strong and she could do a lot of things." The appealing illustrations show her in the summer working as a bulldozer and pulling a steamroller out of a pond. In winter, she is converted to a snowplow and proves her worth to the city during an enormous snowfall. She clears the way for all the workers: police, mail carriers, telephone repair trucks, firefighters, and doctors. Only when all have reached their destinations, thanks to Katy, does she stop to rest. The pictures have an old-fashioned feel, but they and the story hold up beautifully regardless of their age.

Caines, Jeannette. *Just Us Women*. Illustrated by Pat Cummings. 1982. Hard: Harper. Pbk: Harper Trophy. Ages 3–7.

The narrator and her aunt Martha set off on a road trip together, packing the food they like and planning to do whatever they feel like along the way. They walk in the rain in different states, shop at roadside markets, and thoroughly enjoy themselves together. A strong sense of independence pervades this short book, in which the illustrations show the characters as African-American. Great fun.

Caple, Kathy. *The Purse.* **1986. Hard: Houghton, o.p. Pbk: Houghton. Ages 3–7.**

In this humorous story, an enterprising girl buys a purse to replace the metal Band-Aid box she had kept her money in. Once she has thrown away the box, she realizes how much she misses the clanging of coins against the metal, so she sets about to earn enough money to buy another box of Band-Aids. She clearly has the makings of a future businesswoman: She pursues her goal diligently, carefully adds up her earnings, and openly enjoys the sound of money.

Carlson, Nancy. *Harriet and the Roller Coaster.* **1982. Hard: Carolrhoda. Pbk: Puffin. Ages 4–7.**

When Harriet's class plans a trip to the amusement park, her classmate George describes the scary roller coaster and suggests that Harriet will be too scared to ride it. She stoutly asserts she will try it, then worries all night and the next morning. But, predictably, Harriet finds the ride exciting, while it scares George and makes him sick. Harriet ends up riding the roller coaster all day; George spends the day sitting unhappily on a bench. The jacket cover shows a smiling Harriet in a roller-coaster car, so the end is no surprise. Unfortunately the only boy shown is a bully, but the message to girls is admirable, encouraging them to try activities that seem scary.

Carlson, Nancy. *I Like Me!* **1988. Hard: Viking. Pbk: Puffin. Ages 2–5.**

As the title suggests, this bouncy book is a blatant lesson

in self-esteem. A young female pig describes the things about herself that she likes as well as the activities she enjoys doing. She does a cartwheel, paints, rides her bicycle fast, and reads good books. She lists how she takes good care of herself: brushing her teeth, keeping clean, eating good food. Clad in heart-patterned underwear, she admires her round pig body. Finally she recites a few principles important for children to learn, such as getting up again when you fall down and trying again when you make mistakes. It is too bad that her failure followed by success revolves around baking a cake, a stereotypical female accomplishment. However, she does appear a few pages later paddling her own canoe, with a fishing pole beside her. The pictures are cheerful and colorful, and the simple text can provide a good springboard to discussion.

Carlson, Nancy. *Louanne Pig in Making the Team*. 1985. Hard: Carolrhoda. Pbk: Carolrhoda. Ages 3–7.

In this sweet story, Louanne decides to try out for the cheerleading squad, while her smaller friend Arnie wants to try out for the football team. When they practice together, Arnie coaches Louanne on the split jump and cartwheels, which he does much better than she. Louanne, however, excels at football, unlike Arnie. They try to keep up each other's spirits, and even after Louanne fails to make the squad, she swallows her tears to show Arnie a few football tricks. When the coach sees her, he asks her to try out for the football team and she makes it. Inspired, Louanne drags a tearful Arnie over to the cheerleading tryouts. The final pictures show Louanne leading the football team to victory with Arnie leading the cheers. The tidy, colorful pictures suit this story about characters who find the activity that suits them best, regardless of stereotypes.

Chandra, Deborah. *Miss Mabel's Table.* **Illustrated by Max Grover. 1994. Hard: Harcourt. Ages 2–6.**

A cumulative verse starts with Mabel gathering one frying pan, adding two teaspoons of salt, three glasses of milk, and going all the way up to ten dashes of yeast. Then Mabel, who has been pictured traveling through an awakening town on her way to work, whips up some hot pancakes to serve to customers at Miss Mabel's Table, her small restaurant. The upbeat, colorful pictures show a number of other women working on Mabel's route and near her restaurant: a ticket collector, a police officer, a woman pushing a lawn mower, one running a street sweeper, and another climbing a telephone pole. These women plus some men show up at Miss Mabel's Table to eat the sizzling pancakes. Fun to read and look at.

Christelow, Eileen. *Gertrude, the Bulldog Detective.* **1992. Hard: Clarion. Ages 3–7.**

With so many male detectives in children's books, it is good to run across a female dog detective. Because Gertrude loves mystery stories, she decides to go into business as a detective. But her neighbors Roger and Mabel find Gertrude's snooping intrusive. They try to distract her with a misleading note, but it actually leads her to a real mystery. The cheerful, cartoonish illustrations show Gertrude watching for burglars near the art museum, peeking through two holes she has cut in her newspaper. The detective indeed catches two art thieves through careful observation and turns them over to the police. An amusing, upbeat mystery story featuring both a female detective and a female police officer.

Cole, Babette. *Princess Smartypants.* **1987. Hard: Putnam. Pbk: Putnam/Sandcastle. Ages 3–7.**

The cover shows Princess Smartypants zooming along on a

motorcycle with an alligator seated behind her, a clue to her personality. She enjoys doing just what she wants, living in a castle with a collection of outlandish pets. Despite her parents' wishes, she has no interest in getting married: "She enjoyed being a Ms." Inevitably, though, princes appear and she must ward them off with difficult tasks, such as feeding her pets or riding her wild horse. No one succeeds until the arrival of Prince Swashbuckle. In a series of zany pictures, he meets all her demands, to her dismay, for she is sincere in her wish to stay single. So she must resort to a magic kiss, which sends the smug prince away as a gigantic warty toad. In the last picture, the princess lounges happily among her pets, knowing she has rid herself of suitors forever. A humorous counterbalance to the many stories that end with the princess getting married; instead, this one makes single life look very attractive.

Cole, Babette. *Supermoo*. **1993. Hard: Putnam. Ages 3–7.**

This zany picture book introduces an unlikely, clearly female superhero: Supermoo. Supermoo, who flies through the air in a cape and hat, teams up with another female, Calf Crypton, to avert ecological world disasters. Supermoo and Calf Crypton consult the cowputer to gather information. Comic pictures show them fighting off evil insects, picking up ocean tankers with their magnetic hooves, and putting out a fire in an oil well. Their adventures combine excitement and silliness, conveyed through a short, pun-filled text. Children are certain to get a kick out of these supercows and their cowmobile.

Cole, Brock. *No More Baths*. **1980. Hard: FSG, o.p. Pbk: FSG/Sunburst. Ages 3–7.**

Jessie McWhistle, who likes to play in dirt and read with her shoes propped up on the wall, runs away from home one day to avoid taking a bath. She visits her animal friends Mrs. Chicken,

Mrs. Cat, and Mrs. Pig one by one. When she complains about the bath, each friend offers her another way to get clean. Jessie joins Mrs. Chicken in frazzling in the sand but ends up itchy and dirtier than before. She tries to lick herself clean like Mrs. Cat with no success, then joins Mrs. Pig in the mud hole. Looking cranky the whole way, she marches back home to bathe. She ends up clean but still stubborn. When her mother suggests there are worse things than a bath, "aren't there?" Jessie's answer is "Nope." Deliciously messy pictures add to the fun.

Cole, Joanna. *The Magic School Bus in the Time of the Dinosaurs*. Illustrated by Bruce Degen. 1994. Hard: Scholastic. Pbk: Scholastic. Ages 3–8.

Ms. Frizzle, the most dynamic schoolteacher ever, drives a magic school bus on extraordinary field trips in a series of books. In this one, she takes her class back in time to study dinosaurs. As always, she is adventuresome, knowledgeable, and brave. Her students describe her as loving science, lizards, test tubes, slime, mold, and experiments. She has clearly inspired her female students to be as excited about science as she is herself—the girls are every bit as involved as the boys. Although the series is aimed at a slightly older crowd than three- to five-year-olds, the topic of dinosaurs will appeal to them, as will the bright and cluttered pictures. Don't forget to look closely at Ms. Frizzle's amazing clothes!

Other wonderful books include *The Magic School Bus at the Waterworks*, *The Magic School Bus Lost in the Solar System*, and more.

Cooney, Barbara. *Miss Rumphius*. 1982. Hard: Viking. Pbk: Puffin. Ages 3–8.

Miss Rumphius, who is great-aunt to the narrator, resolved

as a girl to travel to faraway places, to live by the sea, and—on her grandfather's advice—to do something to make the world more beautiful. She accomplishes all three, fulfilling her last goal by spreading lupine seed on her piece of the world. One of the most beautiful and inspiring of children's books, which every child should know.

Cousins, Lucy. *Maisy Goes to School*. 1992. Hard: Candlewick. Ages 2–4.

The flaps to lift and tabs to pull in this colorful little book will intrigue children. In it, young mouse Maisy, clad in bright shirt and overalls, spends a satisfying day at nursery school. She draws pictures in a little book and wears a great pirate costume during dress-up time. Adding and subtracting, practicing ballet in a tutu, and feeding the fish complete her day until it is time to go home. Since most simple stories about young children still focus on boys, Maisy is a happy addition to books for toddlers and preschoolers. Cousin's childlike paintings and printing add to the book's appeal. Other books about Maisy include *Maisy Goes Swimming* and *Maisy Goes to the Playground*.

Cowen-Fletcher, Jane. *Mama Zooms*. 1993. Hard: Scholastic. Pbk: Scholastic. Ages 2–5.

In this very brief story, an attractive, smiling mother zooms a young boy around on her "zooming machine." Told from the child's perspective, the story portrays the mother as adventurous and fun-loving. It is only near the end that the audience realizes the zooming machine is a wheelchair. The mother with her "very strong arms" gives her child love and excitement, all the while erasing stereotypes about the disabled.

Crowley, Michael. *Shack and Back.* **Illustrated by Abby Carter. 1993. Hard: Little, Brown. Ages 4–8.**

The Spurwink Gang of four girls and three boys breaks up the day "Crater" Creighton says, "Cooking is for sissy-girls." The girls, who had suggested making mini-pizzas, stalk off in disgust. The other two boys aren't too pleased with Crater, especially when the Broad Cove Bullies challenge them to a bike race. The best Spurwink racer is one of the girls, T-Ball, so the boys plead with her to rejoin them. Crater even grumbles that he's sorry, but the girls, who are busy swinging, won't commit themselves to the race. In the end, the gang is reunited, the fierce T-Ball has shown how unfounded Crater's remark was, and Crater has reluctantly recognized his mistake. These scruffy children in their jeans, T-shirts, and bike helmets seem believable, as does their argument.

de Paola, Tomie. *Strega Nona.* **1975. Hard: Simon & Schuster. Pbk: Simon & Schuster. Ages 4–8.**

This tale set in Italy tells of Strega Nona, which means "Grandma Witch," an old woman whom the town relies upon for cures for their ills and troubles. When she hires a young man, Big Anthony, to do domestic tasks for her, he overhears her speak to her magic pot to produce a meal. But when Strega Nona leaves one day and Big Anthony tries the magic words, he fills the whole town with pasta because he doesn't know the words that will stop the pot. Strega Nona returns and saves the day, then metes out due punishment: Big Anthony must eat up all the pasta. What a woman: wise, clever, and just. A Caldecott Honor Book.

Demarest, Chris L. *No Peas for Nellie.* **1988. Hard: Macmillan. Pbk: Aladdin. Ages 2–6.**

This book would once have been written only about a boy.

Nellie, who hates peas, describes all the things she'd rather be eating—and they all qualify in the vocabulary of the young as "Gross!" She would rather eat "a wet, slimy salamander" or "a hairy warthog." The list goes on and on. The cartoonish illustrations show a grinning girl wearing a pith helmet swinging at some scared aardvarks from a tree, pulling a python by its tail, and sliding down an elephant's trunk sharpening her dinner knife. She doesn't actually eat any of them, and at the end Nellie finds she has unknowingly eaten the detested peas. Her father then reminds her to drink her milk, and she replies that there are other things she'd rather drink! An outright silly romp that will make some children shriek with laughter.

Dorros, Arthur. *Abuela*. Illustrated by Elisa Kleven. 1991. Hard: Dutton. Ages 3–7.

A girl imagines that she and Abuela, her grandmother, fly together above New York City one day. In this splendid trip, they visit the Statue of Liberty, spot friends, and race sailboats. Abuela, with her billowing star-studded skirt, revels in the flying as much as her granddaughter does because she is a woman who "likes adventures." The warmth of the relationship, the bustling beauty of the city, and the joyful romp through the air are perfectly conveyed by extraordinarily vibrant pictures. The simple text includes Spanish words and phrases, defined in a glossary at the back. In the sequel, *Isla*, the two take another flying trip, this one over the Caribbean island where Abuela grew up.

Dunrea, Olivier. *Eppie M. Says*. 1990. Hard: Macmillan. Ages 3–7.

Narrator Ben's favorite person in the world is his big sister Eppie M., who knows everything. Most of what she tells him is wildly inaccurate (for example, that babies fall from the sky on rainy days). Eppie M.'s strong imagination is captured in the comical pictures in which she jumps, flies, dresses up, and invariably has a terrific time. It is unusual and welcome to have a book in which a boy greatly admires a girl and wants to be like her.

Ehlert, Lois. *Mole's Hill*. 1994. Hard: Harcourt. Ages 4–8.

Gloriously illustrated, this woodland tale pits Mole against Fox. Fox, tired of the mess Mole makes when she digs, tells her that he and his friends plan to build a road across her territory in the autumn. Mole defies the threat by digging out more dirt than ever and making a large hill, which she plants with beautiful flowers. When Fox and his friends see it, Fox realizes he cannot destroy it and so asks Mole to dig a tunnel through her hill. Bright flat collages in a large format showcase Ehlert's wonderful sense of color.

Enderle, Judith Ross, and Stephanie Gordon Tessler. *Nell Nuggett and the Cow Caper*. Illustrated by Paul Yalowitz. 1996. Hard: Simon & Schuster. Ages 3–7.

Droll colored-pencil illustrations introduce cowgirl Nell Nuggett, her horse Pay Dirt, and her little dog Dust. Riding with her herd one morning, Nell realizes her best cow Goldie is missing. The sheriff, who claims to be looking for the rustler Nasty Galoot, is no help. So Nell rides off onto the range and finally hears Goldie's "Moo." Nasty Galoot has her cow and, refusing to return her, lassos Nell's dog as well. But Nell, with the help of her piano and her cattle, defeats the rustler. Yelling with triumph and tossing her five-gallon hat in the air, Nell and her herd head home. The creative book design incorporates words and sounds into the pictures, giving this tale of cowgirl victory a distinctive look.

Father Gander or **Douglas W. Larche.** *Father Gander Nursery Rhymes: The Equal Rhymes Amendment.* **Illustrated by Carolyn. 1985. Hard: Advocacy Press. Ages 2–4.**

Father Gander, as the author calls himself, has undertaken to update Mother Goose rhymes. His aim is to promote equality for women, environmentalism, good nutrition, and general responsibility. Some of the verses preserve the rhythm and verve of the original folk rhymes better than others. "Jack and Jill Be Nimble" expands easily to have Jill jumping, too, and "Humpty Dumpty" is put back together again by women and men. Many of the rhymes give a traditional verse, then add another featuring the opposite sex. "Wee Willie Winkie" has a second verse about "Wee Wendy Winkie," and "Little Bo Peep" is followed by "Little Joe Peep." Others are changed more drastically: Georgie Porgie kisses the girls and "makes them sigh," then stays to play with the boys. The stiff color drawings compare poorly with some of the beautifully illustrated versions of Mother Goose. However, for those tired of Peter, Peter Pumpkin Eater beating his wife, this volume is worth browsing through for its more successful rewritten rhymes.

Faulkner, Matt. *The Moon Clock.* **1991. Hard: Scholastic. Ages 3–7.**

Highly original illustrations and typeface in different sizes give this book an unusual look. When Robin stays home from school to avoid a bully, a flamboyant Viennese soldier named Kolshinsky magically appears and asks her help in defending his city against invaders. They swirl through the air on his horse and land above the city on a huge clock. Robin sings to Kolshinsky's army to wake them up, then leads them into battle. After a vigorous fight with pillows, Robin confronts the enemy leader and makes him surrender. She returns home, sad to leave but braver and more confident. An odd, energetic book with many funny details.

Florian, Douglas. A *Chef*. 1992. Hard: Greenwillow. Ages 2–5.

This simple book follows a female chef through her day as she selects foods, checks deliveries, plans menus, supervises her staff, and of course, cooks. It is especially good to see men depicted working for a woman. At the end, male as well as female chefs are shown working in hospitals, hotels, the military, schools, and restaurants.

Florian, Douglas. A *Potter*. 1991. Hard: Greenwillow. Ages 2–5.

Clad in a work shirt, jeans, boots, and a denim apron, this capable potter kneads clay, throws it on a wheel, paints it, and fires it in a kiln. Simple, colorful pictures show pottery products: cups, mugs, bowls, bottles, planters, and plates. Very few words combined with the simple pictures make this a good choice for young children.

Friedman, Aileen. *The King's Commissioners*. Illustrated by Susan Guevara. 1994. Hard: Scholastic. Ages 3–7.

This humorous tale with its vivid illustrations concerns a king who is confused. He has appointed so many royal commissioners, such as the Commissioner for Things That Go Bump in the Night, that he can't keep track of them. With the help of his two advisers, he tries to count them as they file into the throne room. Interrupted by his jaunty red-haired daughter, the king loses track and then cannot understand his advisers' tallies. One has counted by twos, the other by fives. So his daughter has the commissioners line up in rows of ten, then explains how the same results can be reached by twos or fives. Her confused father finally understands, thanks to the princess. A long note for adults discusses how children learn mathematics, and how to use the book with them. A highly palatable way to reinforce counting skills, complete with funny pictures and a smart princess.

Gauch, Patricia Lee. *Christina Katerina & the Box*. Illustrated by Doris Burn. 1971. Hard: Coward, McCann, o.p. Pbk: Putnam/Sandcastle. Ages 3–8.

Christina, with her flyaway hair and disheveled clothes, enjoys action. When a new refrigerator arrives at her house, she commandeers the cardboard box and applies her imagination to it. First she makes a castle, with the help of her father, but her rambunctious friend Fats kicks it over. Christina converts the box, now on its side, to a clubhouse decorated with skull and crossbones. Then it becomes a racing car that she races wearing helmet and goggles—and always wins. When the box gets flattened on the ground, she turns it into a summer mansion and hosts a ball. Christina is full of energy and ideas, well worth reading about. Other books about her adventures include *Christina Katerina and the Great Bear Train* and *Christina Katerina and Fats Watson's Finest Hour*.

George, Jean Craighead. *To Climb a Waterfall*. Illustrated by Thomas Locker. 1995. Hard: Philomel. Ages 4–8.

The simple text, worded in the second person, gives directions on how "you" might find and climb a waterfall, directions followed by a girl in the pictures. The luminous oil paintings, reminiscent of the Hudson River School, show the barefoot girl walking, swimming, and climbing in a beautiful woods. She meets a painter and a writer, both male, who are trying to capture the beauty of the waterfall. Various animals appear in the paintings: a deer, a bear, an eagle, and more. The hike is a difficult one, and the girl works hard to reach the magnificent view captured in the final picture. Poetic text and exquisite paintings make this a beautiful book.

Gerrard, Roy. *Jocasta Carr, Movie Star*. 1992. Hard: FSG. Pbk: FSG/Sunburst. Ages 5–8.

This offbeat book presents a strong, independent young woman, Jocasta Carr, who is a movie star. When her talented dog Belle is kidnapped, Jocasta sets off in her bright red hydroplane to rescue her. She flies all over the world, surviving several disasters, and succeeds in saving her dog while punishing the kidnappers. The two of them then return to their lives of luxury as movie stars. Highly stylized pictures reminiscent of old movies will appeal to some children and adults. Some readers will find the verse stilted, but others will enjoy the whole quirky package.

Gibbons, Gail. *Marge's Diner*. 1989. Hard: Crowell. Ages 4–8.

Marge owns and runs a popular small-town diner with efficiency and good humor. From the start, she appears doing all kinds of work, from pouring coffee to paying bills and making decisions about menus and supplies. Marge has men and women working for her who obviously respect her. On her way home after a long day, during which her husband and daughter have come to the diner for dinner, Marge makes a night deposit at the bank. Here is a successful small businesswoman who deals with money and is appreciated by her family and employees—a neglected species in children's books.

Gomi, Taro. *Coco Can't Wait*. 1984. Hard: Morrow, o.p. Pbk: Puffin. Ages 2–5.

In this charming book from Japan, Coco and her grandmother decide to journey to visit each other on the same day. Unbeknownst to them, their paths cross when one takes a bus and the other a train, then one a taxi and the other a truck. Both determined, Coco hops on her scooter and Grandma on her motorbike; finally they meet halfway with great signs of joy. The story is told mainly through the clean-lined, expressive illustrations. Young children find the close encounters funny and the final meeting very satisfying.

Greene, Carol. *The Old Ladies Who Liked Cats*. Illustrated by Loretta Krupinski. 1991. Hard: Harper. Pbk: Harper Trophy. Ages 3–7.

To give a lesson on ecology, Charles Darwin made up a story about clover and cats, according to the author's note at the beginning of this tale. Scientists have added to the original story, and now this author has changed it further. The result is a beguiling tale about an island that prospers thanks to its ecological balance. Well-nourished sailors, who drink milk from cows who eat good red clover, protect the island. Long-tongued bees pollinate the clover, while their honeycombs are protected from field mice by cats. Each night the old ladies let their cats out to chase the mice. But when the mayor trips on a cat and rules that the cats must stay in at night, it weakens the sailors, and invaders take over the island. What to do? The old ladies, who understand the island ecology, have the answer and solve the problem. When the mayor awards medals to the sailors, the sailors give them to the "real heroes," the gray-haired women surrounded by their cats. The message never overwhelms the nicely illustrated story.

Greenfield, Eloise. *Africa Dream.* **Illustrated by Carole Byard. 1977. Hard: Crowell. Pbk: Harper Trophy. Ages 3–7.**

"I went all the way to Africa / In a dream one night," begins this poetic book about an African-American girl and her imaginary journey. Soft-edged, timeless black-and-white drawings create a magical atmosphere as she visits cities and villages, dances and sings. A particularly effective picture shows her meeting her grandfather, who forms a circle for her with his long arms. More poetry than story, but poetry about a brave girl on an adventure.

Grifalconi, Ann. *Darkness and the Butterfly.* **1987. Hard: Little, Brown. Ages 3–8.**

During the day, young Osa is not afraid of anything. She climbs huge trees and explores the African valley where she lives. Yet she is afraid of the darkness of night. One day in her wanderings, she comes to the home of the Wise Woman and climbs a ladder to help her hang strings of herbs from the roof poles. When the Wise Woman admires Osa's bravery, Osa confesses her one fear and then falls asleep. In a dream she chases a small butterfly who is not afraid of the dark, and then floats through the dark air like the butterfly. After she wakes up, Osa announces she is no longer afraid and she walks home bravely through the dark. Lushly colored pictures develop the setting in this story of newly found courage.

Grimes, Nikki. *Meet Danitra Brown.* **Illustrated by Floyd Cooper. 1994. Hard: Lothrop. Ages 6–10.**

This poetry collection about a "splendiferous" girl named Danitra Brown looks like a picture-story book, with one poem and a glorious picture on each double-page spread. An admiring friend of Danitra Brown's supplies the voice for each poem, and appears with Danitra in the pictures. The two jump rope and bicycle together, share problems and pleasures. They both prefer wearing jeans to wearing dresses, and Danitra likes to wear purple because it's the color that queens wear in Timbuktu. Maybe, says her friend, Danitra is a princess. Aiming high, Danitra plans to win the Nobel Prize someday for her writing. An outstanding combination of art and poetry about two splendid African-American girls.

Haas, Irene. *The Maggie B.* **1975. Hard: McElderry. Pbk: Aladdin. Ages 3–8.**

Maggie combines the best of traditionally female and male tasks when she wishes for a ship for a day to be "alone and free" but with "someone nice" along. She finds herself and her baby brother James on her own delightful ship with its little warm and snug cabin. As this nearly perfect day progresses, she cleans, cooks, plays with James, paints a portrait of him, fishes, and plays the fiddle. She also makes the ship secure against a storm, which they weather nicely in their warm cabin. Maggie is definitely the ship's captain, but some may find her idea of the ideal day too domestic, too centered around baby James and food. Others may see her as making her own choices, which happen to include the pleasures of babies and meals. In either case, it is a beautifully written text, accompanied by appealing pictures that a child may enjoy poring over.

Hayes, Sarah. *Mary Mary.* **Illustrated by Helen Craig. 1990. Hard: McElderry. Ages 3–7.**

Mary is so contrary that everyone calls her "Mary Mary" from the nursery rhyme. But she is also fearless enough to visit the local giant, who terrifies everyone in town. The other children, boys as well as girls, "followed her as far as they dared."

In her direct way, she manages to help the miserable giant straighten up his house and his life, and turns him into a giant playground for the children to enjoy. A wonderful final picture shows Mary with the giant, relaxing after a successful day, which, they agree, "she had managed." Not to be missed.

Hazen, Barbara Shook. *Mommy's Office.* **Illustrated by David Soman. 1992. Hard: Atheneum. Ages 3–6.**

When a girl visits her mother's office, she notices that her mother's job has some similarities to the girl's work at school. Her mother does paperwork, and the girl does, too, only hers is with crayons. Her mother takes a coffee break not unlike snack time at school and gives a presentation that reminds the girl of show-and-tell. The book demystifies the office workplace and conveys the message that women are at home there just as the girl is at home at school. A bit heavy-handed, this book nevertheless serves its purpose well.

Hendrick, Mary Jean. *If Anything Ever Goes Wrong at the Zoo.* **Illustrated by Jane Dyer. 1993. Hard: Harcourt. Pbk: Harcourt/Voyager. Ages 3–6.**

Leslie and her apparently single mother go to the zoo each Saturday. There Leslie tells all the zoo workers she sees that if "anything ever goes wrong at the zoo," they should send the animals to her house. Sure enough, one night the zoo floods, and the workers bring the animals to Leslie's house. The monkeys perch on the swing set, the alligator stretches out in a bathtub full of water. The elephant keeper Joanna drives up in a huge truck with three elephants, who go into the garage. When the zookeepers come the next day to retrieve the animals, women are shown handling the lion and the goats. The presence of so many women working with the animals is gratifying, as is the tolerant spirit of

Leslie's mother as she asks her daughter to check with her first the next time she asks friends home.

Henkes, Kevin. *Chester's Way*. 1988. Hard: Greenwillow. Pbk: Puffin. Ages 3–7.

One of the best books in this section, this story opens by introducing Chester and Wilson, two rigid but likeable mice who are best friends. Then the flamboyant Lilly moves into the neighborhood. She likes to wear Band-Aids all over herself to look brave; she always carries a loaded squirt gun. The two friends ignore Lilly until one day she saves them from some bullies, thanks to one of her many disguises. From then on the three are great friends and Lilly puts a new sparkle into their safe but dull routines. She is the daring and inventive one of the threesome, the leader in their adventures, and one of the liveliest picture-book characters ever, male or female.

Henkes, Kevin. *Julius, The Baby of the World*. 1990. Hard: Greenwillow. Pbk: Mulberry. Ages 4–8.

The mouse girl Lilly from *Chester's Way* is back and as incorrigible as ever. Witness the dust jacket: Lilly, wearing her Groucho Marx disguise along with red cowboy boots, is leaning over her brother's crib trying to scare the baby. Some adults will find Lilly too negative about poor Julius, "the germ of the world" as she calls him. But others will howl at her distinctive voice as she yells out to a pregnant woman, "You will live to regret that bump under your dress." In the end she charges to the defense of her brother when someone else insults him— and the last picture shows both of them in Groucho glasses. An outstanding combination of great story and illustrations. In a third delightful book, *Lilly's Purple Plastic Purse*, Lilly can hardly contain her excitement about school, her teacher Mr. Slinger, and her new plastic purple purse.

Henkes, Kevin. *Sheila Rae, the Brave*. 1987. Hard: Green-willow. Pbk: Puffin. Ages 3–7.

Sheila Rae is the idol of her younger sister Louise. When Sheila Rae eats fruit cocktail, she makes believe the cherries are the "eyes of dead bears" and eats five at a time. She giggles at the principal and steps on every crack in the sidewalk. But even Sheila Rae has her weaknesses; one of them emerges when she walks home from school a new way and gets lost. Her normal refrain of "I am brave, I am fearless" fails to raise her spirits. Luckily the more timid Louise has secretly followed her and knows exactly how to get home. Louise leads the way, stepping on every crack herself, and when they get home she has the joy of Sheila Rae's praise: "Louise, you are brave. You are fearless." As if such an outstanding plot weren't enough, charming pictures add detail and humor to the story.

Hoban, Russell. *A Birthday for Frances*. Illustrated by Lillian Hoban. 1968. Hard: Harper. Pbk: Harper Trophy. Ages 3–7.

The intrepid Frances resents all the fuss over her little sister Gloria's birthday, but then she herself makes a fuss because she hasn't bought Gloria a present. When she does buy her a Chompo candy bar, she finds it difficult not to eat it or at least squeeze it a lot. In the end, Frances rises above most of the temptation and gives Gloria the whole bar. Frances is very funny, making up little songs and spelling out words incorrectly but expecting her parents to recognize them. Fun for adults and children.

Hoffman, Mary. *Amazing Grace*. Illustrated by Caroline Binch. 1991. Hard: Dial. Ages 3–8.

The jacket introduces the reader to the exuberant Grace, grinning on the front and dancing on the back. She is a girl who loves playacting as Joan of Arc, Anansi the Spider, or Aladdin. Charming watercolors also show her as an explorer, a warrior, a pirate, and a doctor. But when her classmates tell her she cannot be Peter Pan in the school play because she is black and a girl, Grace needs all the encouragement her mother and grandmother can give her. She regains her self-confidence when her grandmother takes her to see a talented black ballerina. "I can be anything I want," the girl thinks, and goes on to be a stunning Peter Pan. An outstanding story.

Honeycutt, Natalie. *Whistle Home*. **Illustrated by Annie Cannon. 1993. Hard: Orchard. Ages 3–6.**

This young girl has a strong mother and aunt in her life. When her mother drives into town in her red truck, jauntily captured in the colorful acrylic paintings, her aunt Whistle and the girl go apple-picking with her dog Dooley. Aunt Whistle, famous for her whistle, which can rustle up ground-hogs and pigs and sheep and skunks, reassures her niece that she can whistle Dooley home when he's run off after a rabbit. She also lovingly assures the girl that she doesn't need to whistle up the girl's mother, because she is sure to come home on her own—and she does.

Hopkinson, Deborah. *Sweet Clara and the Freedom Quilt*. **Illustrated by James E. Ransome. 1993. Hard: Knopf. Pbk: Random House. Ages 5–8.**

Striking paintings in rich colors illustrate this story of a girl who escapes slavery through her own ingenuity and daring. Taken from her mother and sent to another planta-tion, Clara finds a friend in fellow slave Rachel, who treats her like a daughter. Rachel, worried that fieldwork will wear Clara out, teaches her to sew and gets her a job in the Big House as a seamstress. From her chair in the sewing room

Clara overhears bits of information about the layout of the plantation, the countryside around it, and the Underground Railroad. In a stroke of brilliance, she fashions a quilt that will serve as a map, and she adds landmarks and roads as she hears about them. Not only does it enable her to escape, rescue her family, and follow the North Star to Canada, but the map serves as an aid to others around the plantation. An inspirational story about a resourceful girl and the others who take risks to help her.

Hughes, Shirley. *Up and Up*. **1979. Hard: Lothrop. Ages 2–5.**

In this entrancing wordless book, a girl decides she wants to fly and, after trying various methods, receives a huge magic egg that gives her the power. She has a perfectly splendid time, pursued all the while by a growing crowd of people on the ground, starting with her astounded parents. She is a naughty child who makes faces through an upper-story window at children in a classroom and thumbs her nose at a man determined to catch her with his hot-air balloon. She finally descends, utterly pleased with herself—and who wouldn't be? A wonderful portrayal of a fantasy many children share.

James, Betsy. *Mary Ann*. **1994. Hard: Dutton. Ages 3–7.**

Amy, whose short hair and casual clothes give her a unisex look, is sad because her best friend Mary Ann is moving away. As a small consolation, she names a praying mantis Mary Ann and takes conscientious care of her. But inevitably the insect dies after laying her eggs. A sad Amy and her parents go off to visit the human Mary Ann and her parents, and the girls have a wonderful, active time together. And when Amy returns home, lo and behold, the eggs have hatched without the terrarium screen on to hold the praying mantises in, and the house is filled with young insects, "hundreds and hundreds of Mary Anns." Besides offering a particularly warm picture of a family, this delightful book shows a thoughtful and spirited girl who is enthusiastic about the natural world and insects. Her jump of joy when she sees the newly hatched insects is a pleasure to see.

Jeram, Anita. *Contrary Mary*. **1995. Hard: Candlewick. Ages 2–5.**

The theme of this simple book is that little girls can be contrary and still be loved. The young mouse Mary starts the day by putting her cap on backward and her shoes on the wrong feet. When her mother calls to ask if she is awake yet, Mary answers, "No." On the way to the store with her mother, Mary refuses to get under the umbrella, dancing instead in the rain. Later she rides her bike backward and takes a walk on her hands. All day, her mother looks bemused but remains affectionate, then joins in the fun at bedtime. A snappy combination of story and pictures for the youngest listeners.

Jeram, Anita. *Daisy Dare*. **1995. Hard: Candlewick. Ages 2–5.**

The young mouse Daisy, dressed in overalls and polka-dot shirt, does things that her three friends—two boys and Contrary Mary—don't dare to do. She climbs trees to get apples, walks along a high wall, and eats a worm. On a dare she takes a bell off the collar of a huge cat. After a scary moment, she escapes into the house with her friends, who sing her praises. Daisy, hoisted on their shoulders, beams with pride and doesn't mind admitting she is scared sometimes. The short text, small format, and jaunty little mice will appeal to young children.

Johnson, Angela. *The Girl Who Wore Snakes.* **Illustrated by James E. Ransome. 1993. Hard: Orchard. Ages 3–7.**

When a zookeeper visits Ali's class with a snake, Ali immediately volunteers to hold it. In fact she wears it all day long, to the consternation of some of her classmates. Radiant paintings show a smiling African-American girl who revels in her role as "the girl who wore the snake." Soon she buys her own snakes and wears them at home. Her parents, friends, and teacher tolerate her new pleasure but don't share it. Then one day she discovers that one of her aunts also understands the attraction of snakes. The story aptly contradicts stereotypes about girls being afraid of snakes, while the illustrations make the snakes Ali loves look beautiful.

Jonas, Ann. *The Trek.* **1985. Hard: Greenwillow. Pbk: Mulberry. Ages 4–7.**

A girl's vivid imagination turns her walk to school into a trek through the jungle. The clever illustrations subtly change the ordinary landscape into exotic flora and fauna: bushes look like gorillas and tree trunks like elephants. She meets her friend midway and they continue the trek hand in hand. While not all of the pictures are successful, children enjoy searching the pages for the animals identified at the back of the book. This daydream of exploring dangerous territory is an unusual one for girls in picture-story books, where boys tend to have the role of explorer.

Jukes, Mavis. *I'll See You in My Dreams.* **Illustrated by Stacey Schuett. 1993. Hard: Knopf. Ages 5–8.**

This moving story features a girl who would like to say good-bye to her dying uncle by skywriting the word "Good-bye" outside his hospital window. In her imagination, she sets off in a worn leather jacket and a silk scarf through the woods to an old biplane. In a businesslike way, she checks the controls, instruments, and gas, and taxis down the grass runway. Paintings capture the glory of flying in the gorgeous colors of dusk. After skywriting outside the hospital, she flies over the ocean and writes the words "I love you" and "I'll see you in my dreams." But the dream ends and the girl and her mother are sitting in a commercial airplane, thinking about their upcoming visit to the girl's uncle. Leaving the plane, the girl looks into the cockpit at the female first officer. At the hospital she finds the courage she needs to visit her dying uncle. An unusual, dreamlike book with a powerful message about different types of courage.

Keats, Ezra Jack. *Maggie and the Pirate*. 1979. Hard: Four Winds. Pbk: Scholastic. Ages 4–8.

Maggie, who lives on a river and paddles wherever she goes, treasures her cricket Niki and the house her father made for him. But then Niki is stolen by someone who leaves a note: "The pirate was here." Maggie leads her two faithful friends, a boy and a girl, through the darkening evening in search of the thief. When she finds him, she launches herself at the pirate— an unhappy boy—"trying with all her strength" to rescue Niki. Though the cricket dies, the book ends on a peaceful note. Terrific pictures show Maggie as a wild-haired, expressive hero who is fearless in her search for her pet.

Keller, Holly. *Geraldine's Blanket*. 1984. Hard: Greenwillow. Pbk: Mulberry. Ages 2–5.

Geraldine has no intention of giving up her blanket, no matter what her parents want. When her exasperated mother tells her that the frayed blanket looks silly, Geraldine replies, "Then don't look at me." But when she receives a new doll meant to replace the blanket, Geraldine supplies her own solution: she makes the blanket into a dress for the doll. This very simple story creates a strong female character, a plot that engages young children, and a clever resolution. A gem.

Geraldine shows her stubborn streak again in *Geraldine's Big Snow* and *Geraldine's Baby Brother*.

Kidd, Nina. *June Mountain Secret*. 1991. Hard: Harper. Ages 3–7.

On the cover of this book, a girl and her father are fishing, with the girl standing in a river clad in full fishing gear. At first they have no luck, and Jen is frustrated, but she forgets her anger in the fun of climbing a tree and sliding down a boulder. The second time they try, Jen lands a shimmering rainbow trout. After admiring the fish, she returns it alive to the water. Sun-dappled watercolors highlight the animal and plant life on land and in the water, some labeled with their names. A sparkling book that makes fly-fishing look exciting and accessible to girls.

Kimmel, Eric A. *Charlie Drives the Stage*. Illustrated by Glen Rounds. 1989. Hard: Holiday. Ages 5–8.

In an old Western town, Senator McCorkle is looking for a stagecoach driver to help him catch a nearby train. The only person willing to take the risks is small, smooth-cheeked young Charlie Drummond, whose one condition is that once they leave, they won't turn back. The senator agrees, but has his doubts when they barely miss an avalanche. A raging river and two different attacks keep things lively, but nothing stops Charlie's skillful driving. Due to no fault of Charlie's, they miss the train—and have to try to catch up with it. Scruffy, vibrant pictures capture the exciting ride and the eccentric Western characters. The final page reveals that, to the senator's amazement, the driver's first name isn't Charles—it's Charlene. A fast-paced story with a feminist twist.

Kimmel, Eric A. *Four Dollars and Fifty Cents*. Illustrated by Glen Rounds. 1990. Hard: Holiday. Pbk: Holiday. Ages 5–8.

Widow Macrae intends to get the four dollars and fifty cents that cowboy Shorty Long owes her. She cannot run her Silver Dollar Café if customers don't pay up, so she picks up her rolling pin, hitches up her horses, and heads out to the Circle K ranch. When his pals see her coming, they whip together a coffin for Shorty to climb into. Widow Macrae is suspicious, so she offers to take the coffin back to town for a burial. The ragged sketches smudged with color, perfectly suited to the story, show the widow and Shorty's coffin at the graveyard, where she announces that she intends to watch the body all night. The midnight arrival of robbers leads to an unpredictable ending. Rollicking pictures and homespun language tell an action-packed story about one determined businesswoman in the Old West.

Kiser, SuAnn. *The Hog Call to End All!* Illustrated by John Steven Gurney. 1994. Hard: Orchard. Ages 3–6.

Not many girls are likely to win a hog-calling contest, but young Minerva manages to do just that. She brings her hog Tillie to the county fair, hoping to win a blue ribbon for once. Before the hogs are judged, Minerva has time to enjoy the fair, laughing her way through the haunted house, trying all twenty-two kinds of five-alarm chili, and hitting the target at the dunking booth. She is a capable girl not easily fazed. At the hog-calling contest, a comic picture shows her opening her mouth incredibly wide and belting out, "Suuuuu-eee!" The call has wild results and wins Minerva a blue ribbon. Energetic illustrations add funny details to this tale of an unconventional girl and her female hog.

Kline, Suzy. *SHHHH!* Illustrated by Dora Leder. 1984. Hard: Albert Whitman. Ages 2–6.

A young girl finds that everyone in her life is constantly telling her to be quiet: "SH!" they say. She solves her frustration beautifully by tiptoeing to her backyard and making lots of wonderful noise with her voice and her activities. She yells and screams and whistles, while the pictures show her swinging and climbing trees and jumping in leaves and playing with her dog, all with great enjoyment—which readers will share.

Krause, Ute. *Nora and the Great Bear.* 1989. Hard: Dial, o.p. Pbk: Puffin. Ages 3–7.

Everyone in Nora's village is afraid of the great bear but longs to be the one to capture it. Little Nora decides to try and begins to train for it even though others make fun of her. Engaging watercolors show her hitting a punching bag and practicing with bow and arrow, a skill she perfects. Nora joins the hunt and learns all the necessary skills: building traps, tracking, running fast, listening carefully. One day she finds bear tracks in the snow, follows them, and encounters the huge bear. Though scared, she looks it in the eye and recognizes its beauty. The bear leads her back to camp, then disappears. She feels rewarded for all her preparation, even though the adults do not seem to believe her story. The last picture shows Nora, her head sticking out of her tent, seeing the bear again in the moonlight. Children will especially enjoy seeing the smallest of the villagers accomplish what no one else has.

Kunstadter, Maria A. *Women Working A to Z*. 1994. Hard: Highsmith. Ages 4–8.

In this unique alphabet book, each letter stands for a job held by a real woman. For example, A is an airplane pilot named Betty Jean, shown in photographs as a girl and an adult. One page is devoted to each letter, with a paragraph about the woman's childhood and a sentence about her current work. The jobs range from traditional to unusual: mother, grandmother, nurse, engineer, judge, race-car driver, surgeon, and more. The women vary in age and ethnic group. A useful book, nicely put together.

Lasker, Joe. *Mothers Can Do Anything*. 1972. Hard: Albert Whitman. Ages 4–8.

For a book written more than twenty years ago, the text of this holds up very well and the illustrations barely look dated. The title-page picture sets the scene, showing Whistler's mother sitting across from a white-haired woman in what seems to be a race-car driver's outfit. The book describes many mothers and a few grandmothers doing a variety of jobs: police officer, principal, painter, judge, dentist. The double-page spreads alternate between black-and-white and color. The final line "Mothers can do anything!" shows a woman astronaut floating in space, while the cover shows an animal trainer patting a lion and bear. The jobs include a few too many on the exotic side, but the book can lead to a discussion of other work closer to home.

Lasky, Kathryn. *Pond Year*. Illustrated by Mike Bostock. 1995. Hard: Candlewick. Ages 3–6.

Two six-year-old girls who call themselves "pond buddies and scum chums forever" love to spend time at the shallow pond near their houses. Not the least bit squeamish, they like to catch bugs, make mud cookies, and braid friendship rings from dried scum. Appealing watercolors show them wading during the summer, looking for muskrats at night in the fall, and skating in the winter. They collect frogs' eggs and crawdads, examine dead bugs under a magnifying glass, and let salamanders crawl up their arms and legs just for fun. Lovely illustrations, poetic text, and two terrific girls make this an all-around winner.

Lattimore, Deborah Nourse. *Frida Maria: A Story of the Old Southwest*. 1994. Hard: Harcourt. Ages 4–7.

Frida Maria longs to ride the horse Diablo in the upcoming fiesta, to her mama's horror. Her mother wants Frida to be ladylike, and the girl tries, but she finds it hard to get interested in sewing and baking. When the fiesta finally arrives, Frida Maria seizes the chance to ride Diablo, racing to win a bet and save her family a lot of money. In the end even her mother recognizes that Frida has important talents, ladylike or not. Vigorous, colorful paintings, filled with the architecture of the Southwest, match Frida Maria's strong character.

Lee, Jeanne M. *The Song of Mu Lan*. 1995. Hard: Front Street. Ages 4–8.

This brief Chinese poem tells of Mu Lan, who rides off to war in her father's place. She disguises herself as a man and proves her valor during twelve years in the emperor's army. When offered a reward for her deeds, she asks only to return home. Her comrades ride with her and, once at her home, are shocked to learn she is a woman. The poem's final verse points out that when two rabbits run together, "No one can tell which is male, which is female." Lovely delicate watercolors add important details and setting to the verses, which also appear in Chinese calligraphy on each page. A final note explains that this folk poem probably dates to the fifth century, and is still learned by schoolchildren and sung in operas in China.

Lionni, Leo. *An Extraordinary Egg*. 1994. Hard: Knopf. Ages 3–6.

Lionni himself is extraordinary in his ability to keep producing wonderful books decade after decade. In this new gem, a frog named Jessica, who is "full of wonder," discovers an egg while she is out exploring. When she rolls it home to her friends, they say it is a chicken egg, and even when a small alligator hatches, they think it's a chicken. The alligator, also a female, becomes close friends with Jessica. One day a bird tells the alligator that her mother is looking for her and leads the two friends to a happy reunion between the alligator and her mother. Touches of humor will appeal to young children, as will the terrific pictures and story of friendship. A most unusual book to have two female animal friends as main characters.

Lionni, Leo. *Tillie and the Wall*. 1989. Hard: Knopf. Pbk: Dragonfly. Ages 3–6.

Tillie, the youngest of the mice, persists in trying to scale a wall that all the other mice ignore. Her attempts fail until she sees a worm digging and gets the idea of tunneling under the wall. Surprised to find ordinary mice on the other side, she receives a great welcome from them and leads them back to meet her friends and family. From that day on, mice from both sides honor Tillie as the one "who first showed them the way." Lionni employs his characteristic collages to add humor and visual beauty to an inspiring story.

Little, Jean. *Jess Was the Brave One*. Illustrated by Janet Wilson. 1991. Hard: Viking. Pbk: Puffin. Ages 3–6.

Claire would like to be brave, like the heroes and heroines

in her grandfather's stories, but she knows she isn't. Her younger sister Jess is much less afraid of things. Jess doesn't mind shots or big fierce dogs. She likes to climb high in trees and watch scary shows on television. She even likes thunderstorms. All of these things scare Claire. Yet one day Claire proves she is indeed brave. She hears Jess screaming and goes outside, where she discovers some older children have taken Jess's teddy bear. To her own surprise, Claire confronts the bullies, concocting a believable story about her two strong cousins who are about to arrive. Loud and courageous, Claire gets the teddy bear back. The realistic illustrations show Claire enjoying her triumph and the admiration of her younger sister. Now there are two brave girls in the family.

Lotz, Karen E. *Can't Sit Still*. Illustrated by Colleen Browning. 1993. Hard: Dutton. Ages 2–5.
A high-spirited African-American girl twirls her way around her urban neighborhood because she just can't sit still. In autumn, she does somersaults and rides her bicycle, while in winter she plays in the snow on a welcome snow day. Spring finds her dancing with her umbrella and drawing pictures on the roof. In summer she runs through the water from the fire hydrant, skips around on the sidewalk, and rides the Ferris wheel in the evening. Only the voice of her mama—"you up there child well get down right now"—seems to keep this exuberant child from soaring through the air. Vibrant pictures complement the poetic text about a buoyant city girl.

Luenn, Nancy. *Nessa's Fish*. Illustrated by Neil Waldman. 1990. Hard: Atheneum. Ages 4–8.
When Nessa and her grandmother, who appear to be Inuit, are ice fishing away from home, the grandmother falls ill. Nessa protects her and their catch of fish, scaring away a

fox and warding off a bear with a song. Particularly impressive is the way she dominates the lead wolf of a pack by making herself tower above it and stare it in the eye. Beautiful, luminous watercolors make this a pleasure to look at as well as read.

Luenn, Nancy. *Nessa's Story*. Illustrated by Neil Waldman. 1994. Hard: Atheneum. Ages 4–8.

Another beautiful book about the Inuit girl Nessa, this one concerns the legendary beast called a silaq, a gigantic, hairy creature rarely seen. Nessa, who is looking for a story of her own, finds an enormous egg and sits against it in the fog. When she hears mysterious noises in the fog, she ignores her fear and jumps to defend the egg. But the noises turn out to be the sounds of the silaq emerging from the egg. The beast disappears when the sun gleams through the fog, just as legend predicted. When Nessa returns to camp to tell her story, everyone listens to her, a powerful metaphor for being taken seriously. Glorious watercolors create a sense of magic in which Nessa's experience seems possible. A lovely book in word, picture, and message.

Lyon, George Ella. *Mama Is a Miner*. Illustrated by Peter Catalanotto. 1994. Hard: Orchard. Ages 4–8.

A truly unusual book, this shows a mother working at the dangerous job of mining and explores how her young daughter feels about her mother's job. Scenes alternate between the warmth of an ordinary home and the darkness of the mine. Her children do homework at the kitchen table and get tucked in lovingly at night, but they also know their mother works hard at a dirty job to put food on the table. Soft-edged watercolors merge the world of home and the world of the mine, as they are merged in the mother's life and the daughter's imagination. On the final page is the picture of a miner labeled "Mama" the girl has drawn under her covers at night.

Lyon, George Ella. *Together*. Illustrated by Vera Rosenberry. Hard: Orchard. Pbk: Orchard. Ages 2–6.

Two girls imagine having lots of good times together, "dreaming the same dream." Joyful watercolor and ink pictures expand the simple poem, showing one dark-haired, dark-skinned girl and another blond, light-skinned one. When the poem says they are fighting a fire together, the pictures show one driving a fire truck and the other putting out a fire from a dragon's mouth. They also sail, fish, and ride dolphins together. At the end we see them driving horse-drawn chari-ots into the sky, as always, having a great time together. A tribute to friendship and imagined adventure.

Mahy, Margaret. *A Busy Day for a Good Grandmother*. Illustrated by Margaret Chamberlain. 1993. Hard: McElderry. Ages 3–7.

The intrepid Mrs. Oberon is delivering a special cake to her teething grandchild via her trail bike, racing raft, Piper Cherokee airplane, and skateboard. Along the way, she fights off alligators and ice vultures. After teaching her son the cake recipe, she's on her way home again to settle happily in bed with her seven cats. The story is a wild adventure, the illustrations are suitably zany, and the dust jacket of Mrs. Oberon doing a wheelie on her bike will capture the interest of children.

Mahy, Margaret. *The Man Whose Mother Was a Pirate*. Illustrated by Margaret Chamberlain. 1986. Hard: Viking, o.p. Pbk: Puffin. Ages 3–6.

There has never been such a flamboyant, devil-may-care pirate as Sam's mother. Sam himself is a shriveled-up little man in a brown suit who works as a bookkeeper. His mother, clad in a wild combination of colors and patterns, topped off with skull-and-crossbones earrings, announces that they must visit the sea. When they reach the water, sedate Sam tosses off his primness and frolics wildly in the sand. He doesn't have to think twice when a ship captain invites the mother to be his bo'sun and Sam to be his cabin boy. Off they paddle to the ship, the son suddenly as carefree as his pirate mother. Silly but entertaining.

Marshall, James. *The Cut-Ups*. 1984. Hard: Viking. Pbk: Puffin. Ages 5–8.

In this slight story illustrated with comic pictures, Spud Jenkins and Joe Turner are the cutups, incorrigible boys who drive adults crazy. But Mary Frances Hooley, who drives a sports car she built and named after herself, impresses even these two hard cases. She offers them a ride in the spaceship she has constructed and gets them into trouble by having them land in a nasty neighbor's yard. While the angry man pursues the boys, Mary Frances rescues some sports equipment that he had confiscated from her and other neighborhood kids. She has tricked the tricksters, who richly deserve it. Mary Frances, shown as a redheaded, sturdily built girl with green sunglasses, is a force to be contended with.

Martin, C.L.G. *Three Brave Women*. Illustrated by Peter Elwell. 1991. Hard: Macmillan. Ages 3–7.

Caitlin, her mother, and her grandmother, who share a fear of spiders, each tell a story about being afraid. Then Caitlin decides to overcome her fear and asks the other two for help. They wrinkle their noses but pitch in. They all crawl under the porch, where Caitlin discovers a huge, black spider. Though a bit scared, they persist and capture the spider. "We are three brave women," Grammy declares. Caitlin quickly digests the lesson that confronting fear can overcome it, and plans to catch a mouse and dig up some worms, also with the help of her mother and grandmother. The theme that girls learn timidness, sometimes from their mothers, and can unlearn it is summed up in Caitlin's last comment that "my grandchildren aren't gonna be afraid of anything!" Expressive illustrations record Caitlin's transformation from a sobbing child to a girl proudly flexing her muscles and leaping through the yard. Terrific.

Mayer, Mercer. *There's Something in My Attic*. 1988. Hard: Dial. Pbk: Puffin. Ages 2–5.

Like the better-known *There's a Nightmare in My Closet*, this concerns a child confronting her fears. Her bugaboo is a large, almost cuddly creature who has stolen her teddy bear. Wearing her nightgown, cowboy boots, and a cowboy hat, she successfully lassos the creature, but it manages to escape before her parents see it. "I'll just have to get my bear back tomorrow," she concludes. Persistent, brave, and good with a lasso—what more can you ask?

McCully, Emily Arnold. *The Bobbin Girl*. 1996. Hard: Dial. Ages 7–10.

This picture-story book deals with a subject most appropriate for older children: the working conditions for female millworkers in the mid-1800s. It focuses on a ten-year-old named Rebecca who works in a textile mill removing full bobbins of yarn and replacing them with empty ones. Her mother runs a boardinghouse for the workers, so Rebecca hears a lot of talk about the mills and their problems. When one of the workers who lives at the boardinghouse gets injured by a machine, the mill owners fire her. Next, the owners announce that wages will be cut. Judith, a young woman whom Rebecca admires, calls a meeting to fight back against the owners and leads a walkout. When the workers in Rebecca's workroom hesitate to follow Judith, Rebecca speaks out and leads the way. A lot of information, such as why various women came to work at the mills, is packed into this story. Elegant illustrations add to the sense of time, place, and character. An author's note explains that Rebecca was based on a real girl, and gives more details about the mills and the women who fought against unfair working conditions.

McCully, Emily Arnold. *Mirette on the High Wire*. 1992. Hard: Putnam. Ages 5–9.

This gloriously illustrated book, which won the Caldecott Medal, is set in Paris a hundred years ago. Mirette, whose mother runs a boardinghouse popular with performers, becomes determined to walk the tightrope when she sees a guest named Bellini practicing in their courtyard. Bellini, a world-famous tightrope walker who has lost his nerve, agrees to teach her because he is impressed with her perseverance. Her belief in him inspires Bellini to attempt a dangerous crossing high above a nearby street. When he freezes at the last minute, Mirette saves the day by starting to walk from the opposite end of the rope. The brilliant paintings make this story of a daring girl unforgettable.

McDonald, Megan. *Insects Are My Life*. Illustrated by Paul Brett Johnson. 1995. Hard: Orchard. Ages 3–7.

The budding young entomologist Amanda Frankenstein is crazy about all insects. She collects them, studies them, tries to protect them, and even imitates them sometimes. She argues with her brother, whose passion is dinosaurs, declaring, "Insects are fascinating. Insects are my life!" When Amanda starts school, she trades inventive insults with an unpleasant boy who teases her, but finally finds a promising friend, another girl with a strong interest in nature. The apt illustrations capture Amanda's enthusiasm and add touches of humor and interest. Amanda is an endearing character with a mind of her own.

McDonough, Yona Zeldis. *Eve and Her Sisters: Women of the Old Testament.* **Illustrated by Malcah Zeldis. 1994. Hard: Greenwillow. Ages 5–8.**
Boldly colored paintings accompany descriptions of fourteen women from the Old Testament. A paragraph or two describes each woman, highlighting the female role in the predominantly male Bible. One of the braver women featured is Deborah, who became a judge thanks to her wisdom and who helped fight a battle against the enemies of the Israelites. After that battle, another woman named Jael killed one of the enemy leaders by striking him with a tent pin and hammer as he slept. Ruth and her mother-in-law Naomi are shown traveling alone on a long journey, a feat the old woman Naomi was willing to try on her own if need be. Other women include Abigail, who negotiates for her husband's safety, and the Queen of Sheba, who approaches King Solomon as an equal and makes him prove his wisdom to her. Vibrant folk paintings dominate the book. An unusual approach to the Bible, this colorful work brings to the fore the overlooked role of women.

McKissack, Patricia C. *Flossie & the Fox.* **Illustrated by Rachel Isadora. 1986. Hard: Dial. Ages 3–8.**
This irresistible tale features a little girl named Flossie who must deliver a basket of eggs to a neighboring farm. Her mother warns her about a fox around who will do "most

anything to get at some eggs." Sure enough, Flossie meets him immediately, and proceeds to distract him with her teasing. She claims not to be afraid of him because, she says, she doesn't believe he is a fox. Indignant, the fox tries again and again to convince her. Unafraid, Flossie keeps him at bay until she reaches her destination, where a hound is waiting to pursue him. Told in a readable dialect and accompanied by appealing pictures, this is a wonderful story.

McKissack, Patricia C. *Mirandy and Brother Wind.* **Illustrated by Jerry Pinkney. 1988. Hard: Knopf. Ages 5–8.**
Luminous watercolors, full of motion, illustrate this story of a determined girl who captures the wind. When Mirandy wants to win the junior cakewalk, Ma Dear tells her an old belief that if you catch Brother Wind, he will do your bidding. Mirandy fails to catch him twice, but the third time she succeeds and locks him up. Now she has to decide if she wants to dance with Brother Wind himself or her friend Ezel. Vibrant pictures show children and adults dressed in their finest at the cakewalk, a traditional African-American dance contest. In the end Mirandy proves herself kind as well as clever. A Caldecott Honor Book.

McKissack, Patricia C. *Nettie Jo's Friends.* **Illustrated by Scott Cook. 1989. Hard: Knopf. Pbk: Knopf. Ages 4–8.**
Joyful, slightly blurred pictures evoke a time past in this story about a resourceful girl. Nettie Jo needs to sew her doll a dress that will be presentable at a wedding, but she has no needle. While she is looking for one and gathering stray things into a burlap sack, Nettie Jo helps three animals solve their problems. She happens to have the perfect answer for each in her sack. As in many folktales, her ingenuity and generosity lead to a happy ending. The final picture shows a smiling

African-American girl dancing in the moonlight with her doll and her sewing needle, while three comical animals dash away in the background.

McLerran, Alice. *Roxaboxen*. Illustrated by Barbara Cooney. 1991. Hard: Lothrop. Pbk: Puffin. Ages 5–8.

This is truly a gem among books, combining a poetic, evocative text and stunning illustrations. Roxaboxen is a city some children have created near their homes in the desert. Dominant among these friends is Marian, who serves as mayor and sometimes as general. Although boys play at Roxaboxen, girls seem most important. The pictures show girls gathering rocks, "driving" steering wheels, riding stick horses (for which there is no speed limit), and holding down their Fort Irene. One fine picture shows a girl, Frances, relaxing with an air of propriety and confidence in her own spot outlined by colored glass: "a house of jewels." Based on a true story about the author's mother and her friends in Yuma, Arizona, seventy years ago, this beautiful book describes a magical place with room for girls to lead and create.

McNaughton, Colin. *Captain Abdul's Pirate School*. 1994. Hard: Candlewick. Ages 4–8.

In this zany picture-story book, told in diary format, Maisy Pickles's parents send her to Pirate School because she likes art and books too well, and she isn't tough enough. The faculty at Captain Abdul's Pirate School are scruffy male pirates with names like Poop Deck Percy Ploppe and Riffraff Rafferty. The children, boys and girls dressed in pirate uniforms, make cannonballs and swords in arts and crafts class and learn how to read treasure maps in geography. The pirates encourage them to lie, cheat, and cut in line. But when Maisy overhears the pirates' plan to kidnap and ransom them just before parents' day, the children mutiny under Maisy's leadership. Maisy ends up as the swashbuckling captain of her own pirate ship, who steals only from other pirates. Animated cartoonlike pictures cluttered with funny details fill the large book format, just the right accompaniment to this story, which turns the idea of school on its head.

McPhail, David. *Annie & Co.* 1991. Hard: Holt. Ages 2–5.

Annie has learned from her father, who has a repair shop, how to fix just about everything. So one day she fixes up a wagon, nails on it a sign, "Annie & Co. We Fix Anything," and sets off with her cat, Bill, and her pony, Bub, having persuaded her father to let her go out in the world and find things to fix. She has a series of adventures and solves some surprising problems for the people and animals she meets. Annie is wonderfully competent and inventive, an outstanding example of an independent girl who is at home with tools and confident of her abilities.

McPhail, David. *Ed and Me.* 1990. Hard: Harcourt. Ages 3–6.

The little girl who tells this story appears on the title page sitting on the roof of a truck. The truck, known as Ed, used to belong to a family friend, then "came to live with us." She tells of all the enjoyable times she has with Ed, going into town for ice cream, sitting on his tailgate for picnics, decorating him for a parade. In the cozy pictures, she is shown helping her father load Ed with hay and later with firewood and then pumpkins. She even pitches a tent in the back of the truck one night and stays until her flashlight batteries run out. As winter approaches, she helps her father build a shed for Ed. Encouraged by her father, this small girl does everything you would expect a farm boy to do, even swinging on a rope to jump into a pond. A unique portrayal of a young girl and the truck she loves.

McPhail, David. *Emma's Vacation.* **1987. Hard: Dutton. Pbk: Puffin. Ages 2–5.**

After a day of commercial pleasures in restaurants and amusement parks, Emma insists on enjoying some of the family vacation outdoors. When her parents ask, "What can we do here?" she leads them wading in brooks, fishing, berry picking, tree climbing, picnicking, and hiking. This short book, with few words, will warm the hearts of parents and children who find their greatest pleasure in nature. Children will also enjoy the message that Emma, a child, has something to teach her parents and that she does so successfully.

Meddaugh, Susan. *Beast.* **1981. Hard: Houghton, o.p. Pbk: Houghton. Ages 2–5.**

Anna is the youngest in her family and the bravest. When she spots a big furry beast coming out of the forest, the rest of the family immediately declares it a dangerous, bad beast. Her father tries unsuccessfully to shoot it and decides it must be tricky as well as dangerous. Anna, however, wants to know more before she makes up her mind. Like a scientist, she learns more about the beast, and discovers it is far from dangerous. Anna, who has red hair and wears a red dress, is a girl who promises to go far thanks to her inquiring spirit. Simple drawings of the small, determined girl and the huge furry beast will delight readers.

Meddaugh, Susan. *Hog-Eye.* **1995. Hard: Houghton. Ages 3–7.**

A young pig is telling her family the story of why she

didn't go to school that day. Cartoon balloons add the funny comments of her family as she tells the tale. After getting on the wrong school bus, she says, she was captured by a wolf, who decided to make her into soup. Children will enjoy the discrepancy between what the pig describes and what the cartoon-like pictures show; for example, she reports they went to the wolf's "terrible, gloomy cave," but the pictures show a cozy little house. The pig, a quick thinker, goads the wolf into using a recipe he can't read. Each ingredient she mentions causes him big problems when he goes to fetch it, especially the "green threeleaf" that gives him a terrible rash. She convinces the wolf she has the power to release him from the itching, and so escapes. A tale very high in child appeal with droll illustrations.

Meddaugh, Susan. *Martha Calling*. 1994. Hard: Houghton. Pbk: Houghton. Ages 3–7.

The first page of this funny book shows the dog Martha up in the air catching a Frisbee thrown by her owner, Helen. Martha, amazingly enough, can speak when she has been eating alphabet soup, and she loves to talk, especially on the telephone. One day she answers a radio quiz correctly and wins a free weekend for four at the Come-On-Inn. Because the inn doesn't allow dogs, Martha goes dressed as an old lady, a disguise she almost gives away when she leaps to catch a Frisbee at the inn. When Martha's pose is revealed, she complains loudly about the hated words "No Dogs Allowed," wringing the hearts of visiting dog owners. The inn changes its policy—and hires Martha as the dining room hostess. Martha rates high as a canine heroine: She's energetic, talented, and far from shy. The cartoonlike pictures, with plenty of talk balloons, are hilarious. Martha first appears in the funny *Martha Speaks*.

Merriam, Eve. *Mommies at Work.* **Illustrated by Eugenie Fernandes. 1989 revised edition. Hard: Simon & Schuster. Pbk: Aladdin. Ages 3–7.**

A useful look at the jobs, blue-collar and professional, that some mothers hold outside their homes. Typical of the text are lines such as "Mommies with telescopes. Mommies punching tickets on trains." Women appear working in grocery stores, offices, auto plants, and airports. There are dancers, teachers, doctors, truck drivers, and even tightrope walkers. The cheerful illustrations are multicultural and show warm relationships between the mothers returning from work and their children.

Miller, M.L. *Dizzy from Fools.* **Illustrated by Eve Tharlet. 1985. Hard: Picture Book Studio. Ages 3–6.**

Sprightly little round-faced people populate a traditional kingdom in which only boys can grow up to be court jesters, or fools, as they are called. When the princess questions this policy, her mother insists that it's always been like that. The princess still cannot see why girls can't be "funny and wise," a jester's role. So when the king holds auditions for a new fool, she disguises herself and tries out. Turning double cartwheels, playing a tiny tuba, and stumping the king with two riddles make her the top candidate. In the end she proves her point and wins the job. A simple story about a clever girl who breaks tradition.

Minarik, Else Holmelund. *The Little Girl and the Dragon.* **Illustrated by Martine Gourbault. 1991. Hard: Greenwillow. Ages 2–5.**

In this story, a dragon escapes from a little girl's book and begins to swallow her toys. She quickly becomes indignant, standing with her hands on her hips and a scowl on her face as he eats her puzzles. Pointing a finger at him, she orders the dragon to give all the things back, "and right away, too!" The creature looks snide until he realizes that the girl has him in a corner; she plans to sit on the book he is from and not let him go home until he gives back her toys. He finally complies and she lets him back in the book, then perches triumphantly on her bed with the book secure under one of the bedposts. The colored-pencil illustrations create an original dragon with pink wings and horns and a flamelike tongue. A top-notch simple story about an unflappable little girl.

Moss, Lloyd. *Zin! Zin! Zin! A Violin*. Illustrated by Marjorie Priceman. 1995. Hard: Simon & Schuster. Ages 3–8.

This wonderful introduction to an orchestra combines a witty rhymed text and outstanding illustrations. Five of the ten orchestra members are women who play the trumpet, cello, flute, oboe, and harp. The players in the multicultural group resemble their instruments: The trumpeter's skirt flares out like a trumpet, while the flute player herself is long and thin. A subplot with a dog, two cats, and a mouse will delight younger children, while older ones will effortlessly absorb information about musical instruments. Named a Caldecott Honor Book for Priceman's clever, highly original illustrations. Bravo!

Moss, Thylias. *I Want to Be*. Illustrated by Jerry Pinkney. 1993. Hard: Dial. Ages 4–7.

Glorious watercolors combined with poetic text celebrate a girl's dreams of what she wants to be. Pinkney's light-filled illustrations show her running, leaping, dancing, flying a kite, swinging, and poised at the top of a slide. A magical quality pervades the book as the girl jumps rope "with strands of rainbow" and flies her kite far beyond the earth.

She wants to be everything: big and strong, fast and tall, wise but willing to learn. The pictures show her as African-American, although the text doesn't specify—a glowing child in overalls and dresses. A joyful celebration with memorable illustrations.

Munsch, Robert N. *The Paper Bag Princess*. Illustrated by Michael Martchenko. 1980. Hard: Annick. Pbk: Annick. Ages 4–7.

This story of a princess who rescues a prince certainly conveys a worthy message. When a dragon steals the prince and ruins all the princess's pretty clothes, she resorts to wearing a paper bag and sets off to rescue her fiancé. She tricks the dragon and releases the prince, only to have him grouse at her about what a mess she looks. She replies that he looks like a prince but is acting like "a bum," and they part ways with the princess romping off into the sunset. Although the writing is choppy and the pictures unexceptional, the theme is right on target.

Narahashi, Keiko. *Is That Josie?* 1994. Hard: McElderry. Ages 2–5.

This simple book asks questions about a little girl named Josie, and answers by comparing her to an animal. "Is that Josie running fast through the grass?" "No, it's a cheetah. There she goes—wait for us." In the watercolor picture, the girl is running, with a more transparent cheetah beside her. As the story progresses, the animals named become larger and more powerful, from a fox and turtle to a hippopotamus and a crocodile, strong images for a young girl to aspire to. Take note of the wonderful endpapers, with Josie on one side in various positions and different animals on the other imitating her.

Nash, Ogden. *The Adventures of Isabel.* **Illustrated by James Marshall. 1991. Hard: Little, Brown. Pbk: Little, Brown. Ages 3–8.**

Two great humorists come together to create one of the bravest, most entertaining girls in children's books. No fearful creature can get the best of Isabel, who conquers a bear, witch, giant, doctor, and nightmare in this wonderful poem. Marshall's red-haired Isabel perfectly suits Nash's words. She is an inspiration to all readers, as she teaches them how to "banish a bugaboo." Appropriately, she is surrounded in the pictures by admiring, even dumbfounded, children who clearly look up to her. Girls and boys could use dozens more role models like Isabel. A book with very high child appeal.

Newman, Lesléa. *Heather Has Two Mommies.* **Illustrated by Diana Souza. 1989. Pbk: Alyson Wonderland. Ages 3–7.**

In this story about a girl whose two caring mothers are lesbians, the women serve as strong role models. One is a doctor who lets Heather listen to her own heartbeat with a stethoscope; the other is a carpenter who gives Heather a small hammer to use on the table they are building together. While a bit stilted in picture and text, this is valuable for its attention to a neglected topic and for its warm spirit.

Oram, Hiawyn. *Reckless Ruby.* **Illustrated by Tony Ross. 1992. Hard: Crown. Ages 3–6.**

A wild-eyed, red-haired girl is diving into a goldfish bowl on the cover of this funny book, a hint of what is to come. Poor Ruby suffers from overly solicitous parents who want to "wrap her in cotton wool and only bring her out for glittering banquets" because she is so precious. Hearing their plans to protect her and then marry her to a prince, Ruby consults her friend Harry for advice. He suggests getting reckless, and she throws herself headlong into the project, jumping off walls, balancing on bicycle handlebars, walking on tightropes, and trying to swallow fire. Ruby's exploits grow ever more outrageous until her parents no longer find her precious and scrap their plans to marry her to a prince. The final picture shows her wearing a helmet and zooming off a skateboard ramp.

Paton Walsh, Jill. *When Grandma Came*. Illustrated by Sophy Williams. 1992. Hard: Viking. Pbk: Puffin. Ages 2–5.

Grandma compares her granddaughter Madeleine to all the exciting things she has seen on her travels: whales and polar bears and hippos and more. The soft illustrations show the grandmother in the Arctic, Africa, Australia, India, and Egypt. Nowhere has she seen anything as "heavenly-and-earthly" as her granddaughter. By the final picture of this loving story, baby Madeleine has grown old enough to borrow Grandma's binoculars and satchel, looking ready to travel herself. Poetic text, wonderful theme.

Peet, Bill. *Encore for Eleanor*. 1981. Hard: Houghton. Pbk: Houghton. Ages 3–6.

Eleanor the elephant has been a star performer in the circus, accustomed to crowds roaring "Encore!" after her act. But she has grown old and unsteady, and finally the circus boss sends her off to live in a zoo. Unhappy without a job to do and missing her fancy circus clothes, Eleanor mopes in her barn all day. But one afternoon a teenage girl sets up an easel near Eleanor's fence and starts to draw. The artist loses her temper when the rhino she is sketching rolls over. She stomps away, leaving her materials behind, and Eleanor decides to try drawing. She picks up charcoal with her trunk and quickly sketches a clown face. The returning teenager exclaims with delight, but the officious zoo director insists that a "dumb animal" could not have drawn the picture. The "super-intelligent" Eleanor proves him wrong with a quick, skillful drawing of a lion, and she becomes a star once more. One of the few books about a female by this popular author.

Pinkney, Brian. *JoJo's Flying Side Kick.* **1995. Hard: Simon & Schuster. Ages 3–7.**

The jacket picture of JoJo in her Tae Kwon Do clothes performing a flying side kick will attract readers immediately. JoJo must break a board with a flying side kick in order to earn her yellow belt. The challenge makes her so nervous, she tells her granddaddy, "I'm freakin' out." Remembering his boxing days, he advises her on footwork. A friend with Tae Kwon Do experience says to yell loudly. And her mother, clad in a tennis dress, advises her to visualize her goal. JoJo puts it all together and a forceful picture shows her triumph. JoJo and her family are African-American in this unusual story about a girl mastering a martial art while she also masters her own fears. A real winner by an award-winning illustrator.

Pinkwater, Daniel. *Aunt Lulu.* **1988. Hard: Macmillan. Pbk: Aladdin. Ages 3–7.**

Author and illustrator Daniel Pinkwater is truly an original. Here he has created a strong-willed librarian in Alaska who delivers books to gold miners via her dogsled. When she decides to move back to New Jersey, her parting with the miners is politely unsentimental, for she finds them nice but "boring." However, when her fourteen huskies start crying, she agrees to take them with her. Aunt Lulu's strong character and dry voice make up for the thin plotline. The pictures are full of humorous touches, such as the irresistible pink-rimmed sunglasses she and the dogs wear in New Jersey.

Pomerantz, Charlotte. *The Piggy in the Puddle*. Illustrated by James Marshall. 1974. Hard: Macmillan. Pbk: Aladdin. Ages 2–7.

A rollicking, rhyming story about a naughty girl pig who won't get out of a mud puddle. No matter how much she is scolded by her parents and brother, she won't budge. She ignores their complaints and their pleadings and their advice to use lots of soap (to which she answers, "Nope"). In the end, she is having such a merry time that her family decides to join her. A "squishy-squashy, mooshy-squooshy" story that is almost a tongue twister, this little book is not to be missed. As always, James Marshall's illustrations add character and humor to the text.

Priceman, Marjorie. *How to Make an Apple Pie and See the World*. 1994. Hard: Knopf. Pbk: Random House. Ages 3–7.

An outstanding book that tells the story of a girl who wants to make an apple pie but finds the grocery store closed. So she takes a journey around the world to pick up the various ingredients she needs. She cuts a dashing figure in many countries on all sorts of transport, from bicycle to balloon to airplane. Lively pictures, witty prose, and a great sense of adventure fulfill the promise of the dust jacket, on which the girl is merrily parachuting through the air with a cow and a chicken and her cooking supplies.

Rabe, Berniece. *The Balancing Girl*. Illustrated by Lillian Hoban. 1981. Hard: Dutton, o.p. Pbk: Dutton. Ages 4–8.

Margaret, who relies on her wheelchair or crutches, prides

herself on her ability to balance things. But her classmate Tommy belittles the structures she builds from blocks and sometimes knocks them down. When the class wants to help raise money at a school carnival, Margaret has a clever idea that uses her skills and raises more money than any event. Even Tommy is finally impressed. Margaret is a girl who knows how to maximize her strengths and enjoys her triumphs.

Rathmann, Peggy. *Officer Buckle and Gloria.* **1995. Hard: Putnam. Ages 3–6.**

Officer Buckle is an earnest, boring safety officer who puts schoolchildren to sleep with his safety tips. But when he teams up with the dynamic police dog Gloria, children sit up and pay attention. Behind Officer Buckle's back, Gloria acts out the dire consequences of ignoring his tips. When he advises children not to swim during electrical storms, she soars in the air with her hair on end. Her acrobatics delight the audience but dismay Officer Buckle when he finally realizes she is upstaging him. The clever, funny pictures, which won the Caldecott Medal, show Gloria's antics, which are never mentioned in the text. Young readers enjoy being in on the secret well before Officer Buckle is. A surefire hit.

Ray, Mary Lyn. *A Rumbly Tumbly Glittery Gritty Place.* **Illustrated by Douglas Florian. 1993. Hard: Harcourt. Ages 2–5.**

A young girl muses on the gravel pit across the road, using her imagination to transform it into a mountain she can climb and a beach without an ocean. She thinks about what it was like in the past and how it may be a pasture in the future. She loves the rocks she finds there and carries them home by the armload. Even her dog is shown with a pile of rocks on its back. Lovely watercolors, with hand-lettering for the brief text, capture her enthusiasm and her vision. An admirable example of a girl who appreciates dirt and stones.

Riggio, Anita. *Beware the Brindlebeast*. 1994. Hard: Boyds Mills. Ages 3–7.

On All Hallows' Eve, Birdie, a poor but optimistic old woman, is walking home past the old burying ground when, to her surprise, she almost trips over a kettle full of gold. She starts pulling it home through the dusk and suddenly realizes the pot of gold has turned into a barrel of apples. But she sees this has benefits, too, and cheerfully continues on her way. When the apples become a pumpkin, Birdie again sees the transformation in the best light. Outside her cottage, the pumpkin turns into a terrible monster, the Dread Brindlebeast that all her neighbors fear. Fearless, Birdie is even slightly amused by the monster, and her courage brings unexpected rewards. Bold oil paintings show a hearty, white-haired woman who enjoys life. Perfect for children who enjoy being scared— a little.

Ringgold, Faith. *Tar Beach*. 1991. Hard: Crown. Pbk: Random House. Ages 4–8.

Rich illustrations in a folk-art style show eight-year-old Cassie Lightfoot flying through the night above the George Washington Bridge. As she says in the poetic narrative, she feels powerful in the air and magical when she sleeps out on Tar Beach, the rooftop of her apartment building. Most of all she feels free. She wishes she could use the power she feels to save her family from hard times. But if she cannot do that, Cassie can at least take her brother with her and teach him to fly. The strength of this unusual book is the extraordinary artwork, based on a story quilt shown at the back of the book. A Caldecott Honor Book.

Rockwell, Harlow. *My Doctor.* **1973. Hard: Macmillan, o.p. Pbk: Aladdin. Ages 2–6.**

In this simple book, a young boy describes his visit to his doctor, who is a woman. He goes through the steps of his physical: being weighed, having his blood pressure taken, and more. Uncluttered pictures supply information about what the office and instruments look like. The sensible-looking doctor, whose hairstyle looks only slightly dated after more than twenty years, wears a white coat with a stethoscope in her pocket. The child, who makes no comment on the fact that the doctor is a woman, concludes simply, "She is a nice doctor." A useful introduction to going to the doctor, and instructive for those children who still believe all doctors are men.

Rose, Deborah Lee. *Meredith's Mother Takes the Train.* **Illustrated by Irene Trivas. 1991. Hard: Albert Whitman. Ages 3–7.**

Meredith spends the day in child care while her mother goes off to a job in the city, taking the train there and back. Each double-page spread contrasts Meredith's day with her mother's. The girl chases bubbles while the mother fields phone calls. They each think of the other during the day and are happy to be together in the evening, when the two are shown preparing dinner and eating together. Although the rhyming text is slightly stiff, the watercolor and pencil pictures are cheerful and lively, and the theme is a welcome one, aimed here at young children.

Rosenberg, Liz. *The Carousel.* **Illustrated by Jim LaMarche. 1995. Hard: Harcourt. Ages 4–8.**

Two sisters, remembering words their mother had said when she was alive, visit a carousel on their way home one day in winter. When they hear horses whinnying inside, they venture in, mount their favorites, and race into the sky, with the other horses galloping behind. The horses act wild, because the carousel is broken, so the girls fetch their mother's toolbox, for she "had been someone who could fix anything" and who sometimes took apart appliances just for fun. The narrator, pictured sitting among the pieces of the dismantled carousel machinery, carefully inspects it until she fixes the problem. Then her sister lures the mad horses back by playing a song their mother used to play on the flute. The final picture shows them safely with their father, all thinking about their mother. The story conveys warmth and love despite the gloomy winter night and the sense of loss. It emphasizes the girls' courage and resourcefulness, an inheritance from their strong mother.

Rosenberg, Liz, collector and reteller. *Mama Goose: A New Mother Goose.* **Illustrated by Janet Street. 1994. Hard: Philomel. Ages 2–5.**

Parents tired of the sexism in traditional nursery rhyme collections will welcome this cheery volume. On the title page, an efficient-looking woman is at her desk typing, with a big goose nearby. Illustrations show active girls and boys, light- and dark-skinned, clad in everyday clothes, playing in modern settings. Some of the rhymes have been altered in a smooth manner that keeps their rhythm and spirit. Others haven't been changed, and only the pictures suggest a new interpretation. For example, "Star bright, star light," in its familiar form, is accompanied by a picture of some boys and girls lying on a hill looking up at the stars, near a girl who is swinging on a tire swing. The originators of the collection have reached their goal of producing a Mother Goose that parents can read "without wincing." An agreeable alternative to the traditional nursery rhyme books.

Sadler, Marilyn. *Elizabeth and Larry.* **Illustrated by Roger Bollen. 1990. Hard: Simon & Schuster, o.p. Pbk: Simon & Schuster. Ages 3–5.**

It's hard to resist a book about a woman with a pet alligator. Elizabeth receives Larry by mistake in a box of oranges from Florida and decides to keep him as a pet. They get along beautifully. Larry teaches Elizabeth to dive for fish, they play poker and old maid, and Larry helps with the housekeeping. But over the years, Larry begins to feel lonely for others like himself, so Elizabeth buys him a one-way airline ticket to Florida. But who can live without a favorite alligator? Elizabeth buys herself a one-way ticket too and is soon perched on a floating chair in a swimming pool, surrounded by alligators. She may look like a conventional old woman, knitting and drinking tea, but in the end she ignores convention and makes her own choices.

Samton, Sheila White. *Jenny's Journey.* **1991. Hard: Viking, o.p. Pbk: Puffin. Ages 2–6.**

Jenny draws a marvelous boat with a dog figurehead, then sets sail in it to visit her friend who has moved away. The text is a letter describing her travels, with just a sentence or two on each page. First, the Statue of Liberty, an ice-cream cone in her hand, asks where Jenny's going as she rides through the harbor. Jenny sleeps at night under the stars, greets the rising sun, and has her loneliness swept away by dolphins and seagulls. She reassures a concerned voice from a huge ocean liner that she is fine, which she proves by weathering a storm alone. At last her journey ends at an island where the dark-skinned

Jenny greets her happy, light-skinned friend. The joyful colors of the pictures match the mood of this imaginary journey.

Sasso, Sandy Eisenberg. *But God Remembered: Stories of Women from Creation to the Promised Land.* **Illustrated by Bethanne Andersen. 1995. Hard: Jewish Lights. Ages 6–10.**

Taken from the midrashic tradition, which extends stories in the Bible, this lovely book portrays strong women whose stories are not well known. It tells of Lilith, who came before Eve but argued with Adam when she insisted on equality. The second tale is about Serach, a harpist who knew all the ancient stories and composed music to go with the words. Bityah, also called Meroe, was a pharaoh's daughter who raised and influenced the future leader Moses. Last are the five daughters of Zelophehad, women who wandered the wilderness with their people and changed the law so that women could inherit property if a man had no sons. Graceful paintings show women who appear dignified rather than pretty, a fitting choice.

Saul, Carol P. *Someplace Else.* **Illustrated by Barry Root. 1995. Hard: Simon & Schuster. Ages 4–7.**

All her life Mrs. Tillby had lived in the same place and wondered what it would be like to live elsewhere. So one day she takes off in her old green truck to visit each of her grown children and see how she likes life where they live: in the city, at the seashore, and in the mountains. Then she tries other places as well, including an adobe hut and a riverboat. This cardigan-clad, white-haired woman has a strong case of wanderlust. Luckily, as she heads back home pondering the fact that no place suits her, Mrs. Tillby spots a silver trailer for sale, which she buys and hooks to her truck. Evocative paintings show her tooling along in an old-fashioned truck, learning to ski, and finding the home of her dreams.

Schotter, Roni. *Captain Snap and the Children of Vinegar Lane*. Illustrated by Marcia Sewall. 1989. Hard: Orchard. Pbk: Orchard. Ages 3–7.

Old-fashioned, beautifully colored prints give a feeling of time gone by to this story about some children and a taciturn neighbor. Bravest of the children on Vinegar Lane is Sody, the littlest of all. When the gang sneaks up on the house of cranky Captain Snap, she's the one to march right up and ask him how he's doing. But all he ever does in reply is snap his lower lip. One day when Captain Snap doesn't appear, Sody leads the way to peer in his window. Seeing him lying uncovered on a mattress, Sody and the children run off to get him blankets and food. Sody, of course, delivers the heavy stew pot to the door and knocks. The end is a happy one, as Captain Snap turns out to be far more interesting than the children expected. The original illustrations are the highlight of this story about an old man and a brave girl.

Schwartz, Amy. *Bea and Mr. Jones*. 1982. Hard: Bradbury. Pbk: Aladdin. Ages 3–7.

Bea is tired of kindergarten and her father is tired of his job, so they change places one day, with Bea donning her father's coat and tie. Mr. Jones proves himself to be a big help at school, while Bea snags a promotion at work with her advertising slogan for crackers. They decide to make it a permanent arrangement, and Bea quickly becomes president of toy sales. She has the brisk manner of an executive and carries herself with such confidence, despite the huge suit, that somehow the story doesn't seem as absurd as it sounds. Charming black-and-white illustrations, and fun all around.

Sendak, Maurice. *Higglety Pigglety Pop! or, There Must Be More to Life.* **1967. Hard: Harper. Pbk: Harper Trophy. Ages 4–8.**

Based on a short nursery rhyme in which a dog eats a mop, this small chapter book follows the adventures of Jennie, a Sealyham terrier. Although she has everything, it doesn't seem to be enough, so she sets off into the world to seek her fortune. She would like to be the leading lady for the World Mother Goose Theater but she needs experience first. Her experience consists of working as nurse to a baby and saving him from a roaring lion. Sendak's charming black-and-white illustrations grace each chapter and a long series of them illustrates the play Jennie finally acts in. Text and illustration weave the story and play together in a dreamlike way in this offbeat book from an eminent illustrator.

Sharratt, Nick. *Mrs. Pirate.* **1994. Hard: Candlewick. Ages 2–4.**

A red-haired, pink-cheeked smiling woman wearing a pirate's hat beams out from the cover of this little book. Bright illustrations show everything Mrs. Pirate buys when she shops one day, alternating between cozy, everyday items and accoutrements for a pirate. First she buys an apple pie, then an eye patch. Most amazing of all, she buys "buttons for her coat" and then "a big sailing boat." At last she sets sail on her boat, which is stocked with all her purchases. A very brief text, bright pictures, and a jolly pirate theme will appeal to many small children. Great fun.

Shaw-MacKinnon, Margaret. *Tiktala.* **Illustrated by László Gál. 1996. Hard: Holiday. Ages 6–9.**

Set in the Far North, this story is about a girl who wants to be a soapstone carver, a traditional occupation among her people. The wisest woman of the village advises the girl to go in search of a spirit helper. Although she is afraid, Tiktala undertakes the quest, during which she turns into a harp seal. Traveling with another seal, she learns how dangerous humans are to seals, especially the pups. An act of physical courage turns Tiktala back into a human being and sends her home, ready to begin her life as a carver. Stiff paintings in subtle colors depict a cold world of snow and ice. Slightly sentimental, with a strong message about ecology, this story is noteworthy for the fact that a girl, not a boy, goes on a spiritual quest.

Sisulu, Elinor Batezat. *The Day Gogo Went to Vote: South Africa, April 1994.* Illustrated by Sharon Wilson. 1996. Hard: Little, Brown. Ages 6–9.

On the cover of this picture-story book is a quote from Nelson Mandela, "Inspiring and moving"—an apt description of the book's impact. Set in South Africa in April 1994, it tells of an old South African woman from the viewpoint of her young granddaughter Thembi. Gogo, which means grandmother, has never had the opportunity to vote due to the political system of apartheid. She announces to her surprised family that she fully intends to vote, even though she never leaves the family's yard. Concerned about her health, they argue against her plan, to no avail. Someone loans her a car and driver, and Gogo insists that Thembi come, too. A spirit of celebration pervades the trip to the voting booth and the rest of the day, and Thembi becomes aware of the importance of voting. Warm pictures of a loving family and a happy event make this story and its message accessible to children.

Slawson, Michele Benoit. *Apple Picking Time.* Illustrated by Deborah Kogan Ray. 1994. Hard: Crown. Ages 3–6.

Not many children have a chance to earn money, so the

narrator in this nostalgic book is excited about going to pick apples for pay. Soft-edged pictures show a young girl on a ladder with her canvas bag strapped onto her stomach. Her ambition is to fill a bin this year for the first time. She picks all day through the increasing heat, and finally hears the sound she has been waiting for, a girl's voice calling, "Full." She gets her ticket punched and rushes off to cash it in. Her parents and grandparents express their pride at her efforts, and that night she dreams of filling two bins next year. A quiet story that encourages girls to work hard with a goal in mind.

Smucker, Anna Egan. *No Star Nights*. Illustrated by Steve Johnson. 1989. Hard: Knopf, o.p. Pbk: Knopf. Ages 6–9.

"When I was little, we couldn't see the stars in the nighttime sky because the furnaces of the mill turned the darkness into a red glow." So begins this beautifully illustrated book about growing up in a mill town in West Virginia. The narrator is a girl whose father works at the steel mills. She plays baseball, goes to Pittsburgh Pirate games as a special treat, and climbs the slag heaps, huge hills of glassy refuse from the mills. Set in the 1950s, the story gives examples of girls who enjoy sports and adventures that dirty their blue jeans. These girls are as curious as any boy about the mills dominating their lives. Evocative oil paintings show both the beauty and the bleakness of life in the mill town. One of the few children's books with an industrial setting, this is all the more unusual because it focuses on girls.

Steig, William. *Brave Irene*. 1986. Hard: FSG. Pbk: FSG. Ages 3–7.

This is one of Steig's few books with strong females. Irene's mother, a seamstress, has finished a beautiful ball gown for the duchess but is too sick to deliver it. Her daughter insists on braving the wintry weather, tucks her mother in bed, and sets out to deliver the dress. She battles the snow and a particularly nasty wind, and is almost buried in a snowdrift, but finally makes it to the palace by cleverly using the dress box as a sled. When things look the worst, Irene draws on her inner resources "in an explosion of fury" and triumphs. It would be preferable if Irene braved the blizzard for something other than a ball gown, but Steig's talent is such that the story rises above this limitation.

Stevenson, James. *Rolling Rose*. 1992. Hard: Greenwillow. Ages 2–5.

Baby Rose has a chair on wheels, dubbed the Rosemobile, that she rolls around the house in. One day when her family is too busy to pay attention to her, Rose rolls out the door and into the garden, then rolls to the gate and down the sidewalk. Intent on her adventure, Rose rolls too fast for anyone to catch her. Soon other children in their rolling chairs, boys and girls, join the parade that Rose leads down a road and into the country. In Stevenson's comic watercolors, the children look very pleased with themselves. When it starts raining, they roll on home. An exuberant adventure about very young children, and in particular about one bold girl.

Stock, Catherine. *Sophie's Knapsack*. 1988. Hard: Lothrop. Ages 2–5.

Sophie's parents take her on her first backpacking trip, an overnight hike up a mountain. Although young, she carries her own knapsack, collects pinecones for the fire, and even leads the way sometimes. She does not let the steepness of the mountain deter her, refusing her father's offer of a ride. Her reward is the joy of reaching the peak, which feels to her "like the top of the world." This simple text and soft watercolor pictures make the idea of hiking an attractive one.

Thomas, Iolette. *Mermaid Janine*. Illustrated by Jennifer Northway. 1991. Pbk: Scholastic. Ages 2–5.

Janine, a sturdy little African-American girl, starts swimming lessons and enjoys them right away despite stinging eyes and a few mouthfuls of water. The upbeat pictures follow her progress as she learns to jump in and retrieve a brick from the pool bottom. When she complains about her slow progress, her father offers to take her to the pool for extra practice. She starts eating vegetables and skipping rope to get stronger. Janine reaches her goal of swimming the length of the pool, thanks to her hard work and determination. A happy story featuring parents who encourage their daughter in her interests.

Thompson, Kay. *Eloise*. Illustrated by Hilary Knight. 1955. Hard: Simon & Schuster. Ages 4–8.

Eloise is one of a kind in the world of children's books. She tears around her home, the Plaza Hotel in New York, as if it were a playground. Sometimes she takes two sticks and drags them along the walls, disturbing guest after guest, or if she wants to make a "really loud and terrible racket," she "slomps" her skates along the walls. She saws her doll in half for the excitement of imagining an ambulance and surgery. She drives her tutor crazy by imitating his every word and gesture. Her room could hardly be messier. At the same time she has a loving, jolly relationship with her nanny and appears certain that everyone in the hotel is glad to see her. The hilarious text is matched by funny, apt illustrations. The incorrigible Eloise deserves her years of popularity. Other books include *Eloise in Paris*, *Eloise in Moscow*, and *Eloise at Christmastime*.

Turkle, Brinton. *Do Not Open.* **1981. Hard: Dutton. Pbk: Puffin. Ages 3–7.**

Miss Moody and her cat live by the beach, where Miss Moody loves storms and the treasures they deposit on the sand. One day she discovers a bottle and opens the stopper, releasing a huge, fearsome creature that gets bigger and more fearsome when it realizes that Miss Moody is not afraid. To get rid of it, she tricks the creature into becoming a mouse and the cat eats it. For children who love scary books, this one has a truly ugly monster and a very brave woman, a great combination.

Tusa, Tricia. *Miranda.* **1985. Hard: Macmillan. Pbk: Aladdin. Ages 4–7.**

Scraggly drawings introduce young piano player Miranda and her motley assortment of relatives. Aunt Lorraine, Grandma Belle, and the rest love to listen to Miranda play Bach, Haydn, and Mozart. She willingly plays the school anthem for her teacher and scales for her piano teacher. But one day she hears the irresistible sound of boogie-woogie on the street and realizes that's what she wants to play for herself. Pictures show her practically dancing on the piano as she throws herself into the beat. But, alas, everyone else objects to the noise, and Miranda finally refuses to play anything if she cannot also play boogie-woogie. In the end, her relatives and teacher relent, and she plays both classical and boogie-woogie with enthusiasm. A zany tribute to the piano and one strong-minded girl.

Tyler, Anne. *Tumble Tower.* **Illustrated by Mitra Modar-ressi. 1993. Hard: Orchard. Ages 3–7.**

In this lighthearted tale by well-known author Anne Tyler, Princess Molly the Messy finds herself at odds with her much tidier parents and brother. Completely belying any notion that girls are naturally neat, Molly strews her clothing all over her room and leaves dishes and old food lying about. She even has an orange tree grown from an orange she never ate. Molly answers her family's complaints by insisting, "It's my own private room, and I like it just the way it is." In the end, her family comes to appreciate Molly's habits when the rest of the castle floods. They seek refuge in her tower room, where they have no problem finding clothes and food for all. After this episode, her parents start to be a bit messier themselves. Charming pictures make the family and messiness even more vivid.

Van Allsburg, Chris. *The Widow's Broom*. 1992. Hard: Houghton. Ages 5–9.

When the widow Minna Shaw aids a witch who has fallen into her cornfields, the witch leaves Minna her old broom. Soon the broom is helping merrily with the chores and even playing the piano in the evening. Minna's straitlaced male neighbors are scandalized and label the broom evil, although their wives point out what a big help it is around the house. Minna and the broom hatch a plot to best the interfering men, and the final scene shows the contented widow and her broom safe and cozy in their little farmhouse. The remarkable brown-and-white pencil illustrations perfectly suit the spirit of the story, set in the fall, and give the broom a jaunty personality. An enchanting book by an award-winning illustrator.

Vaughan, Marcia. *Whistling Dixie*. Illustrated by Barry Moser. 1995. Hard: Harper. Pbk: Harper Trophy. Ages 3–7.

Dixie Lee is a little girl with no fear and an indulgent mother. First she finds a little alligator and brings it home, saying to her mother, "I 'spect I'll keep it for a pet." Her mother objects until Dixie Lee points out it can eat the "churn turners," slimy creatures that steal buttermilk from the churn. Next Dixie Lee, who dashes around in overalls with a slingshot in her pocket, finds a snake that can scare off the bogeyman and a little owl that can keep the mist sisters from floating down the chimney. Skillful watercolors create a mischievous Dixie Lee and the scary creatures that haunt her house.

Vigna, Judith. *Boot Weather*. 1989. Hard: Albert Whitman. Ages 2–5.

Snow means boot weather to Kim, and off she goes on adventures. Her real pastimes, playing in the snow and on playground equipment, are echoed by imaginary escapades. When she climbs up a slide she pictures herself mountain climbing. Zooming down the slide, she sees herself sledding down a steep mountain. She imagines herself as an astronaut, a hockey player, a construction worker, and an explorer. She gets shot from a cannon and takes off with Santa in his sleigh. A brief text and appealing watercolor pictures convey her morning of fun.

Waber, Bernard. *Gina*. 1995. Hard: Houghton. Ages 3–7.

Gina, who loves sports, has a problem. She has moved into a new apartment building that has no girls near her age, but dozens and dozens of boys. At first they ignore her, and she must content herself with playing with her cat, drawing pictures, and reading sports books. But one day she demonstrates her baseball skills, and suddenly she has lots of friends. Although much happier, she still misses her female friends from the old neighborhood and keeps hoping for girls to move into the building. Waber's lively comic pictures are far stronger than the stilted rhyming text, and the final scene where Gina dons a dress is a bit disconcerting. Still, she is an unusually athletic girl for any children's book, and likeable, too.

Walsh, Ellen Stoll. *Hop Jump*. 1993. Hard: Harcourt. Pbk: Harcourt. Ages 2–5.

In this superb book, a frog named Betsy prefers to try something new while all the other frogs spend their time hopping and jumping. She imitates leaves she sees falling and soon she is leaping and turning and twisting—and dancing. Remarkable cut-paper collages in greens and blues capture Betsy's movements and her excitement. While at first the other frogs disdain anything new, they become so intrigued that they try dancing, too. The expansive pictures turn into a celebration of movement that practically flies off the page. Don't miss this one.

Westcott, Nadine Bernard, adapter. *The Lady with the Alligator Purse*. 1988. Hard: Little, Brown. Pbk: Little, Brown. Ages 2–7.

This adaptation of a familiar jump-rope rhyme jumps with joy. The whimsical pictures are perfect for the upbeat text about a lady with an alligator purse who cures Tiny Tim after he eats up all the soap. Her remedy, in contrast to the medicines recommended by the (male) doctor and (female) nurse, is—to the pleasure of the children listening—pizza! A perfect ending to the short rhyme shows the lady, her alligator purse, and a healthy Tiny Tim sliding merrily down the banister. Here is a woman who knows how to have fun in a way children appreciate.

Wiesner, David. *June 29, 1999*. 1992. Hard: Clarion. Ages 4–8.

The slight plot of this book is a vehicle for its ingenious illustrations. Holly Evans, a very capable girl, is conducting a science experiment for school, studying the effects of sending vegetable seedlings into space. She appears first at home launching her experiment, with a picture of Einstein on her bulletin board and the periodic table of elements on the wall behind her. She is sending seedlings on cardboard trays out the window, borne aloft by small helium balloons. Soon giant vegetables appear in the sky throughout the country. In one wonderful picture, people rein in giant red peppers. A gigantic broccoli plant appears in Holly's yard, and she builds a treehouse in it. She is shown clipping newspaper articles about the vegetables and keeping a chart of where they've appeared. She is baffled because some of the vegetables are not the same ones she sent into space, but a true scientist to the end, she is "more curious than disappointed." A final picture of some equally puzzled space aliens solves the mystery for the reader.

Williams, Linda. *The Little Old Lady Who Was Not Afraid of Anything*. Illustrated by Megan Lloyd. 1986. Hard: Harper. Pbk: Harper Trophy. Ages 3–7.

A plucky old woman goes out to gather herbs and nuts in the forest one day. On her way home in the dark, she finds herself followed by a pair of shoes that go "CLOMP, CLOMP," which are joined by a pair of pants that go "WIGGLE, WIGGLE" and so on. She starts running only when a scary pumpkin head yells, "BOO, BOO!" Safe in her house, she plucks up her courage to answer the door, and unafraid, gives the collection of items a piece of advice. Next morning in her garden stands a scarecrow made up of all the scary items. A cumulative tale popular with children.

Williams, Vera B. *Music, Music for Everyone.* **1984. Hard: Greenwillow. Pbk: Mulberry. Ages 3–8.**

Glowing colors fill this book about a girl and her friends who form a band. Rosa, who tells the story, wants to help earn money now that her grandmother is sick. Remembering that her other grandmother used to play music at parties and weddings for pay, Rosa forms the Oak Street Band with three friends. Rosa plays the accordion, Leora the drums, Jenny the fiddle, and Mae the flute. The four girls, encouraged by relatives, practice together and successfully perform at their first paid job. Williams's beautiful watercolors show a multicultural group of four girls in a working-class environment, banding together for fun and profit. One of the few children's books featuring an all-girl band, this is a gem. Other beautifully illustrated books about Rosa include *A Chair for My Mother* and *Something Special for Me*.

Williams, Vera B. *Three Days on a River in a Red Canoe.* **1981. Hard: Greenwillow. Pbk: Mulberry. Ages 3–7.**

In this original work, the narrator, her brother, her mother, and her aunt take a three-day canoe trip together. To plan it, the mother and aunt happily pore over maps of canoe trips they took before the children were born. The four camp at night, and the narrator learns about camping as well as canoeing. Her new knowledge appears in illustrations of how to tie half hitches and put up a tent. The story, which feels like a scrapbook about the trip, also includes maps, recipes, and labeled drawings of the fish they see. Fun to read and look at, this outstanding book about females outdoors will have the reader longing to take a canoe trip.

Wilsdorf, Anne. *Philomene.* **1992. Hard: Greenwillow. Ages 3–6.**

The fun starts on the endpapers, which show young Philomene hamming it up in different poses. She is dressed in a sailor dress and a big straw hat with a blue ribbon, but she is also wearing red high-top sneakers. Swinging a bright red purse, she ventures into the forest one day to prove that no witch lives there. In disbelief, Philomene sees a purple-clad witch riding a huge monster swoop down on her. After the witch carries her back to a castle and puts her to work, Philomene joins forces with the monster to outsmart the witch. Cartoonlike illustrations present the lighthearted battle between good and evil, in which evil gets turned into a frog.

Yee, Paul. *Roses Sing on New Snow: A Delicious Tale.* **Illustrated by Harvey Chan. 1992. Hard: Macmillan. Ages 5–8.**

Maylin cooks in her father's restaurant in Chinatown but gets no credit for her hard work and talent, since her father tells everyone that his two sons do the cooking. When the governor of South China visits, Maylin creates a delicious dish she names Roses Sing on New Snow. The governor loves it so much he wants the two sons to teach his cook the recipe, but of course they fail. When Maylin's father confesses that Maylin invented it, the guests are "astounded to hear that a woman had cooked this dish." Maylin shows herself the equal of the governor and gains fame throughout Chinatown. Witty watercolors add detail to the setting and characters in this charming tale.

Yolen, Jane. *Owl Moon.* **Illustrated by John Schoenherr. 1987. Hard: Philomel. Ages 4–8.**

This exquisite book, which won the Caldecott Medal for

its pictures, is about a girl who goes out owling at night with her father for the first time. It is winter and the child (who is identified as a girl in the jacket copy but not the text) is bundled up against the cold. She doesn't complain about the weather because her older brothers have warned her that you have to keep quiet "and make your own heat" and be brave. The persistence of child and father is finally rewarded by the sight of a great horned owl, beautifully depicted in watercolors. What a magical experience for a young girl, to be out on an adventure on a winter night—and this book fully conveys the magic.

Young, Ed. *Seven Blind Mice*. 1992. Hard: Philomel. Ages 3–7.

While this Caldecott Honor Book is most notable for its exquisite design and artwork, it also features a female mouse who solves a problem six male mice couldn't. Each of the seven mice sets off on a different day to figure out what the new Something is that has appeared by their pond. Each mouse misinterprets the part of the Something he touches. The first one, for example, feels the animal's leg and reports that it's a pillar. Readers will figure out that the Something is an elephant, as the girl mouse does when she sets off last and explores the whole animal instead of just one part. A remarkably beautiful and cunningly wrought book.

2

Folktales

Fairy tales with passive female characters like Cinderella and Sleeping Beauty have become metaphors for women who believe that a Prince Charming will enter their lives and make everything perfect. Parents who want to send a different message will find the books described in this chapter invaluable. The heroines in these tales offer a welcome alternative to Disney's insipid, glamorous fairy-tale females. Even in these books, the girls and women tend toward the beautiful, but they also take the lead and have adventures, instead of waiting to be rescued.

In addition to folktales, this chapter includes fairy tales and parodies. Folktales come from an oral tradition in which they are passed down through time, changed by tellers along the way. There is no specific author for such tales, although collectors and retellers attach their names to published versions. Technically speaking, fairy tales are stories that resemble folktales but are written by an identified author who draws from traditional folklore for structure, style, and content. Katherine Paterson's *The King's Equal*, which falls into this category, is an original story that sounds like a traditional tale. In recent years, a number of books have parodied well-known folktales using a type of broad humor that appeals to many children. *Ruby* and *Cinder Edna*, for example, are light-hearted spoofs of "Little Red Riding Hood" and "Cinderella."

These books are for a wide range of ages; again, the age range given indicates listening level, not reading level. Many of the folktales work well for reading aloud because of their exciting plots and honed language. Many are beautifully illustrated, too. Most can also be read alone by good independent readers, although the vocabulary tends to be too difficult for beginning readers.

The first section of this chapter contains illustrated versions of single tales, which resemble the picture-story books in the previous chapter. Most are thirty-two pages and can be read in one sitting. The next section includes collections of folktales, books with fifteen or more stories gathered together. These longer volumes present a valuable contrast to traditional collections of folktales in which men and boys play the leading roles.

Single Tales

Aardema, Verna. *Borreguita and the Coyote: A Tale from Ayutla, Mexico.* Illustrated by Petra Mathers. 1991. Hard: Knopf. Ages 3–8.

A little female lamb named Borreguita outwits a hungry coyote again and again in this Mexican folktale. Illustrations in vivid hues show an innocent, curly-haired white lamb staring guilelessly at the evil-eyed coyote as she talks him out of eating her. First she advises waiting until she is fatter, then fools him again with two other schemes. In the last trick, Borreguita combines cleverness and physical force in a feat that sends the coyote slinking away for good. Borreguita is young and female, and very clever indeed. Outstanding illustrations and a satisfying plot.

Aardema, Verna. *Rabbit Makes a Monkey of Lion: A Swahili Tale.* Illustrated by Jerry Pinkney. 1989. Hard: Dial. Ages 3–8.

Twice Rabbit steals honey from Lion's supply, and twice she tricks him—"makes a monkey of him"—and gets away. The second time her companion is Turtle, who escapes by tricking Lion into putting her into a pond. Thus, two smaller females triumph over a fierce male lion. The third time she considers stealing, Rabbit decides that judgment is the better part of valor and stays home. Lush pencil and watercolor illustrations in yellows, greens, and browns add humor and beauty. The rhythmic storytelling makes this Swahili tale perfect for reading aloud.

Barry, David, adapter. *The Rajah's Rice: A Mathematical Folktale from India*. Illustrated by Donna Perrone. 1994. Hard: Scientific American Books for Young Readers. Ages 5–8.

A girl named Chandra is at the center of this retelling of a folktale set in India, illustrated with warm, textured pictures. Chandra loves elephants, so she enjoys her job of bathing the Rajah's elephants. She also loves numbers, and everywhere she goes, she counts things. One day while counting the bags of rice that the Rajah collects as rent from hardworking villagers, she gets angry at his greed. She has a chance to remedy the unfair situation when she cures the Rajah's elephants of an illness and he offers her any reward. Cleverly, Chandra asks for rice to be placed on a chessboard: two on the first square, four on the next, eight on the next, and so on, doubling each previous square. To everyone's surprise, the amount of rice is so large that it depletes the Rajah's supply by the fifth row of the chessboard. A diagram on the last page explains this principle of "powers of two," showing a chessboard with symbols on it. When the Rajah realizes he cannot keep his promise, Chandra asks him instead to give the villagers the land and take only the rice he needs. A heroine, she has used her superior math skills to outwit the male ruler and help her people.

Blia Xiong. Adapted by Cathy Spagnoli. *Nine-in-One, Grr! Grr!* Illustrated by Nancy Hom. 1989. Hard: Children's Book Press. Ages 2–6.

In this entertaining Hmong tale from Laos, a tiger goes to a male god and asks how many cubs she will have. Rather carelessly, the god replies, "Nine each year," but tells the tiger that she must remember that number for the prophecy to happen. So the tiger makes up a rhyme and recites it: "Nine-in-one, Grr! Grr!" She is overheard by the clever Eu bird, another female, who asks the tiger what her rhyme means. The answer dismays the bird, who realizes the island will soon be overrun with dangerous tigers. So the bird distracts the tiger, who forgets her rhyme. The bird teaches it back to her as "One-in-nine, Grr! Grr!" thus saving the island's animals from being crowded out by tigers. Colorful silk-screened artwork that draws from Hmong stitchery enhances the tale.

Bull, Emma. *The Princess and the Lord of Night*. Illustrated by Susan Gaber. 1994. Hard: Harcourt. Ages 5–8.

The eye-catching jacket of this original fairy tale shows a girl resolutely riding a galloping horse. She is a princess who lives under an unusual curse: She must get everything she wants or her parents' kingdom will be destroyed. On her thirteenth birthday, the princess decides to take her fate into her own hands and sets off on a journey with some of her magical possessions. She gives one after another of these to people in need, and in exchange for her magic cloak, a man gives her a magic ring. With the ring she bravely defeats the Lord of the Night, the one who originally cursed her. By the end she has obtained what she wanted most through her own initiative. Lovely watercolors and an elegant design add to this story about a strong princess.

Carey, Valerie Scho. *Tsugele's Broom*. Illustrated by Dirk Zimmer. 1993. Hard: Harper. Ages 4–8.

Tsugele is a hardworking girl who lives with her parents in the village of Potsk. When her loving parents want her to marry, she declares that she will not marry until she finds a man as reliable as her broom. Her parents ignore her and arrange for two different suitors to visit, but one turns out lazy and vain, and the other, just plain lazy. So Tsugele decides to go out into the world. She gets a job she enjoys as a housekeeper, but the kind couple she works for also want her to get married. As luck would have it, she manages to keep her original vow to marry someone as reliable as her broom when her broom comes to life as a hardworking man. The bright illustrations, with their folk-art quality, perfectly capture the nature of this funny, warm tale.

Cohen, Caron Lee, reteller. *Sally Ann Thunder Ann Whirlwind Crockett*. Illustrated by Ariane Dewey. 1985. Hard: Greenwillow. Pbk: Mulberry. Ages 4–8.

Colorful language describes the tall-tale heroine and her exploits in a text suited to those readers ready for easy chapter books. A wild-maned Sally Ann, wearing a live snake for a belt, skins bears, outruns foxes, and jumps over the Grand Canyon with her eyes shut. Simple, bright pictures show her fighting off wolves, mountain lions, and eagles. The bulk of the short book centers around Sally Ann's encounter with the braggart Mike Fink, who bets her husband Davy Crockett that he can "scare her teeth loose." Fink dresses up as an alligator, but he doesn't scare Sally Ann a bit; he just makes her furious. This is one tough woman.

de Paola, Tomie. *Fin M'Coul: The Giant of Knockmany Hill*. 1981. Hard: Holiday. Pbk: Holiday. Ages 3–7.

In de Paola's cheerful illustrations, the giant Fin M'Coul, his lovely great wife, Oonagh, and the enemy Cucullin barely fit on the pages, they are so huge. Red-haired, freckled Fin learns how smart his wife is when Cucullin comes looking to fight Fin and Oonagh fools him. First she has Fin dress up as a baby and climb into the cradle, and she bakes iron pans into loaves of bread. When a bellowing Cucullin arrives, she feeds him the bread, which breaks his teeth. After two more tricks, Cucullin, the fiercest giant around, loses his strength, and Fin is safe. The comical story, the appealing illustrations with their lovely borders, and the giant heroine result in a first-class Irish tale.

Dewey, Ariane. *The Tea Squall*. 1988. Hard: Greenwillow. Pbk: Mulberry. Ages 4–7.

What a gathering when six tall-tale heroines get together for a "tea squall"! Bright colorful pictures show them in frenzied action, one arriving pulled by a wild turkey, another atop an alligator, and a third on a wildcat's back. They swap exaggerations in true tall-tale style: The winter was so cold, for example, that ice cream came out when the cow was milked. The huge feast that Betsey Blizzard serves takes four pages to describe, and not a crumb is left at the end. Simple and fun, this is one of the few books available about tall-tale heroines.

Emberley, Michael. *Ruby*. 1990. Hard: Little, Brown. Pbk: Little, Brown. Ages 5–9.

Ruby is a mouse with a mouth on her that will make many children shriek with laughter and some adults frown with disapproval. Her mother sends her, clothed in a red hood, to walk through Boston to deliver cheese pies to Granny and her neighbor Mrs. Mastiff. She trudges through the crowded city with her head in a book. When a scuzzy-looking reptile confronts her on the way, Ruby tells him, "Buzz off, barf breath." A well-dressed cat rescues the pies from the reptile, then tries to trick Ruby into telling him where Granny lives—an urban twist on the Red Riding Hood story. But Ruby thinks fast and tricks him instead, sending him to a dire fate. The pictures and text are filled with irreverent humor, such as the No Parking sign that reads, "Don't Even Think About It." Smarter than the original Red Riding Hood, Ruby is a wisecracking heroine in this new version of the old story.

Ernst, Lisa Campbell. *Little Red Riding Hood: A New-fangled Prairie Tale.* **1995. Hard: Simon & Schuster. Ages 3–7.**

Another modern Red Riding Hood, this one wears a red sweatshirt with a hood as she zooms around on her bicycle. On the way to deliver muffins to her grandmother, she does get taken in by the nattily dressed wolf, but her sturdy grandmother does not. Looking for an "ancient granny," the wolf finds a female farmer who is ready to crush him "like a bug, if need be." The self-possessed grandmother tames the wolf in an unexpected way, leading to a funny ending. Ernst's deft illustrations extend the clever text in this fresh version.

Forest, Heather. *The Woman Who Flummoxed the Fairies.* **Illustrated by Susan Gaber. 1990. Hard: Harcourt. Ages 3–7.**

Captivating, round little fairies flit through this story, decorating the initial letter on each page, hiding in flowers and flying around in their world. The king of the fairies has discovered an excellent bakerwoman and has his fairies capture her. But the bakerwoman knows that if she bakes him a cake, the king will never let her go home, because her cakes are so good. So she insists the fairies fetch a series of things she needs from her home. Humorous pictures show her husband and baby watching in astonishment as flour and eggs float out the window, followed later by the cat and dog. Knowing how fairies hate noise, she has them bring her baby, too, and the husband follows behind. When they are all gathered in the fairy's home, the bakerwoman provokes the most noise possible from the dog, cat, and baby until the king of the fairies can take no more. He settles for having her bake him a cake at her home, and rewards her generously. The illustrations enhance the magic and humor of this tale about a woman who gets the best of the fairy king.

Garfield, Leon. *The Saracen Maid*. Illustrated by John O'Brien. 1994. Hard: Simon & Schuster. Ages 5–8.

The dust jacket of this original fairy tale shows a young woman climbing down knotted sheets from a window in a Middle Eastern city. Five short chapters, amply illustrated with watercolors, tell the story of a scatterbrained young man named Gilbert who lives "in the year eleven hundred and something or other." When he travels from England to Asia for his father's business, pirates kidnap him and sell him to a rich merchant in Tyre. The merchant hopes to ransom Gilbert, but Gilbert cannot remember his father's name. The merchant's daughter, the Saracen maid, befriends him in his dungeon cell; they fall in love and she helps him escape. She cleverly follows him to London and they are reunited. Thanks to the Saracen maid, who is undeniably brighter and more resolute than her sweetheart, the two live "long and happily" in this lighthearted tale.

Helldorfer, M. C. *The Mapmaker's Daughter*. Illustrated by Jonathan Hunt. 1991. Hard: Bradbury. Ages 5–8.

In this original fairy tale, the mapmaker's daughter Suchen longs to go on an adventure to a land called Turnings. A witch's spell encircles Turnings, and Suchen aspires to break the spell. She gets her chance when the king's son ventures forth and doesn't return, and his father seeks help from the mapmaker. Suchen persuades them to let her try to rescue the prince. She takes three gifts with her from her father, gifts that ultimately help in her quest. Although the rescue itself seems too easy, the book's conclusion avoids the usual romantic clichés. The last of the picturesque illustrations shows Suchen not in a wedding gown but astride a horse, dressed for her next adventure.

Hong, Lily Toy. *The Empress and the Silkworm*. 1995. Hard: Albert Whitman. Ages 4–8.

Charming stylized pictures accompany this legend about Si Ling-Chi, a Chinese empress said to have discovered how to make silk. According to the story, more than four thousand years ago the empress was taking tea when a cocoon fell from a mulberry tree and began to unravel in the heat of the tea. Si Ling-Chi saw its possibilities as thread that could be woven into strong, beautiful cloth. Although the emperor's male advisers laughed at her scheme, the empress proved herself right: After months, workers under Si Ling-Chi's supervision finally produced a magnificent silk robe for the emperor. A note at the end explains the origins of the legend and gives information about the process of making silk.

Hooks, William H. *The Three Little Pigs and the Fox*. Illustrated by S. D. Schindler. 1989. Hard: Macmillan. Ages 5–9.

"This story happened a long time ago, way back when the animals could still talk around these parts," begins this tale from the Great Smoky Mountains. As in the traditional tale, a mother pig sends her three children off into the world, but in this version her third child is a girl pig named Hamlet. Hamlet's older brothers go off, one at a time, and get caught by the "mean, tricky old drooly-mouth fox" to be eaten later. But Hamlet is brighter and braver than her brothers. She wards off the fox and builds herself a strong house. Then she tricks him into telling her where her brothers are and sends him down the river in a churn. Hamlet then sets the brothers free and they all return home happy and hungry. The story's Appalachian language has a rollicking rhythm and flavor, perfect for reading aloud.

Isaacs, Anne. *Swamp Angel*. Illustrated by Paul O. Zelinsky. 1994. Hard: Dutton. Ages 4–9.

Here is a new figure in the tradition of tall tales: Angelica Longrider, known as Swamp Angel. Born in 1914 in Tennessee, "the newborn was scarcely taller than her mother and couldn't climb a tree without help." When she was two, she built her first log cabin, and when she was twelve, she rescued a whole wagon train from a swamp and earned her nickname. In the main adventure, she pursues a giant bear and eventually defeats him after a series of outlandish skirmishes. Zelinsky's witty paintings, done on wood veneer, so beautifully extend the story that the book was named a Caldecott Honor Book. The last we see of the folk heroine, she is dragging the enormous bear pelt behind her on her way to more open territory. *Swamp Angel* is a mighty good addition to the American tall tale.

Jackson, Ellen. *Cinder Edna*. Illustrated by Kevin O'Malley. 1994. Hard: Lothrop. Ages 4–8.

There's nothing subtle in this funny retelling of the Cinderella story. In an updated setting, the mopey Cinderella and the self-reliant Cinder Edna live next door to each other. They both have to work for their wicked stepmothers and stepsisters, but Cinder Edna uses the toil as a chance to master a few tasks. She also makes money on the side working for neighbors. Unlike Cinderella, Edna is no beauty, but "she was strong and spunky and knew some good jokes." When the king announces a ball, Cinderella calls on her fairy godmother, but Cinder Edna wears a dress bought with her extra earnings. The traditional girl goes by pumpkin, Edna by city bus. Although Edna finds the prince dull as can be, his brother Rupert, who runs a recycling plant, is just her type of man. And so, Cinderella ends up with the dull but handsome prince and Edna with an intelligent man who shares her interests and values. The last line: "Guess who lived happily ever after." Boisterous, exaggerated pictures add to the fun.

Keams, Geri. *Grandmother Spider Brings the Sun: A Cherokee Story*. Illustrated by James Bernardin. 1995. Hard: Northland. Ages 4–8.

Children enjoy reading about someone very small who saves the day, such as little Grandmother Spider who succeeds where the bigger, male Possum and Buzzard couldn't. Their task is to fetch some sun from the light side of the world to brighten up the dark side, where the animals live. After Possum and Buzzard fail, the other animals scoff when Grandmother Spider volunteers, even though she has done many things in her time to help them. But she persists and sneaks by the fearsome Sun Guards to deliver the light. Witty illustrations in acrylic and colored pencil develop the personality of each animal, from sly Coyote to feisty little Spider.

Kellogg, Steven. *Sally Ann Thunder Ann Whirlwind Crockett: A Tall Tale*. 1995. Hard: Morrow. Ages 4–9.

In another book about Sally Ann Thunder Ann Whirlwind Crockett, with zanier pictures than Cohen's book on the same subject (listed previously), Sally Ann lives up to her name from the start. Just after birth she proclaims, "I can out-talk, out-grin, out-scream, out-swim, and out-run any baby in Kentucky!" And she proves it on the spot by outrunning her nine older brothers. When she turns eight, she sets off for the frontier and new challenges such as skinning bears and wrestling alligators. Who could she marry but the most famous outdoorsman in the country, Davy Crockett? From beginning to end, the frenzied, funny pictures show Sally Ann beating all opponents and having a good time at it. A good match to the many tall tales about frontiersmen.

Kimmel, Eric A. *The Four Gallant Sisters.* **Illustrated by Tatyana Yuditskaya. 1992. Hard: Holt. Ages 5–9.**

This charming variation on a fairy tale, apparently adapted from the Grimms, features four sisters seeking their fortunes after their mother dies. Each, disguised as a man, apprentices herself to learn a trade: tailoring, hunting, sleight of hand, and stargazing. Each sister excels at her choice and leaves after seven years with a special gift from her master. They go to serve the king, and from there rescue a princess and four princes captured by a dragon. Their special gifts in combination with their courage save the day. Back at the castle, the princes say of their rescuers, "We never had truer friends or more valiant companions," and in the end each sister agrees to marry one of the princes. A remark by the rescued princess denigrating women mars the text, but overall, this is a fairy tale with unusually strong heroines.

Kimmel, Eric A., adapter. *Rimonah of the Flashing Sword: A North African Tale.* **Illustrated by Omar Rayyan. 1995. Hard: Holiday. Ages 5–9.**

Although this North African version of "Snow White" features the usual wicked stepmother, the heroine diverges from the usual story by being strong and fearless. After she escapes from the death ordered by her stepmother the queen, Rimonah joins a group of bedouins. As the years pass, she grows in bravery until she rides "with the reckless daring of a bedouin horseman." Excellent with both dagger and sword, she grows in fame, which eventually brings her to her stepmother's notice. No longer safe with her comrades, Rimonah eventually takes refuge in a cave with forty thieves, honest people who have suffered under the queen. Rimonah rides with the thieves and as the boldest of all becomes known as "Rimonah of the Flashing Sword." Reverting to a passive plotline, Rimonah nearly dies and is only rescued from her glass coffin by the prince of her dreams. However, she then rescues her father and defeats her stepmother. Ornate, fanciful pictures create a setting reminiscent of the Arabian Nights. An unlikely version of a familiar tale with a strong, sword-wielding heroine.

Knutson, Barbara. *How the Guinea Fowl Got Her Spots: A Swahili Tale of Friendship*. 1990. Hard: Carolrhoda. Pbk: Carolrhoda. Ages 3–7.

An unusually attractive design and illustrations of watercolor and ink on scratchboard make this tale a visual treat. The simple story tells of two female friends, Nganga the Guinea Fowl and Cow. Nganga, a glossy black bird at the beginning, saves Cow from an attack by Lion, and the next day, saves her friend again. In thanks, Cow sprinkles milk over Nganga's shiny black feathers and gives the guinea fowl the white speckles it has today. Not only is her coloration beautiful, but it saves her from Lion, who doesn't recognize her. Borders of African designs, large typeface, and lots of white space add to the outstanding visual appeal of this story about two female friends.

Le Guin, Ursula K. *A Ride on the Red Mare's Back*. Illustrated by Julie Downing. 1992. Hard: Orchard. Pbk: Orchard. Ages 5–9.

A brave girl sets off through the wintry woods to try to rescue her brother, who has been stolen by trolls. When she meets her first troll, the wooden toy horse she's brought magically becomes life-sized and helps her with her quest. They gallop through the darkness and snow to the troll's High House, where the brother is a prisoner. While the red mare distracts the trolls, the girl courageously saves her brother. Though the horse turns back into a toy, the girl leads her brother safely on the long journey home. Lovely watercolors, which show some truly ugly trolls, grace this beautifully designed book, making it a pleasure to read and look at. A brave girl aided by a stalwart female animal is an unusual, welcome combination.

Merrill, Jean. *The Girl Who Loved Caterpillars*. Illustrated by Floyd Cooper. 1992. Hard: Philomel. Ages 5–9.

In this twelfth-century tale from Japan, the girl named Izumi becomes known as "The Girl Who Loved Caterpillars." Her aristocratic parents would have preferred that she act more sedate and concentrate on more seemly pastimes, but Izumi is fascinated with creatures that squirm, crawl, or hop. She fills her room with them and befriends scruffy boys who bring her more. She defies other conventions as well, refusing to pluck her eyebrows or blacken her teeth, as the fashionable young ladies do. She takes a lot of criticism, which unfortunately comes mostly from other females. She earns the admiration of a nobleman, but romance holds no appeal for Izumi: She ignores the nobleman to ask a peasant boy for fresh leaves for the caterpillars. No fairy-tale ending for this budding scientist with a mind of her own.

Mills, Lauren. *Tatterhood and the Hobgoblins: A Norwegian Folktale*. 1993. Hard: Little, Brown. Pbk: Little, Brown. Ages 3–8.

This version of Tatterhood, though too wordy, does present a refreshing heroine born from her mother's eating a weed, while her twin sister, Isabella, comes from a flower. Delicate, dreamlike illustrations show her clothed in a patched cape and mounted on her goat, holding a wooden spoon high. When hobgoblins come to the castle and replace Isabella's beautiful head with the head of a calf, Tatterhood sails away with Isabella to retrieve her sister's head. Then they sail on for three years "to many splendid lands" just for the fun of exploring. A shipwreck leads to a final adventure and a romantic ending. The pretty illustrations don't do justice to Tatterhood's strong character, nor do they make the hobgoblins look adequately scary. Although Isabella rarely takes initiative, Tatterhood gets full marks for ingenuity, courage, and self-confidence.

Oughton, Jerrie. *The Magic Weaver of Rugs*: A Tale of the *Navajo*. Illustrated by Lisa Desimini. 1994. Hard: Houghton. Ages 5–8.

When cold and hunger beset their people, two Navajo women go on a quest to seek help. Spider Woman, hearing their pleas, lassos them with a web and lifts them to her high canyon wall. There she teaches them how to weave on a loom she constructs from four large trees. The women, under Spider Woman's directions, weave a rug from all the colors of the world. But they doubt and question her, and consequently weave an imperfect rug. Quick to anger, Spider Woman will not give them the rug but sends them on their way, saying they have the gift they need. Returning to their people, the two women teach them how to weave beautiful rugs, which eventually they trade for food and other necessities. A haunting tale, powerfully illustrated in rich colors, this attributes the origin of Navajo rugs to two brave women and the mythological Spider Woman.

Paterson, Katherine. *The King's Equal.* **Illustrated by Vladimir Vagin. 1992. Hard: Harper. Pbk: Harper Trophy. Ages 5–10.**

In this splendid original fairy tale, an arrogant, selfish prince receives a strange blessing from his dying father: "You will not wear my crown until the day you marry a woman who is your equal in beauty and intelligence and wealth." Since the prince thinks so highly of himself, his ministers cannot come up with a bride he will accept. When a peasant named Rosamund appears, aided by a magic wolf, the prince discovers that she is more than his equal. He must earn her hand in marriage through a year of living in the mountains that she comes from. The brave Rosamund proves to be a much more industrious, successful ruler than the absent prince, who returns a wiser man. Ornate illustrations by a Russian artist add to the fairy-tale quality of this charming book.

Peterson, Julienne, reteller. *Caterina, the Clever Farm Girl: A Tale from Italy.* **Illustrated by Enzo Giannini. 1996. Hard: Dial. Ages 4–8.**

The heroine of this Tuscan folktale is a farmer's daughter named Caterina who has more sense than her father or the king whom she marries. Her father finds a gold mortar and takes it to the king, who, as Caterina predicted, wants a gold pestle to go with it. When the farmer brags that his daughter predicted the king's reaction, the king makes an impossible request of her, to which she gives a witty response. He tries to trick her with a new request, and she tricks him instead. They marry but the king finds her independent thinking threatening. When she questions one of his decisions, he orders her to return to her father—but she tricks him again. From then on they rule together and pass judgment together in the court.

Described as not a great beauty, Caterina relies on her intelligence. Pleasant illustrations draw on the Tuscan countryside and buildings for inspiration.

Roth, Susan L. *Brave Martha and the Dragon*. 1996. Hard: Dial. Ages 3–7.

Roth's distinctive collage art sets the scene in a small village in France. The villagers' troubles begin when first some goats, then some pigs, then some sheep disappear at night. When the mayor keeps watch one night, he sees a wild green and red dragon, depicted in eye-catching cut-paper art. The villagers are debating what to do when a young woman named Martha arrives, barefoot and singing. The baker and his wife offer her shelter, but she climbs through the window at night and chases the dragon. Despite the dragon's attempts to scare her, Martha yells at him, lassos him with her sash, binds him up, and locks him in a dungeon, to the lasting gratitude of the villagers. In the town of Tarascon, they still celebrate Martha's brave deed each year with a special festival.

San Souci, Robert D. *The Samurai's Daughter*. Illustrated by Stephen T. Johnson. 1992. Hard: Dial. Ages 5–10.

Set in medieval Japan, this tale revolves around Tokoyo, the daughter of a samurai warrior. Her father schools Tokoyo, his only child, in the arts of the samurai, such as shooting a bow and riding a horse. He also instills in her the samurai's sense of honor. When she gets older, she dives with the amas, women divers who are better than men at harvesting abalone and oysters. One day, at the command of their lord, soldiers seize her father to imprison him on an island. Tokoyo arms herself with a dagger and follows, disguised as a peasant. After a dangerous journey she reaches the island. There she takes the place of a young woman about to be sacrificed to a sea serpent and succeeds in killing the serpent and by chance also freeing her father from exile. Powerful paintings show her diving with the dagger in her teeth and attacking the huge white monster. A tale of courage and strength, not to be missed.

San Souci, Robert D. *Young Guinevere.* **Illustrated by Jamichael Henterly. 1993. Hard: Doubleday. Ages 6–10.**

Young girls fascinated by the Arthurian legends will find little in them about brave women. This is an attempt, not completely successful, to flesh out the character of Guinevere, based very loosely on folklore and literature. It mainly concerns a dangerous ride she takes to enlist King Arthur's help when her father's kingdom is under attack. On the ride, accompanied by a wolf, she must kill a fierce monster before she can cross the Perilous River. She succeeds and wins the heart of her future husband. A thin plot, accompanied by paintings in which Guinevere never looks less than beautiful—but this tale does serve to fill a literary vacuum.

Schields, Gretchen. *The Water Shell.* **1995. Hard: Harcourt. Ages 5–8.**

Drawing on elements from Polynesian folklore, this original tale opens on an island paradise, Kua-i-Helani, a place of unchanging perfection. The Water Shell, a magic egg deep in the ocean, protects the island from the darkness and danger that surround it. But the fierce Fire Queen sends soldiers to get the egg and ruin Kua-i-Helani. In the chaos that follows, the girl Keiki learns she must save her people and land. With help from a male shark, a female spider, and three women warriors,

Keiki confronts the Fire Queen and wrests the Water Shell from her. When Keiki releases the magic in the egg to re-create her land, she realizes the future will hold change and she herself changes into a young woman. Elaborate water-colors, brimming with flora and fauna, will appeal to those who like their art ornate. The writing is similarly ornate, full of details from mythology explained in the author's note. Although not for everyone, this story does have mainly female characters, good and bad.

Shepard, Aaron. *Savitri: A Tale of Ancient India*. Illus-trated by Vera Rosenberry. 1992. Hard: Albert Whitman. Ages 5–8.

This legend drawn from the *Mahabharata*, a classical San-skrit epic of India, tells of the princess Savitri. Beautiful and intelligent, Savitri intimidates the local men, so she leaves home to find a husband worthy of her. But the man she chooses, Prince Satyavan, has only one year to live, according to a prediction. Firm in her love, Savitri marries him anyway. When Yama, the god of death, comes to take the sleeping Satyavan, Savitri follows them. Yama is impressed with her courage and endurance, and grants her three favors, anything but Satyavan's life. On the third favor, Savitri tricks Yama and the god returns her husband to her. Delicately colored illustra-tions decorate this tale.

Singer, Marilyn. *The Painted Fan*. Illustrated by Wenhai Ma. 1994. Hard: Morrow. Ages 5–9.

When the cruel Lord Shang, ruler of the Land of the Seven Caves, learns from a soothsayer that the only thing he has to fear is a painted fan, he orders all fans burned. Years later he falls in love with a brave farmer's daughter named Bright Willow and takes her to his palace. But unknown to him, she packs her only valuable possession, a painted fan. When the lord finds out she has fallen in love with one of his servants, he threatens to kill the servant unless Bright Willow brings him a great pearl guarded by a demon. Armed with her courage and the fan, Bright Willow defeats the demon and then uses the demon to defeat the cruel lord. Having ended the suffering of her people, Bright Willow weds the man she saved, and they are happiest of all. Lovely, expansive water-colors complement this romantic story about a brave woman who causes the downfall of a tyrant.

Stamm, Claus. *Three Strong Women: A Tall Tale from Japan.* **Illustrated by Jean and Mou-sien Tseng. 1990. Hard: Viking. Pbk: Puffin. Ages 4–9.**
Walking on a country road one day, a famous wrestler called Forever Mountain sees a round young woman, Maru-me, and cannot resist tickling her. Although she giggles in response, she also clamps down on his hand and to his shock he cannot get free. She pulls him along the road and announces she will take him home to make a truly strong man out of him. At her family farm they see her mother, who is carrying a cow, and her little old grandmother, who easily pulls up a tree that's in her way. The mother and grand-mother agree that Forever Mountain appears to be quite feeble, but they will help train him for an important wres-tling match in three months. They start him out wrestling with the grandmother, who is least likely to injure him acci-dentally. When he can finally hold her down for thirty sec-onds, although he still cannot defeat the other two women, he is ready to go wrestle before the emperor. The appealing dust jacket shows a huge wrestler held up effortlessly in the air by the three women, conveying the spirit of this terrific tall tale.

Stewig, John Warren. *Princess Florecita and the Iron Shoes: A Spanish Fairy Tale.* Illustrated by K. Wendy Popp. 1995. Hard: Knopf. Pbk: Knopf. Ages 5–9.

Here is a reversal of the Sleeping Beauty story, one in which a princess wakes a sleeping prince. Princess Florecita hears from a bird about an enchanted prince who can only be rescued by a maiden who wears out a pair of iron shoes. Determined to undertake this quest, Florecita has a pair of iron shoes made and sets out one night on her adventure. She braves a dark forest, scorching sun, soaking rain, and bitter cold on her journey. Her feet ache badly, but she pushes on and walks so far that one day she has worn the iron shoes clear through. She enters the castle of the prince and awakens him. They agree to marry and return to her parents, who had feared Florecita dead. Although the wedding guests admire Florecita's determination, they also comment on her beauty and selflessness rather than her bravery and strength. The illustrations also emphasize her beauty and romanticize the story. However, Florecita is still tougher than most of the females in fairy tales are.

Uchida, Yoshiko, reteller. *The Wise Old Woman.* Illustrated by Martin Springett. 1994. Hard: McElderry. Ages 4–8.

When a cruel young lord in this Japanese folktale decides that all the old people of his village must be taken to the mountainside to die, one old woman hides in a secret room instead. A local warlord threatens to conquer the village unless the young lord can perform three impossible tasks. The lord presents the challenge to all the wise men of the village, to no avail. The wise old woman, who learns of the challenge from her son, is able after careful thought to complete the three tasks and save the village. Her deed convinces the young lord that he has made a mistake about old people. The woman gets three bags of gold, and she and her son prosper "all the days of their lives." The airbrush and ink illustrations, which resemble Japanese woodcuts, are richly colored and dramatic.

Wisniewski, David. *Elfwyn's Saga*. 1990. Hard: Lothrop. Ages 5–8.

Wisniewski's amazing cut-paper illustrations, full of intricate details, are the highlight of this original tale. The story, based on Icelandic lore, tells of the girl Elfwyn, who is beloved by the Hidden Folk, the fairies. Although she is born blind due to a curse on her family, the Hidden Folk guide her so that she can run and ride horses at full speed without danger. When an enemy gives her people a magic crystal that makes them neglect their work and grow dissatisfied with their lives, only Elfwyn is immune to its powers. So she removes the crystal with the help of her horse and splinters it into the many pieces that now make up the Northern Lights. As a result, Elfwyn gains great honor among her people and is called Elfwyn the Second-Sighted.

Wisniewski, David. *The Wave of the Sea-Wolf*. 1994. Hard: Clarion. Ages 4–8.

In another book with remarkable cut-paper illustrations, Wisniewski draws from the motifs of Pacific Northwest native peoples to create this original tale. Tlingit princess Kchokeen resolves to see Gonakadet, the Sea-Wolf, because anyone who sees him receives wealth and honor. Disobeying her mother's warning not to go near the mouth of the bay, Kchokeen falls into the hollow trunk of a great tree. While her friends are going for help, a great sea-wave lifts her out and she sees the marvelous vision of Gonakadet, which no girl had ever seen before. As a result of her vision, Kchokeen can predict the coming of destructive waves and advise fishermen when the water will be safe. Thanks to her, her village prospers. When a French ship threatens the village, Kchokeen saves her people by leading a party of warriors in a war canoe and luring the French ship into a fatal sea-wave. The distinctive illustrations convey the power of the sea-wave and the expansive beauty of the Northwest. Well worth seeking out.

Yep, Laurence, reteller. *The Shell Woman and the King: A Chinese Folktale*. Illustrated by Yang Ming-Yi. 1993. Hard: Dial. Ages 4–8.

Delicate, beautifully colored paintings illustrate this adaptation of an eighteenth-century Chinese tale in which a good man named Uncle Wu marries Shell, a woman who comes from the sea. When he brags that she can change herself into a shell, the greedy king hears of it and wants Shell for himself. She refuses but agrees to fetch the king three wonders to keep him from killing Uncle Wu. She brings him the hair of a toad and the arm from a ghost, but when the king wants "luck by the bushel," Shell turns the tables on him and saves her husband. In the last scene, she leaps on the back of a large magic dog, holds out her hand to her husband to help him up, and they ride away to freedom.

Yolen, Jane. *The Emperor and the Kite*. Illustrated by Ed Young. 1988. Hard: Philomel. Pbk: Philomel. Ages 4–8.

Exquisite illustrations, made to resemble Chinese cut-paper art, extend this story of a young girl who rescues her father, the emperor. Tiny Djeow Seow, as the youngest of the emperor's eight children, has long been ignored and learns to entertain herself flying her kite. One day, sitting unnoticed, she sees villains steal her father away and hide him in a tower. While her siblings weep and sigh, Djeow cleverly uses her kite to supply her father with food and comes up with a way to save him. In return, she gets the attention and love she has longed for, sits by his side while he rules, and succeeds him as ruler. A delightful story about someone small who accomplishes something big. A Caldecott Honor Book.

Yolen, Jane. *Tam Lin.* **Illustrated by Charles Mikolaycak. 1990. Hard: Harcourt. Ages 7–10.**

Accompanied by graceful, romantic illustrations, this story based on an old ballad tells of Jennet MacKenzie, who saved a man from death. Jennet, a headstrong girl known for saying what she thinks, is determined to reclaim the castle that belonged to her ancestors. Ignoring her parents' protest, she sets off to the castle on her sixteenth birthday. There she encounters Tam Lin, a young man from the past who is to be sacrificed that night by the fairies unless someone is caring enough and strong enough to save him. Although it means wrestling with dangerous beasts, Jennet succeeds. Here is a tale in which a female does the rescuing and the fighting. It is she, not the man she saves and marries, who later restores the castle for their descendants. She is a true heroine, depicted as more resolute than beautiful.

Young, Ed. *Lon Po Po: A Red-Riding Hood Story from China.* **1989. Hard: Philomel. Ages 4–8.**

Watercolor and pastel illustrations arranged in panels that echo Chinese art create an atmosphere of drama in this version of the Red Riding Hood story. A mother leaves her three children home, warning them not to let anyone in, but the

younger children let in a wolf who claims to be their grandmother. Fortunately the eldest and cleverest child, a girl
named Shang, sees through the disguise. She outwits the wolf
by luring him up a tree to eat gingko nuts and dropping him in
a basket to the ground, where his heart breaks to pieces. A
Caldecott Medal winner for its striking, powerful pictures.

Collections

Bruchac, Joseph, and Gayle Ross. *The Girl Who Married the Moon: Tales from Native North America.* **1994. Hard: BridgeWater. Pbk: Troll. Ages 7–11.**

Of these sixteen stories about Native American women, only five of them feature truly strong heroines. In most of the others, the central character is female but not notably brave or intelligent. The tales, which come from a number of tribes, are organized geographically into four regions. In the Northeast, "Arrowhead Finger" and "The Girl Who Escaped" both have strong female leads who are captured by enemies but escape unharmed. In a tale from the Southeast, "The Girl Who Helped Thunder," the protagonist is a skillful hunter who gets great power from the old man Thunder, then uses the power to save her people. The Cherokee story "Stonecoat" stands out as the most unusual tale. In it, seven women who are menstruating sap the energy from an evil monster because they represent the power to bring new life, which is stronger than the power to destroy. A legend from the Cheyenne, "Where the Girl Rescued Her Brother," is based on an actual battle between the Cheyenne and the American army, during which a woman galloped into the action to save her brother from death. A collection with too few strong heroines, but a step in the right direction.

Hamilton, Virginia. *Her Stories: African American Folktales, Fairy Tales, and True Tales.* **Illustrated by Leo and Diane Dillon. 1995. Hard: Scholastic/Blue Sky. Ages 8–14.**

This beautifully made book combines elegant design with

outstanding illustrations. The carefully chosen details—dust jacket, quality paper, graceful typeface—make it a pleasure just to hold. Hamilton also does a masterful job at retelling the folktales and legends she has brought together, all of which feature African-American women. Her intent, however, is not to concentrate on strong heroines, so only a few of the stories provide role models. Of those that do, the lighthearted "Malindy and Little Devil" offers a sassy, happy girl who sells her soul to the devil but tricks him when he comes to collect it. In another, "Woman and Man Started Even," the first man tries to get the upper hand by appealing to God, but the first woman outsmarts him. The legend of Annie Christmas describes her as the biggest woman in the state of Louisiana, a keelboat operator on the Mississippi who could outfight any other boatman. Some powerful characters in other stories are evil, such as the her-vampire and the bog hag. Still other tales are about more ordinary women who deal with mistakes, jealousy, and sometimes, magic. This is a groundbreaking collection, the first book to gather together stories about African-American girls and women.

Lansky, Bruce, editor. *Girls to the Rescue: Tales of Clever, Courageous Girls from Around the World*. 1995. Pbk: Meadowbrook. Ages 5–10.

To offset the many fairy tales about helpless maidens, this collection of ten stories focuses on fairy-tale heroines. Five are adaptations of traditional tales, the other five original stories. Perhaps the most unusual is "Savannah's Piglets," about a black pioneer girl who manages a farm on her own, relying on her many outdoor skills, when her father leaves. "The Royal Joust" features a girl who competes in a jousting tournament disguised as her brother. The few princes who appear are either pleasant but ineffectual, or more selfish than attractive. The girls use their wits and sometimes their physical strength to gain what they want. Although fairy tales written today don't have the timeworn smoothness of traditional tales, these provide a useful alternative to most of the folklore children hear. *Girls to the Rescue, Book #2* contains ten more stories about courageous girls.

Lurie, Alison, reteller. *Clever Gretchen and Other Forgotten Folktales*. Illustrated by Margot Tomes. 1980. Hard: Crowell. Ages 5–12.

A number of books have gathered together folktales about strong female protagonists from around the world. There is a lot of overlap among the books, although each contains some tales the others do not. Lurie's collection of fifteen tales focuses on European tales more than the others do. It is the most accessible to younger readers, and has the most appealing illustrations. In these polished retellings, the girls face ordeals, rescue friends and loved ones, solve problems, and fight battles. There's Mollie Whuppie, who fools a giant three times; the Maid Maleen, who escapes from a doorless, windowless tower; and Mizilca, who fights for the sultan disguised as a man. In a few, females other than the heroine are nasty creatures, and in many the final reward is marriage, but they are all a welcome change from "Cinderella" and "Sleeping Beauty." Margot Tomes' apt drawings depict ordinary-looking girls undertaking extraordinary tasks.

Minard, Rosemary. *Womenfolk and Fairy Tales*. Illustrated by Suzanna Klein. 1975. Hard: Houghton. Ages 5–12.

As one of the earlier collections of folktales about heroines, this has more stories of female strength than most among its twenty-two tales. The succinct retellings read aloud well and many are accompanied by a stylized black-and-white drawing. They come from places all over the world, including Japan, China, Persia, and Africa, although information about the origin of each story is scant. The heroines are ordinary people and princesses who draw on their own wits and courage. Many marry at the end of the stories, but always to men who respect them. A solid group of stories that break fairy-tale stereotypes.

Phelps, Ethel Johnston. *Tatterhood and Other Tales*. Illustrated by Pamela Baldwin Ford. 1978. Hard: Feminist Press. Pbk: Feminist Press. Ages 6–13.

"Tatterhood," the first story in this collection of twenty-five tales, is outstanding. Wild Tatterhood loves adventures and doesn't care what others think of her. "She was strong, raucous, and careless, and was always racing about on her goat." When a troll puts a calf's head on her twin sister, Tatterhood sails off with her sister to remedy it. She succeeds and also finds a man who admires her insistence on making her own choices. Another particularly good tale is "Kupti and Imani," in which a king's daughter insists she can make her own fortune and builds up a business until she is as rich as her father. This is an impressive collection with well-chosen stories, a thoughtful introduction, and useful endnotes.

Phelps, Ethel Johnston. *The Maid of the North: Feminist Folk Tales from Around the World*. Illustrated by Lloyd Bloom. 1981. Hard: Holt. Pbk: Holt/Owl. Ages 6–13.

This second collection by Ethel Johnston Phelps offers twenty-one tales with female heroes, including three told by Native American peoples. It is a nicely designed volume, although its small typeface makes it less accessible to young readers than other collections. Familiar tales include "East of the Sun, West of the Moon" and "The Husband Who Stayed at Home," but many of the others will be new to readers. In one particularly good story from West Pakistan, "The Tiger and the Jackal," a farmer's wife disguises herself as a man and frightens away a fierce tiger who had thoroughly scared her husband. "The Twelve Huntsman," a German tale, features twelve young women disguised as men. Their disguises fool a king, who observes, "They handle their bows as well as any huntsmen." Their leader, Katrine, uses logic to get the king to keep his promise to her. Dramatic black-and-white illustrations are scattered throughout the book.

San Souci, Robert D. *Cut from the Same Cloth: American Women of Myth, Legend, and Tall Tale*. Illustrated by Brian Pinkney. 1993. Hard: Philomel. Ages 8–14.

American legends and tall tales about men are easy to find, but those about women are scarce. This collection introduces fifteen hardy, strong-minded women from American folklore. Grouped according to geographical region, the stories include a range of ethnic groups. Some of the tales revolve around exciting adventures, while others offer a mishmash of details without a plot. The vigorous black-and-white scratchboard illustrations have an appropriate folkloric feel. Well documented, this volume is a good start toward filling a gap in children's books about American folklore.

Waldherr, Kris. *The Book of Goddesses*. 1995. Hard: Beyond Words Publishing. Ages 7–14.

Most well-known myths center around gods rather than goddesses, so this volume about twenty-six goddesses from many different cultures offers new material. For each deity, there is a bordered page of uninspired text about her role in the culture, usually including an abbreviated tale. On the opposite page, another border surrounds a portrait of the goddess, clad in a flowing dress in most cases. The highly romantic artwork that dominates the book emphasizes the dreamlike beauty of the goddesses, with little sense of their power or strength. Some attempt has been made to use appropriate clothing and other culture-specific details, although it does seem odd that the Greek goddesses are blond. Mythology continues to be popular with children, who will find the familiar figures of Athena, Diana, and Juno along with many lesser-known goddesses from around the world.

3

Books for Beginning Readers

These books for children who are beginning to read independently (typically ages six to eight) are divided into three categories. The first is Easy Readers, specifically geared toward the early stages of reading. These books use a controlled vocabulary with many words that children can sound out. They also feature illustrations that closely follow the story, providing clues to words the reader doesn't know. Many of these are also suitable for reading aloud to children who do not read yet, which is reflected in the age guidelines.

The second category, Short Novels, offers fare for children ready to try chapter books, but who need guidance in finding stories at an accessible level. Educators call these shorter novels "transitional" books, moving children from the first stages of reading to longer novels. They tend to have large print, an open design, and frequent illustrations. It can be difficult to find transitional books; most children's novels are geared toward slightly more advanced readers who are comfortable with longer books, smaller print, and no pictures. For the children at the upper end of this reading stage, check chapter 4, "Books for Middle Readers," which lists other possibilities for this group.

The final category is Biographies. Most of these books also have large print and lots of pictures. They cover a wide spectrum of women and a few girls: rulers, pirates, scientists, artists, and more. Some are famous, others are little-known historical figures.

Don't limit your choices to this chapter alone. All children at this stage should also be listening to books read aloud, including picture-story books and folktales, most of which are still too difficult for them to read alone. Also check "Books for Middle Readers" for longer books to read aloud, such as the fantasy books about animals, popular with all ages.

Easy Readers

Bang, Molly Garrett. *Tye May and the Magic Brush.* **1981. Hard: Greenwillow, o.p. Pbk: Mulberry. Ages 4–8.**

Orphaned Tye May wants to learn to paint when she sees a man teaching male pupils. When she asks for a brush, the teacher scoffs at the idea of a beggar girl painting. "But Tye May had an iron will." She uses sticks and reeds to develop her skills, and one night in a dream a woman brings her a magic brush. When Tye May paints with it, whatever she draws comes to life, so she kindly creates tools for the poor. But a wicked landlord locks her up to make her paint what he wants. She escapes and tricks her strong male pursuers by drawing a net to capture them. Next she outwits the greedy emperor with her art. This adaptation of a Chinese folktale is illustrated in black and white, with touches of red, in a style reminiscent of Chinese art. Delightful.

Bonsall, Crosby. *The Case of the Double Cross.* **1980. Hard: Harper. Pbk: Harper Trophy. Ages 4–8.**

Marigold and her two friends are tired of seeing the sign "No Girls" on Wizard's private-eye clubhouse, which he shares with three other boys. The girls would like to join, but only on their terms. Thanks to Marigold's plan, they get what they want. Marigold writes a letter in code and delivers it to the youngest of the boys. The code baffles the boy detectives, so Wizard finally concedes that he has been fooled and offers to let them join his club. Only when they all agree it's their club, not his, and the "No Girls" sign is down do they join forces to solve future puzzles. Funny, expressive pictures capture the spirit of the story.

Buck, Nola. *Sid and Sam.* **Illustrated by G. Brian Karas. 1996. Hard: Harper. Ages 4–8.**

In this book for beginning readers, a girl named Sid meets her friend Sam and they sing together. Sid is an exuberant character dressed in a bright shirt, shorts, and red cowboy boots, with binoculars hung around her neck. Sam finds Sid's singing overwhelming and tries to tone her down to no avail. Full of alliteration and wordplay, the simple text rises above most easy-to-read stories in its cleverness and appeal. Whimsical illustrations convey Sid's bounciness and the friendship between her and the more sedate Sam.

Coerr, Eleanor. *The Big Balloon Race.* **Illustrated by Carolyn Croll. 1981. Hard: Harper. Pbk: Harper Trophy. Ages 4–8.**

Based on real people, this easy reader describes a balloon race entered by Carlotta Myers, a leading aeronaut in the 1880s. In the story, Ariel, daughter of Carlotta and balloon maker Carl Myers, falls asleep in her mother's balloon just before a race. Unnoticed by her mother, she awakens only once the balloon is in the air. Ariel's added weight makes it more difficult to win, but the mother-and-daughter team prevails thanks to quick thinking, and they defeat the male aeronaut they are racing. Delightful illustrations show Carlotta the Great formally dressed for her flight but clearly in command as she reads her compass and maneuvers her bright-colored balloon. An outstanding book about a skilled woman.

Cristaldi, Kathryn. *Baseball Ballerina.* **Illustrated by Abby Carter. 1992. Hard: Random House. Pbk: Random House. Ages 4–8.**

In this beginning reader, a gender stereotype is turned on its head. The girl who narrates it loves baseball and worries that her teammates will laugh at her if they find out about her ballet lessons. Her mother thinks that baseball is for boys and that her daughter should be doing more "girl things." The narrator hates pink; her mother thinks it's a good color for girls. At ballet class, when they practice positions, the narrator in her baseball cap announces that the only position for her is shortstop. But at their dance recital, she combines ballet and baseball as she leaps to recover a crown that flies off her friend's head. Her male and female teammates in the audience cheer, and she realizes ballet can be fun—although not as good as baseball. Although the mother leaves something to be desired, the narrator is an appealing modern girl who slaps high fives and makes the best of a situation she hasn't chosen.

Cushman, Doug. *Aunt Eater's Mystery Vacation*. 1992. Hard: Harper. Pbk: Harper Trophy. Ages 4–8.

Aunt Eater the anteater loves to read mystery novels and to solve real mysteries. In four short chapters, she encounters four mysteries while on vacation. The puzzles are simple enough that the reader might solve them. Humorous pictures depicting different types of animals as characters show a dowdy Aunt Eater who divides her time between reading and action. Mystery stories are popular with beginning readers, and few at this level feature female detectives. Other books featuring the anteater sleuth are *Aunt Eater Loves a Mystery* and *Aunt Eater's Mystery Christmas*.

Hooks, William H. *Where's Lulu?* Illustrated by R. W. Alley. 1991. Hard: Bantam, o.p. Pbk: Bantam. Ages 3–7.

Sweet, comical pictures introduce a young brown-skinned girl who finds a ball, a gift from her dad, when she wakes up one morning. Right away she starts looking for her dog, Lulu, but can't find her anywhere. After checking with everyone in the large household, the girl settles for bouncing her ball against a fence, whereupon Lulu leaps into view and catches the ball in flight. The girl's father joins the girl and her dog in a romping game of catch. A sunny story with large print and a simple plot.

Levinson, Nancy Smiler. *Clara and the Bookwagon*. Illustrated by Carolyn Croll. 1988. Hard: Harper. Pbk: Harper Trophy. Ages 5–8.

In a story set in Maryland in 1905, young Clara, who works alongside her father in the fields, wants to learn to read, but there are no schools for farm children where she lives. When she wants to borrow a book from a store that serves as a book station, her father won't let her. Books, he says, are for rich people, not for farmers. But a determined woman, Miss Mary Titcomb, drives to their farm in the country's first bookmobile. She persuades Clara's father that reading is important, and Clara checks out her first books. Based on facts about the first bookmobile, the four chapters have crisp illustrations that show a friendly, dignified woman driving a horse-drawn carriage alone through the countryside, a pioneer in her profession.

Lewis, Thomas P. *Clipper Ship*. Illustrated by Joan Sandin. 1978. Hard: Harper. Pbk: Harper Trophy. Ages 5–8.

This beginning history book describes a voyage around Cape Horn from New York to San Francisco. Although the captain of the clipper ship *Rainbird* is a man, his wife charts the course using her chronometer and sextant. When Captain Murdock gets sick, his wife declares, "I will sail the ship," and she does. She gives orders and negotiates the journey past an icy Cape Horn and on to San Francisco. Her daughter and son help her, and one picture shows the girl steering the ship with her mother. The children climb one of the masts together, although while sitting at the top the daughter spends her time rolling her hair into curls. On the whole, however, this is an unusually positive portrayal of a woman in the last century, based on true stories about various women who went to sea with their husbands.

Maccarone, Grace. *Soccer Game!* Illustrated by Meredith Johnson. 1994. Pbk: Scholastic. Ages 3–7.

This simple story about girls and boys playing soccer together is written for the very beginning reader. Many pages have only two or three words on them, such as "We run" and "We pass." In the cartoonlike pictures, as many girls as boys participate energetically in the game. To add humor, two dogs clad in uniforms join in the game, one of which wears a hair ribbon. A girl seems to make the goal that wins the game, and she is shown celebrating with one of her male teammates. The pictures clearly show girls enjoying a team sport and boys treating them as full-fledged teammates and opponents.

Marshall, Edward. *Troll Country.* Illustrated by James Marshall. 1980. Hard: Dial, o.p. Pbk: Dial. Ages 4–8.

Elsie Fay Johnson, who has just been reading a book on trolls, is surprised to hear that her mother met one when she was a little girl. Comical illustrations show the mother's story of how she tricked the troll with the use of a mirror. Despite her father's skepticism about the story, Elsie believes her mother and longs to meet a troll herself. She deliberately goes into the dark woods and, sure enough, meets the same troll her mother had. Her mother's trick won't work twice, so Elsie Fay has to think for herself. She pretends she doesn't believe the troll is really a troll and goads him into standing on his head to prove it. While he is preoccupied, Elsie Fay escapes. The mother and daughter, deceptively sweet with their round faces and frilly clothes, are quick thinkers who don't let a big, ugly troll scare them.

Mozelle, Shirley. *Zack's Alligator.* **Illustrated by James Watts. 1989. Hard: Harper. Pbk: Harper Trophy. Ages 4–8.**

Although the main human character in this book is a boy named Zack, the star is a talking female alligator. When Bridget, a present from the boy's uncle in Florida, arrives, she is the size of a key chain, but she becomes full grown when Zack pours water on her. She exudes energy and enthusiasm in the upbeat, colorful pictures. Don't miss the one of her stretched out on the couch, hollering to Zack to bring her some food. She devours a huge plate of food, wrestles with the snakelike garden hose, and plays on all the equipment at the park. When the park policeman tells Zack that Bridget needs a leash and adds, "Keep him under control," Bridget's reaction is an incensed "Him? Well, I beg your pardon. How rude! Hasn't he ever seen a girl gator before?" Any reader will be glad to have met this original girl gator. In the sequel *Zack's Alligator Goes to School*, Zack brings Bridget on a chaos-producing visit to school.

O'Connor, Jane. *Molly the Brave and Me.* **Illustrated by Sheila Hamanaka. 1990. Hard: Random House. Pbk: Random House. Ages 4–8.**

Beth greatly admires her friend Molly, who isn't afraid of anything, it seems. Beth herself is afraid of many things but does her best to hide it. She finds that pretending she's brave sometimes results in an unexpectedly good time. Visiting Molly's country house, Beth has a chance to be the braver of the two and ends up feeling great: "Maybe I really am a kid with guts!" An added plus is that Molly and her parents have dark skin and Beth has light skin, although race doesn't really enter into the story.

Parish, Peggy. *No More Monsters for Me!* **Illustrated by Marc Simont. 1981. Hard: Harper. Pbk: Harper Trophy. Ages 4–8.**

Minneapolis Simpkin wants a pet, a topic on which she and her mother disagree. After a loud exchange of words, not unusual in their relationship, Minneapolis stamps out of the house and runs into a crying baby monster. "Mother never said no to a monster," she tells herself, and takes it home. She hides it, even though her mother loves monster stories and knows a lot about monsters, some of which she learned from her own mother. After a funny scene at the dinner table, Minn and her mother resolve their differences about pets, and Minn braves the dark night to take care of the monster. It is a shame that Minneapolis cries so much, but otherwise she and her mother are a vigorous pair who enjoy each other's company. Sprightly drawings by Marc Simont enhance the story.

Pomerantz, Charlotte. *The Outside Dog.* **Illustrated by Jennifer Plecas. 1993. Hard: Harper. Pbk: Harper Trophy. Ages 4–8.**

Marisol is a model of persistence. She lives with her *abuelito*, her grandfather, in a little house in Puerto Rico. She would love to have one of the stray dogs in the neighborhood as a pet, but her grandfather objects. She befriends one of the dogs and names it Pancho. Slowly and cleverly Marisol convinces her grandfather that a pet dog is a good idea. Endearing pictures extend the personalities of the people and the dog. Marisol is an active girl who sometimes goes fishing with a neighbor. Another neighbor is a friendly woman who owns a little grocery store. With four short chapters and a sprinkling of Spanish words that are defined in the front, this is an outstanding book for young readers.

Rappaport, Doreen. *The Boston Coffee Party.* **Illustrated by Emily Arnold McCully. 1988. Hard: Harper. Pbk: Harper Trophy. Ages 5–8.**

This history book is based on a true event recorded by Abigail Adams in the 1760s. During the Revolutionary War, women whose husbands were fighting asked local merchants to keep down their prices for sugar and coffee to support the war effort. In this fictionalized version, Sarah Homans and her young sister Emma go from store to store in Boston trying to buy sugar. The one merchant who has sugar sells it to someone else who will pay the highest price. When Mrs. Homans and her friends realize that same merchant has hidden away barrels of coffee to sell when the price rises, they rebel. Sarah and Emma march along with the women to demand the key to the merchant's warehouse, where they take the hoarded coffee. Charming illustrations by award-winning artist Emily McCully show how people lived and dressed at the time, and capture the spirit of the group of angry women, an unusual sight in children's books.

Roop, Peter and Connie. *Keep the Lights Burning, Abbie.* **Illustrated by Peter E. Hanson. 1985. Hard: Carolrhoda. Pbk: Carolrhoda. Ages 6–9.**

This fictionalized biography focuses on the courage and determination of a lighthouse keeper's daughter in 1856. When Captain Burgess has to leave their Maine island to fetch his wife's medicine, he leaves his daughter Abbie in charge of the lights that keep ships from being wrecked on the rocky coastline. A huge storm prevents the captain from returning, and for four weeks Abbie has to keep the lights burning in two lighthouses and, with the help of her sisters, care for her sick mother. She gets up at night to scrape ice off the windows so the light can get through. The storm gets so fierce the family moves into one of the lighthouses and subsists on eggs from the chickens Abbie has rescued from the rain. An easy-to-read account of a girl who proved brave in discouraging circumstances and saved the lives of those at sea.

Schecter, Ellen. *The Warrior Maiden: A Hopi Legend.* Illustrated by Laura Kelly. 1992. Pbk: Bantam. Ages 6–9.
In this simple tale, a girl has the courage and presence of mind to save her pueblo from Apache raiders. The men have gone out to the field when Huh-ay-ay hears invaders. She cleverly directs those remaining in the pueblo to make a lot of noise so that the Apaches will think they are hearing warriors. Heart pounding, she slips by the raiders and runs as fast as she can to find the men. She returns with them and they scare away the Apaches, who are climbing the pueblo walls. Every year since that time the Hopi celebrate the harvest and sing the praises of Huh-ay-ay, the Warrior Maiden. Colorful watercolors provide a sense of place in this beginning chapter book.

Short Novels

Ackerman, Karen. *The Night Crossing*. Illustrated by Elizabeth Sayles. 1994. Hard: Knopf. Pbk: Random House. Ages 7–10.

This is the simple story of a courageous Jewish family traveling through the night and bitter cold to escape the Nazis. Young Clara, who knows the pain of wearing a yellow star and being taunted by her old friends, overhears her parents making plans to leave Austria. Soon she, her older sister Marta, and their parents set off on foot, leaving behind almost all they own. When Clara's family is nearly discovered by some soldiers, she realizes how dangerous the journey really is. At the last minute it is up to Clara to think quickly and save the family. This approachable story for young readers captures the point of view of a child who suffers but is lucky enough to escape. Clara's small act of bravery is at the level a child can understand without knowing more about the Holocaust, which is described in more detail in the epilogue.

Adler, David A. *Cam Jansen and the Mystery at the Haunted House*. Illustrated by Susanna Natti. 1992. Hard: Viking, o.p. Pbk: Puffin. Ages 6–9.

The girl detective in this popular series earned her nickname "Cam" from her photographic memory. She can memorize any scene she sees and recall it later in detail. When her aunt loses her wallet at an amusement park, Cam and her friend Eric try to solve the mystery. They eliminate various suspects by combining Cam's talents with some close observation. In the end, Cam solves the mystery and recovers wallets stolen from several people in the park. The park owner, a woman, rewards her with free passes to the park. Short chapters, large print, and frequent illustrations make this an excellent series for readers new to chapter books. A few of the many other titles include *Cam Jansen and the Mystery of the Dinosaur Bones* and *Cam Jansen and the Mystery of the Stolen Diamonds*.

Auch, Mary Jane. *Angel and Me and the Bayside Bombers*. Illustrated by Cat Bowman Smith. 1989. Hard: Little, Brown, o.p. Pbk: Little, Brown. Ages 7–9.

Although the narrator in this beginning chapter book is a boy, third grader Brian Hegney, he relies on his cousin Angel to save him from a big mistake. He has challenged a good soccer team, the Bayside Bombers, to a game the next Saturday, but he doesn't have a team. When he's about to give up, Angel insists he shouldn't quit without a fight. Since she's a much better player than Brian, Angel coaches him and trains a group of second-grade girls and boys. It looks bad for Brian's team until Angel comes up with the plan to distract the other team whenever possible. When the fateful day arrives, their plan pays off. Although each team has more boys than girls, girls play important roles in this quick-moving book. One of the Bombers, Jessie, is an unpleasant girl, but obviously a good player. Angel is a terrific soccer player, a good organizer, and more determined than Brian. Disappointing illustrations show Angel as an oddly insipid-looking girl, constantly hiding behind other children. All in all, though, an unusual, easy sports novel about a girl who leads a team.

Ball, Duncan. *Emily Eyefinger*. Illustrated by George Ulrich. 1992. Hard: Simon & Schuster. Pbk: Aladdin. Ages 7–9.

When the Eyefingers' daughter Emily is born, she has an extra eye at the end of her finger. Although she finds it can be a nuisance, more often it's a big help. She easily finds things hidden under or behind furniture, which comes in handy when her goldfish gets lost. Emily uses her talent to stop a bully from bothering children and to find a lost snake at the zoo. Most exciting of all, Emily's eyefinger allows her to see criminals during a bank robbery when everyone's face is turned to the floor. This upbeat story features a female doctor, police sergeant, head zookeeper, and bank robber, and mentions a carpenter named Ms. Hammer. Emily enjoys being different from other children, viewing her unusual eyefinger as an asset that makes her special. A lighthearted fantasy illustrated with a humorous black-and-white drawing in each chapter. In the sequels *Emily Eyefinger and the Lost Treasure* and *Emily Eyefinger, Secret Agent*, Emily discovers a valuable Egyptian treasure and helps capture a spy.

Berleth, Richard. *Mary Patten's Voyage*. Illustrated by Ben Otero. 1994. Hard: Albert Whitman. Ages 7–10.

This short novel is based on a true story about the clipper ship *Neptune's Car*, which raced two other ships from New York City to San Francisco in 1856. When the ship's captain fell ill with tuberculosis, his eighteen-year-old wife Mary Patten took over as captain. Due to her skills as a navigator, she took the ship safely around Cape Horn through terrible storms. Some of the male sailors considered a woman, especially a pregnant one, incapable of leading the ship and bad luck as well. But Mary Patten persisted and proved herself a talented and knowledgeable sailor. Although the ship came in second in the race, as the sailor who narrates the story proclaims, "She had proven for all time what a woman could achieve against the sea." The U.S. Merchant Marine Academy hospital in New York is named in Mary Patten's

honor. An exciting adventure based on true life, amply illustrated with color paintings.

Bulla, Clyde Robert. *Shoeshine Girl.* **Illustrated by Leigh
Grant. 1975. Hard: Crowell. Pbk: Harper Trophy. Ages 6–9.**
 Ten-year-old Sarah Ida, sent to spend the summer with
her aunt Claudia, feels unwanted and angry. Fiercely independent, she insists on carrying her own luggage and wants the
sense of freedom money gives her. When Aunt Claudia won't
give her money, Sarah Ida decides to earn her own. She gets a
job helping a shoeshine man named Al, who overcomes his
initial skepticism about having a girl do the job. Sarah Ida half
hopes her aunt will forbid her to do such messy work, but
when she doesn't, Sarah Ida works hard and learns a lot. She
even manages the stand alone when Al spends a few days in
the hospital. A terrific short novel about a girl who earns
money and grows in responsibility.

Cleary, Beverly. *Ramona the Pest.* **Illustrated by Louis
Darling. 1968. Hard: Morrow. Pbk: Avon. Ages 7–10.**
 Ramona's great popularity has endured for more than
twenty-five years. She represents the kind of girl who has not
been subdued by adults or the world in general. When
Ramona has a question, such as where the storybook character
Mike Mulligan goes to the bathroom, she asks it, to the admiration of her fellow kindergartners. She careens fiercely
around on her tricycle, converted to a bicycle by removing
one wheel. She loses her temper and can't be swayed when she
has stubbornly made up her mind to do something. When she's
happy she sings it out and twirls with joy. True, her greatest
wish is to please her teacher, but even that is easily forgotten
when she is tempted to pull another girl's curls. Ramona has
some clear notions about differences between girls and boys—

boys are not supposed to want ribbons—but she doesn't seem to limit herself to certain roles. She stomps in the mud with the best of them, a thoroughly likeable and strong-minded child. A popular read-aloud for younger children, too. Other books about the irrepressible Ramona and her escapades include *Ramona the Brave, Ramona and Her Father*, and more.

Duffey, Betsy. *The Gadget War*. Illustrated by Janet Wilson. 1991. Hard: Viking. Pbk: Puffin. Ages 7–10.

Kelly Sparks likes to invent things. Her desk at school is full of tools and gadgets, and her career goal is to be a "Gadget Wiz." The walls of her bedroom hold Peg-Boards covered with every kind of tool. The first black-and-white drawing shows her smiling as she hammers a nail into a small board, surrounded by a pliers, a screwdriver, a ruler, and wire. But when a new boy enters the third grade wearing an inventor's camp T-shirt, Kelly has a rival for the first time. The new boy, Albert Einstein Jones, quickly challenges her, and they each use their inventions to annoy the other. To her mother's dismay, Kelly invents a food-fight catapult, carefully writing down each test result as she tries it out in their increasingly messy kitchen. The gadget war escalates until Kelly inadvertently hits the principal with an orange half. Kelly and Albert both get into trouble, but it also spells the end of their rivalry and the beginning of their friendship. A slight but lively story about an uncommon girl who likes tools and solving problems with them.

Gauch, Patricia Lee. *This Time, Tempe Wick?* Illustrated by Margot Tomes. 1974. Hard: Putnam. Ages 6–10.

This short novel is based on a legend from the time of the Revolution. Temperance Wick was known for her strength and courage even as a child. She could stay at the plow as long as her father and beat him in a horse race. When ten thousand American soldiers occupied Jockey Hollow in Pennsylvania where she lived, Tempe and her family pitched in to help the troops, sewing and cooking and sharing their farm produce. But after most of the army had left, two disgruntled soldiers who stayed behind tried to steal the family horse. Tempe fooled them for days, even taking the musket from one, and saved her horse. Tomes' homespun illustrations suit the story perfectly, giving a lively sense of time and place.

Gregory, Philippa. *Florizella and the Wolves.* **Illustrated by Patrice Aggs. 1993. Hard: Candlewick. Ages 5–9.**

Princess Florizella, dressed in T-shirts, jeans, and boots, would rather ride her horse Jellybean than do anything else. With her friend Prince Bennett, she rides, hunts, swims, climbs trees, and plays games. No one at the palace is surprised when Florizella brings home four orphaned wolf pups, but her parents insist they be returned to the forest soon. With Bennett's help, Florizella tricks the king and queen into believing one of the wolves is a dog, and they let it stay in the palace after it helps save Florizella from a panther. The captain of the royal guards, who is a woman, also helps save the princess. Although this British import has a chatty tone that can get tedious, the heroine is a strong-minded, rambunctious girl who goes her own way. Breezy black-and-white illustrations appear frequently in the seven short chapters.

Griffin, Judith Berry. *Phoebe the Spy.* **Illustrated by Margot Tomes. 1977. Hard: Scholastic, o.p. Pbk: Scholastic. Ages 6–9.**

A short historical novel set in the time of the Revolutionary War, this is based on a true story about an African-American girl. Phoebe Fraunces, whose father ran the most popular tavern in New York City, finds herself working as a housekeeper for George Washington, then commander of the American army. Her father has gotten her the job so she can help prevent an unidentified enemy from possibly killing Washington. She listens to guests and officers, trying to overhear clues. At the last minute, she figures out who the killer is and prevents him from poisoning the future president. Charming illustrations add to this simple story.

Hänel, Wolfram. Translated by J. Alison James. *Lila's Little Dinosaur*. Illustrated by Alex de Wolf. 1994. Hard: North-South Books. Ages 5–9.

Lila loves dinosaurs and knows a lot about them. When she sees an announcement about a dinosaur exhibit at a local museum, she persuades her father to take her to it. She gives her father details about dinosaurs and their habits, since she knows far more than he does. The exhibit features dinosaurs moving and making noise, which Lila thinks is terrific, although her father seems a bit frightened. While examining one of the mechanical dinosaurs, she runs across a real, tiny dinosaur. The friendly, rainbow-striped creature follows her home, and Lila discovers that only children can see it. It gets her into trouble, though, because it smells like old fish and eats a houseplant. Lila is a red-haired, scruffy-looking, alert seven-and-a-half-year-old with an inquiring mind. Children will enjoy her good luck in finding such a wonderful pet.

Hesse, Karen. *Sable*. Illustrated by Marcia Sewall. 1994. Hard: Holt. Ages 6–10.

Tate, who is always wearing overalls, would rather help her father with his furniture-building than work with her mother around the house. Although her mother is against it,

Tate wants more than anything to keep the stray dog that shows up at their mountain home one day. Sable, a lovable but wandering dog, gets in so much trouble with the neighbors that she must be sent away. Tate resolutely constructs a sturdy fence that proves to her parents she is responsible enough to keep Sable. After being lost, the dog finally returns and is welcomed even by Tate's mother.

Hooks, William H. *The Girl Who Could Fly*. Illustrated by Kees de Kiefte. 1995. Hard: Macmillan. Ages 7–10.

A most unusual girl impresses a group of boys and coaches their baseball team to success in this light fantasy. The narrator, Adam Lee, first meets Tomasina Jones, known as Tom, when she moves into his apartment building. He quickly realizes she has magical powers: She can, for example, stop a ball in midair and construct maps that come alive. Although she refuses to play on his team, the Off-Beats, she disguises herself as a boy and coaches them through tough daily practices. When one of the team members almost drowns, Tom saves him and reveals herself as a girl—a girl who can fly. It is refreshing to have the person from outer space be a female, and better still to have her coaching a group of boys.

Jordan, June. *Kimako's Story*. Illustrated by Kay Burford. 1981. Hard: Houghton, o.p. Pbk: Houghton. Ages 5–8.

In this simple story about an African-American girl named Kimako, it looks at first like the seven-year-old will have to stay inside while her mother is at work. But Kimako convinces her mother that Bucks, a friend's dog, will protect her in her tough neighborhood. The girl and dog wander around together having a good time, and Kimako works on her plans for getting a dog of her own. Fresh line drawings on every double-page spread and Kimako's seven poem puzzles for children to solve add to the pleasure of reading this low-key short novel.

Landon, Lucinda. *Meg Mackintosh and the Mystery at the Medieval Castle: A Solve-It-Yourself Mystery.* 1989. Hard: Little, Brown, o.p. Pbk: Little, Brown. Ages 6–9.

In this popular series, the reader can search for clues in the pictures in order to solve the mystery along with Meg Mackintosh. Meg, the rest of the History Club, and their teacher Mrs. Spencer are on a field trip to a castle when a valuable chalice is stolen. Meg immediately starts taking notes and snapping instant photographs; when the police arrive, she is ready to help solve the mystery. Despite her teacher's admonition to let the police take care of the problem, Meg and her friend Liddy go down into the dungeons and conclude that the police are arresting the wrong person. With her usual cleverness, Meg schemes to trick the real criminals into confessing. She is a girl who likes adventure even if it's dangerous, and loves to figure things out. This short mystery, with its many drawings, involves readers in a way appealing to many children. Other equally strong titles in the popular series include *Meg Mackintosh and the Mystery at Camp Creepy* and *Meg Mackintosh and the Mystery in the Locked Library.*

Levine, Caroline. *The Detective Stars and the Case of the Super Soccer Team.* Illustrated by Betsy Lewin. 1994. Hard: Cobblehill. Ages 7–9.

How can the Foxes, a soccer team that seems to be uncoordinated, keep winning games? That is the mystery that narrator Veronica and her friend Ernest must solve. They attend a Fox game where Ernest takes photographs until a player tries to take the camera. The muscular Veronica comes to the rescue and flips the player to the ground. Sure enough, the photographs provide the clue Veronica needs to solve the case. Energetic black-and-white pictures show the two Detective Stars in action in this short, clever story.

MacLachlan, Patricia. *Sarah, Plain and Tall.* **1985. Hard: Harper. Pbk: Harper Trophy. Ages 6–10.**
"I am strong and I work hard and I am willing to travel. But I am not mild mannered." So writes Sarah Wheaton to Anna's father, Jacob, who has advertised for a wife. Anna, her younger brother, Caleb, and their father wait anxiously in their prairie frontier home for Sarah to visit them. When she does, she proves to be all she had said and more. She is kind and she sings; she slides down haystacks, learns to plow, and helps fix the roof. She insists on learning to drive the wagon, then drives it into town one day. Caleb and Anna worry she won't come back, but she does—for always. It is hard to imagine a more beautifully written story. The simple words convey warmth and humor and, most of all, love. Each small incident tells a lot about the characters. When Sarah dons a pair of Jacob's overalls, Caleb protests, "Women don't wear overalls," to which Sarah crisply replies, "This woman does." Anna, who narrates the story, is a strong girl who cares for her brother and works the farm. This Newbery Medal winner is truly a gem, wonderful for reading aloud.

Markham, Marion M. *The Christmas Present Mystery.* **Illustrated by Emily Arnold McCully. 1984. Hard: Houghton, o.p. Pbk: Avon. Ages 7–9.**
Twin sisters Kate and Mickey combine their talents to

solve mysteries. Kate loves science and Mickey, who plans to be a detective, has a keen eye for clues. They are on their way to their uncle's for Christmas when they discover that the photograph they planned to give him is ruined. Among the family's smiling faces appears the face of a boy sticking out his tongue. Kate, who is interested in photography, speculates on how this could be done, and the two of them make a logical list of clues and questions. A local photographer confirms Kate's theory about the photograph and identifies the boy. The solution to the mystery is more psychological than exciting, but the ending is happy. One of the characters, Miss Winks, embodies the stereotype of a silly older woman given to fainting, a minor drawback. A good mystery about sisters who complement each other. They also solve cases in *The April Fool's Day Mystery*, *The Birthday Party Mystery*, and more.

Mathis, Sharon Bell. *Sidewalk Story*. **Illustrated by Leo Carty. 1971. Hard: Viking, o.p. Pbk: Puffin. Ages 7–10.**

The news that her best friend Tanya is being evicted from her apartment stuns nine-year-old Lilly Etta Allen. Tanya's mother, who has a hard time caring for her six children while holding down a job, has missed a few rent payments. She is evicted and her furniture is piled up on the sidewalk. Knowing that an old woman on the street had been saved from eviction by publicity, Lilly Etta forms a plan. She and Tanya contact a reporter, who is impressed by Lilly Etta's initiative. Ultimately, and to everyone's surprise, Lilly Etta's determination pays off for her and her friend. The handful of black-and-white paintings show that the girls are African-American, a fact mentioned only briefly in the text. Lilly Etta, as the reporter says, is "quite a girl"—a loyal friend who is not afraid to speak up.

Minahan, John A. *Abigail's Drum*. **Illustrated by Robert Quackenbush. 1995. Hard: Pippin. Ages 7–9.**

Another tale based on a true story, this recounts the bravery of two girls during the War of 1812. Rebecca and Abigail Bates live with their parents at the Scituate lighthouse on the coast of Massachusetts. Although they work hard at chores, the girls have time to play a little music, Rebecca on the fife and Abigail on a drum. When British sailors land and take their father hostage, the girls come up with a way to save him and prevent the sailors from burning the nearby town. Scared as they are, the sisters rise to the occasion and cleverly turn back the enemy. The cartoonish drawings add little, but the story of bravery stands on its own.

Nabb, Magdalen. *Josie Smith*. **Illustrated by Pirkko Vainio. 1989. Hard: McElderry. Ages 6–9.**

Josie Smith has a lot in common with Beverly Cleary's Ramona Quimby, although Josie lives in Britain and is the only child of a single mother. Both girls specialize in getting into mischief, usually with the best of intentions. In the first of the three stories in this book, Josie wants to buy a present for her mother, so she earns money through odd jobs. She digs and finds worms for a gardener; she searches for bottles to get deposit money; and she sweeps a grocery market. She works hard and aims high, but the flowers she wants cost too much. In the end, everything works out better than expected. In the other stories, Josie runs away (to her grandmother's) after making an unintentional mess in her room, and she secretly adopts someone else's cat. She refuses to be bossed around by older boys in her neighborhood, and manages to outrun them when she has to. Some adults may be uncomfortable with how often Josie talks about getting "smacked," but it never happens. In fact, her mother seems exceptionally tolerant. The large print, frequent pictures, and lively stories make this a good chapter book for less experienced readers.

In the sequels, including *Josie Smith at the Seashore* and *Josie Smith at School*, she continues her everyday adventures.

Nixon, Joan Lowery. ***You Bet Your Britches, Claude.*** **Illustrated by Tracey Campbell Pearson. 1989. Hard: Viking, o.p. Pbk: Puffin. Ages 5–9.**

In this lighthearted tale set in the Old West, Shirley decides she wants to adopt Bessie, sister to her adopted son, Tom. But her husband Claude objects to having a chatty eight-year-old girl in the house. Bessie, however, proves her worth three times by spotting three different criminals, and convinces Claude of the advantages of adopting her. Both Shirley and Bessie are outspoken and clever, and very pleased with the outcome. In fact, Shirley's smile was so bright that "some folks around those parts got up and pulled down their window shades." Told in a sprightly, tall-tale manner, this short chapter book has lively illustrations on each page. Good for young independent readers and for reading aloud.

Oneal, Zibby. ***A Long Way to Go.*** **Illustrated by Michael Dooling. 1990. Hard: Viking. Pbk: Puffin. Ages 6–9.**

Suffragism is the theme of this short novel set in 1917. Lila's grandmother has been arrested for picketing the White House to advocate giving women the vote. Although Lila's parents disagree with her grandmother, Lila finds herself wondering why her younger brother will one day have a voice in governing the country but she won't. Taking up a challenge by a boy she meets, Lila proves to him that she can sell newspapers as well as a boy can, and later convinces her father to let her march in a suffragists' parade. This engaging story gives younger readers a sense of the way life used to be for girls and women, not so long ago.

Paton Walsh, Jill. *Matthew and the Sea Singer*. **Illustrated by Alan Marks. 1993. Hard: FSG. Ages 6–9.**

A girl named Birdy proves herself smart and generous in this brief story. After she pays a shilling to save a boy named Matthew from a harsh master, he goes to live with the local parson, who wants to train his beautiful voice. But a powerful seal-queen steals Matthew away to enjoy his singing and Birdy must negotiate with her. After some scheming, Birdy solves the problem and saves her friend. Poetically written and illustrated with equally poetic watercolors, this is an unusually lovely chapter book. In an earlier book, *Birdy and the Ghosties*, now out of print, Birdy bravely faces a trio of ghosts.

Pfeffer, Susan Beth. *Sara Kate, Superkid*. **Illustrated by Suzanne Hankins. 1994. Hard: Holt. Ages 6–10.**

In this beginning chapter book, eight-year-old Sara Kate finds she has superpowers. She can throw a basketball from any distance and it will always land in the net. When her disgusted older brother complains to their grandmother about it, the grandmother reveals that certain women in the family get such superpowers. Her own include the ability to fly and, for a while when she was a girl, to lift a car with her right hand. But, she warns Sara Kate, the powers come and go unexpectedly and they can cause trouble. When Sara Kate enters a basketball-throwing contest, hoping to win a thousand dollars, she finds out what her grandmother meant. The results are not exactly what she hopes, but Sara Kate ends up happy. A zippy story about a girl and her grandmother with the kinds of powers that boys usually get in fiction. Followed by *Sara Kate Saves the World*, in which she uses her X-ray vision against a school bully.

Pinkwater, Daniel. *Mush, a Dog from Space*. 1995. Hard: Atheneum. Ages 7–10.

The ever-zany Pinkwater diverges from his usual books about boys with this slim novel about a self-reliant girl and an extraordinary female dog. One summer Kelly's family moves from an apartment to a housing development near some woods. While Kelly is walking in the woods one day, she meets a dog from another planet who can talk. The amazing dog goes home with Kelly, fixes herself a peanut butter, lettuce, and tomato sandwich, and agrees to stay in the garage until Kelly can persuade her parents to let her have a dog. Short chapters and bright, funny pictures maintain a lively pace as their friendship develops. Pinkwater's brand of humor doesn't appeal to everyone, but those who enjoy it will be especially pleased to have a book from him about a girl and her dog.

Porter, Connie. *Meet Addy: An American Girl*. Illustrated by Melodye Rosales. 1993. Hard: Pleasant. Pbk: Pleasant. Ages 7–10.

In this entry in the popular American Girls Collection series, life is grim for ten-year-old Addy, a slave during the Civil War. When her father and brother are sold, Addy and her mother try to escape. Although thoroughly frightened, Addy saves her mother from drowning in a creek they must ford. Later she tricks Confederate soldiers into thinking she is a boy and so avoids getting caught. The suspenseful escape by this brave mother and daughter leads them to a safe house, where an old woman helps them. The story closes as they head for Philadelphia, having, as Addy puts it, "taken their freedom," an expression that emphasizes the role runaway slaves took in changing their own fate. Eight pages at the end give a short history of slavery and the Civil War, heavily illustrated with photographs. The story itself has occasional full-page paintings as well as smaller decorations. Although some adults will be put off by the commercial nature of this series, which exists in part to sell dolls and clothing, the girls do have brave adventures. The writing and pictures tend to be stiff, but that doesn't seem to put off young readers. Sequels include *Addy Learns a Lesson* and *Addy's Surprise*.

Ross, Pat. *Hannah's Fancy Notions: A Story of Industrial New England*. Illustrated by Bert Dodson. 1988. Hard: Viking, o.p. Pbk: Puffin. Ages 7–9.

Hannah is tired of being capable. Ever since her mother died and her father stopped working steadily as a wallpaper hanger, Hannah has had to take care of her three younger siblings and do the housework. Fifteen-year-old Rebecca spends the week in Lowell, working at a mill and living in a boardinghouse. One day, wanting to replace Rebecca's ragged traveling sack, Hannah experiments with cardboard and scraps of wallpaper to make a colorful bandbox similar to the hatboxes she has seen. When her father helps her construct the box, the final product is so attractive that Rebecca's friends want to order their own. Hannah and her father concentrate on making the boxes, while Rebecca takes orders and keeps the books. Into each box Hannah fixes a card that reads "Made and sold by Hannah the Bandbox Maker." An enterprising nineteenth-century girl, Hannah makes the most of her talents and improves the lot of her family.

Ruepp, Krista. Translated by J. Alison James. *Midnight Rider*. Illustrated by Ulrike Heyne. 1995. Hard: North-South Books. Ages 7–10.

More than anything, Charlie wants to ride her neighbor's

beautiful horse Starlight along the beach. But unfriendly Mr. Grimm won't even consider her request. So Charlie coolly leaves her house one night and goes through the dark to make her dream happen. By chance, Grimm wakes up and sees her wild ride on the beach, which calls forth his grudging admiration: "That was one brave little girl! And she rode like the devil." Charlie's venture leads to mishap, but all ends well. Her act of defiance is rewarded, a rare event for fictional girls. Expressive watercolors show a disheveled, redheaded girl exulting in her magnificent ride on the beach.

St. George, Judith. *By George, Bloomers!* Illustrated by Margot Tomes. 1976. Hard: Coward, o.p. Pbk: Shoe Tree Press. Ages 6–9.

This short chapter book illustrates why the restrictive clothing worn by women and girls in the mid–nineteenth century became a political issue. Eight-year-old Hannah would like to be able to skate and walk on stilts like her male friends, but her petticoats make it impossible. When her aunt comes to visit wearing bloomers, pants worn under a skirt, Hannah envies her physical freedom. The determined Hannah secretly fashions a torn skirt into bloomers and with her new mobility rescues her younger brother from a near accident. Appealing illustrations and well-written text make this exemplary historical fiction for younger readers. An author's note adds information about women's fight for equality.

Stevens, Carla. *Lily and Miss Liberty*. Illustrated by Deborah Kogan Ray. 1992. Hard: Scholastic, o.p. Pbk: Scholastic. Ages 6–9.

When France gave the United States the Statue of Liberty in 1885, the children of New York were among those who helped raise money for its pedestal. In this short novel, eight-year-old Lily comes up with a creative scheme to make money for this project. She and her grandmother use paper to construct crowns like the statue wears, and Lily and her friend Rachel sell them on the street. When a newspaper carries a picture of the crowns, business takes off. Lily's mother is not enthusiastic about the statue, but Lily is free to disagree with her, for her family believes that freedom of belief is an American tenet. As was common at the time, Lily's grandmother works in a shop sewing garments, as does one of Lily's young female classmates. An appendix gives detailed directions for making your own Liberty crown. A strong early chapter book.

Tripp, Valerie. *Felicity Saves the Day: A Summer Story.* **Illustrated by Dan Andreasen. 1992. Hard: Pleasant. Pbk: Pleasant. Ages 7–10.**

In this entry in the American Girls Collection series, ten-year-old Felicity is visiting her grandfather on his plantation in colonial Virginia. The spirited Felicity is reunited with a horse she once rescued from a cruel owner. When Ben, her father's apprentice, runs away to join the army and injures himself, Felicity rides bareback, jumping a creek on her way, to warn him that he is being pursued. Uncowed by the fact that he is sixteen, she accuses him of cowardice and persuades him to return to her father. A useful appendix gives facts about the time and setting. Other books include *Meet Felicity*, *Felicity Learns a Lesson*, and more.

West, Tracey. *Fire in the Valley.* **Illustrated by Nan Golub. 1993. Hard: Silver Moon. Ages 7–10.**

Eleven-year-old Sarah lives on a California farm with her twin brother, her parents, and her uncle in 1905. She is constantly struggling against her father's view of how a young lady should act. She wants to be riding horses, not sewing. Despite her father's disapproval, she is interested in a local political controversy over an aqueduct that would divert their water to Los Angeles. The issue gives Sarah several chances to test her moral and physical courage. She speaks out against the aqueduct to the highest authority she can think of. She also risks injury by riding bareback at night in an emergency. Sarah has an "independent streak," as her mother calls it, a trait that proves important to the whole family.

Wright, Betty Ren. *The Ghost Witch*. Illustrated by Ellen Eagle. 1993. Hard: Holiday. Pbk: Scholastic. Ages 8–10.
Jenny has good reason to be afraid of the house her mother recently inherited. When she visits it alone, horrible apparitions such as a crocodile and a dragon jump out at her. Jenny finds the source of the haunting, the ghost of an old witch who used to live in the house. Calling up all her courage, Jenny confronts the ghost in hopes of persuading her to haunt some other empty house. Jenny learns that when she needs to, she can be brave. The book is well designed for young readers, who will be drawn into the story by the scary drawings. By a popular author, this story about an increasingly brave girl is certain to be a hit with children who like ghosts.

Biographies

Accorsi, William. *Rachel Carson.* **1993. Hard: Holiday. Ages 4–8.**

This quirky picture-book biography combines colorful paintings with well-chosen facts about Rachel Carson. It highlights her love of nature as a child and her accomplishments as a writer. The text is simple and straightforward, while the pictures are fanciful. It is odd that a book about a naturalist would have paintings of peach and purple turtles and a blue robin. However, since the stylized pictures look like folk art, it probably won't bother most readers. An author's note adds more information about Carson, followed by a list of important dates.

Adler, David A. *Our Golda: The Story of Golda Meir.* **Illustrated by Donna Ruff. 1984. Hard: Viking, o.p. Pbk: Puffin. Ages 7–10.**

Golda Meir played several important roles in the early years of the state of Israel. Her childhood was spent in the harsh conditions of brutally anti-Semitic Russia until she moved to Milwaukee when she was eight. Always a strong-minded girl, Golda ran away to live with her older sister in Denver after her parents insisted she quit school. Back in Milwaukee two years later, Golda became active in Jewish causes, giving speeches on street corners to alert people to the atrocities in Russia, and working to establish a Jewish homeland. She and her husband, Morris Meyerson, moved to Palestine in 1921, where Golda worked for the Jewish labor union. Once Israel was established, Golda served as ambassador to Russia, the first minister of labor, the foreign minister, and finally for five years as the prime minister. This short biography weaves anecdotes from her personal life with descriptions of her accomplishments. Soft black-and-white pencil illustrations and an attractive cover showing a girl giving a speech will appeal to young readers.

Adler, David A. *A Picture Book of Florence Nightingale*. Illustrated by John and Alexandra Wallner. 1992. Hard: Holiday. Ages 5–8.

This simple biography of an important woman in medicine looks like a picture-story book, with attractive line-and-water-color illustrations on every page. Nightingale rejected the privileged life of her family and insisted on studying nursing, not then considered a respectable profession in England. Her role organizing nurses for the British soldiers in the Crimean War won her great honor but also resulted in lifelong ill-health. Back in England, Nightingale dedicated herself to improving nursing and hospital conditions. She was the first woman to receive the Order of Merit from the king of England. A fine introduction to Nightingale and her accomplishments.

Bingham, Mindy. *Berta Benz and the Motorwagen: The Story of the First Automobile Journey*. Illustrated by Itoko Maeno. 1989. Hard: Advocacy Press. Ages 6–9.

In Germany in 1888, Karl Benz, financed and supported by his wife, Berta, developed an early version of an automobile. When he became discouraged by the lack of interest in his invention, Berta Benz decided the project needed publicity and secretly planned a sixty-mile trip with their two teenage sons. They set out one morning, undetected by Karl, and drove the three-wheeled vehicle over rough roads not meant for cars. Berta overcame every setback with ingenuity and perseverance, getting water and fuel and making repairs. Although one of the sons did the driving, Berta directed the successful venture. Her scheme resulted in the kind of publicity that the automobile needed to prove its worth. Large watercolor illustrations add details and setting. Final notes tell more of the story and offer ways to involve girls in technology.

Blos, Joan W., adapter. *The Days Before Now: An Autobiographical Note by Margaret Wise Brown.* **Illustrated by Thomas B. Allen. 1994. Hard: Simon & Schuster. Ages 3–8.**

Soft pastel and charcoal illustrations and a short, lyrical text make this book feel more like a story than a biography. It reflects on the childhood of Margaret Wise Brown, famous for writing *Goodnight Moon, The Runaway Bunny,* and a host of other books for young children. In words adapted by Joan Blos, Brown describes some of the highlights of her childhood, which included moving from Manhattan to Long Island, where she delighted in the beaches and woods, and the greater freedom. She would hitch neighborhood dogs to her sled, chase butterflies, and climb trees. Most extraordinary is her list of pets, starting with thirty-six rabbits. The hazy pictures evoke a bygone time, "the days before now."

Blos, Joan W. *The Heroine of the Titanic: A Tale Both True and Otherwise of the Life of Molly Brown.* **Illustrated by Tennessee Dixon. 1991. Hard: Morrow. Ages 6–8.**

Legend mixes with fact in this story of Molly Brown, a flamboyant woman who survived the sinking of the *Titanic.* Loose, sometimes rhyming verse follows her from her birth, during a big storm in Missouri in 1867, through her exciting life in the West. She moved to the mining boomtown of Leadville, Colorado, when she was eighteen, hoping to get rich. She made her living singing for miners until she married J.J. Brown and began to raise a family. J.J. struck it rich, and the family moved in style to Denver. But after Molly and her husband separated, she decided to see the world, traveling to Hawaii, China, Siam, Tibet, and all through Europe. At the end of a trip to Europe, including a stopover in Switzerland to learn to yodel, she embarked on the *Titanic* for its maiden voyage. When it began to sink, she boarded a lifeboat and kept up the spirits of the others all through the night until they were rescued. She rowed and got others to take a turn; she sang, yodeled, and told stories. Back in America, she was proclaimed a heroine. Large, sweeping illustrations convey the larger-than-life story of Molly Brown, who proved brave in the face of great danger.

Blos, Joan W. *Nellie Bly's Monkey: His Remarkable Story in His Own Words*. Illustrated by Catherine Stock. 1996. Hard: Morrow. Ages 5–9.

In 1889, journalist Nellie Bly started from New York and traveled around the world in seventy-two days. She broke stereotypes about women travelers by traveling light and beating her original goal of seventy-five days. The bestseller she wrote about the trip mentions a monkey she bought in Singapore, the monkey who tells his version of her travels in this unusual biographical picture book. Each double-page spread features a charming watercolor-and-ink illustration of Nellie Bly and McGinty, as she named the monkey. They travel by ship and train through Asia to San Francisco and across the United States. As McGinty tells the story, he takes note of the excitement that greets Nellie Bly at every stop. Once in New York, McGinty goes to live at the New York Menagerie while Nellie Bly resumes her work as a writer. A two-page note entitled "For Those Who Wish to Know More" supplies details about Nellie Bly's life and career. An original approach to a venturesome woman's exciting race against time.

Blumberg, Rhoda. *Bloomers!* Illustrated by Mary Morgan. 1993. Hard: Bradbury. Ages 5–9.

Imagine wearing a dress so heavy it drags through mud and trips you on the stairs. Imagine wearing a corset that makes it hard to breathe freely. Such were fashionable women's clothes in the 1850s. Wearing comfortable clothes, such as the bloomers popularized by editor Amelia Bloomer, was viewed as controversial and even scandalous. Bloomers were loose pants worn under a knee-length dress. They not only allowed for freer movement than conventional dresses, but were a symbol of freedom for women. Political leaders Elizabeth Stanton and Susan B. Anthony, who were striving to win the vote for women, were among those who wore bloomers. Humorous, cheerful pictures illustrate the new garment and show the disadvantages of the old ones in this intriguing episode from women's history.

Brown, Don. *Ruth Law Thrills a Nation.* 1993. Hard: Ticknor & Fields. Ages 4–8.

In simple language and attractive watercolor-and-pen pictures, this book tells the story of Ruth Law, a pilot who tried to fly from Chicago to New York City in one day. On November 19, 1916, she took off alone through the freezing cold and flew 590 miles nonstop to Hornell, New York. After an emergency landing when she ran out of gas, Ruth Law took off again, but stopped short of New York City when darkness set in and she could no longer read her instruments to fly safely. Although she did not meet her original goal, she set a record and was hailed as a hero when she reached the city the next day. This charming picture book conveys the fascinating details of her memorable story. A gem.

Brown, Drollene P. *Sybil Rides for Independence.* **Illustrated by Margot Apple. 1985. Hard: Albert Whitman. Ages 6–9.**

While many children have heard of Paul Revere's famous ride, few know about the dangerous ride of Sybil Ludington in 1777. She was the sixteen-year-old daughter of a mill owner in New York near the Connecticut border. One night a rider brought news to Colonel Ludington, who commanded the local regiment, that British soldiers were burning Danbury, Connecticut. The colonel chose his daughter Sybil to ride a thirty-mile circuit to alert his soldiers. An experienced rider who knew the roads and the soldiers' houses, she galloped through the rainy night, stopping only to yell or pound on doors with a stick. When she reached home again, four hundred men had assembled to march toward Danbury and head off the British. News of her brave deed spread, and George Washington himself came to her house to thank her. Although her contribution was small, Sybil Ludington symbolizes the courage of girls who defended the colonies in whatever ways they could. This fictionalized biography, with its charming black, white, and red illustrations, pays tribute to one of those brave girls.

Carrigan, Mellonee. *Carol Moseley-Braun: Breaking Barriers.* **1994. Hard: Children's Press. Pbk: Children's Press. Ages 7–10.**

Learning about U.S. Senator Carol Moseley-Braun's background makes her impressive career all the more remarkable. She weathered family problems and periods of poverty as well as racism as she grew up in Chicago. This short biography, illustrated with black-and-white photographs, describes her involvement in the civil rights movement and her accomplishments in school. After practicing law, she served for ten years in the Illinois legislature, then was elected as Cook County recorder of deeds. Through most of her career she forged new territory as the first black and first woman to hold various positions. This culminated in her election to the U.S. Senate in 1992, making her the first black woman ever to serve in the Senate. Her outstanding achievements, presented in simple, clear writing, make Senator Moseley-Braun an important role model for all girls.

Coles, Robert. *The Story of Ruby Bridges*. Illustrated by George Ford. 1995. Hard: Scholastic. Ages 5–9.

In 1960, six-year-old Ruby Bridges was the first African-American child to attend William Frantz Elementary School in New Orleans. Feelings ran so strongly against integration that each morning for months armed federal marshals guarded Ruby on her walk to school. She and her teacher were alone in the classroom because parents were keeping their children home in protest. Ruby's calm courage in the face of threatening, yelling crowds of adults was extraordinary. Her family's support and strong religious beliefs kept her going. A final scene shows Ruby praying in front of the angry mob for God to forgive them. An afterword explains that later in the year white children began to return to school and tells a little about Ruby's later life. An inspiring story of a young moral leader.

Easton, Patricia Harrison. *Stable Girl: Working for the Family*. Photographs by Herb Ferguson. 1991. Hard: Harcourt. Ages 5–9.

This photo-essay gives a portrait of a girl working in her

family's stable, where horses are trained for harness racing. Her father trains the horses, her uncle rides them, and her mother keeps the books and does the billing. Danielle and her older sister learn all aspects of the work and do their share at the same time. Danielle runs errands, cleans out the stalls, and bandages the horses' legs. She even has a chance to ride with her dad while he trains a horse, the first step in learning to be a trainer herself. Clear color photographs show scenes from Danielle's day, which ends at the racetrack with her family. It is easy to believe that she might someday be training horses, running the stable, and teaching her own children the family business. An encouraging glimpse into how the world is changing for the better, this is sure to appeal to the many girls who love horses.

Fisher, Leonard Everett. *Marie Curie*. 1994. Hard: Macmillan. Ages 6–9.

Somber grays and blacks illustrate this introductory biography of Marie Curie. The spare text concentrates on the most important facts about her professional life, adding only a few anecdotes and personal details. It also highlights her political involvement as a Pole protesting the rule of Russia in Poland. The grim, powerful pictures convey the nature of Curie's life, beset as she was by physical pain from radiation, the tragedy of her husband's early death, the relentless demands of her research, and the dangerous work she did in the battlefields of World War I. Her triumphs were tempered by the strong criticism she received from male scientists, especially in France. A succinct biography of a remarkable scientist and woman.

Fritz, Jean. *Surprising Myself*. 1992. Hard: Richard C. Owen. Ages 7–10.

Children's book writer Jean Fritz considers herself an

explorer. She likes to travel and explore new places, and to do research and explore the past. Color photographs show her in Alaska, China, Ireland, and the Caribbean, gathering information for her work. She also appears at home, writing and enjoying her family. Charming illustrations from some of her books are scattered through the slim volume. In the short text, Fritz gives a sense of her life and her approach to writing. She chooses apt details to entertain the reader, like the fact that when she goes away, she leaves her manuscript in the refrigerator to protect it from fire. Fritz's fans will enjoy learning more about her, and those who don't know her books will want to seek them out after reading about this lively author.

Greene, Carol. *Elizabeth Blackwell: First Woman Doctor*. 1991. Hard: Children's Press. Pbk: Children's Press. Ages 6–9.

Large print with ample white space between the lines combined with many photographs and etchings make this beginning biography accessible to young readers. It sums up the groundbreaking career of Elizabeth Blackwell, who in 1849 became the first American woman doctor, graduating first in her class. In simple terms, the biography explains the opposition Blackwell faced, how she was rejected by twenty-nine medical schools before being accepted, and how most hospitals in Paris turned down her requests to study at them. Back in New York, Blackwell and two other women doctors opened a hospital for poor women and children that was also the first hospital to train nurses. She insisted on increased cleanliness in her hospital, a policy that resulted in fewer deaths. In 1868, she added a medical college for women, and later opened another in England. Every child should know about Elizabeth Blackwell and her accomplishments, and this biography offers a good, brief introduction.

Horenstein, Henry. *My Mom's a Vet*. 1994. Hard: Candle-wick. Ages 5–10.

This engaging photo-essay introduces children to the work of a veterinarian who treats farm animals. The vet's daughter Darcie is helping her mother for a week during the summer so she can learn how to care for animals and see how her mother makes their living. In the colorful photos, Darcie listens through a stethoscope, watches her mother X-ray a horse's ankle, and holds the tail while her mother and a farmer help a cow deliver her first calf. The girl also helps when her mother dehorns a goat with a hot iron and performs surgery on a cow with a twisted stomach. Although the details of the surgery are barely shown, the fainthearted may want to avoid some of the photographs. This book depicts a competent, strong mother showing her daughter how she does her job.

Kent, Deborah. *Jane Addams and Hull House*. 1992. Hard: Children's Press. Pbk: Children's Press. Ages 7–10.

Photographs and etchings illustrate this simple story of the life and work of Jane Addams, winner of the 1931 Nobel Peace Prize. Addams decided early in her life to help those less privileged than she, and in 1889 she opened Hull House in the midst of a Chicago slum. The settlement house provided a nursery for the neighborhood women's children, education in the English language for adults, and cultural events for everyone. Addams became increasingly political, lobbying for an end to child labor and a reform of working conditions. She broadened her scope to strive for peace during World War I, a controversial position. Thousands of Chicagoans attended her funeral, a tribute to her influence in that city. An inspiring story of a generous woman undeterred by setbacks.

Krull, Kathleen. *Wilma Unlimited: How Wilma Rudolph Became the World's Fastest Woman.* **Illustrated by David Diaz. 1996. Hard: Harcourt. Ages 5–9.**

Striking collage illustrations suit the drama of Wilma Rudolph's life. The winner of three Olympic gold medals in track in 1960, Rudolph had an unlikely childhood for a future Olympian. She was born prematurely, weighing only four pounds, and she was crippled from polio as a child. Through relentless hard work and exercise, she regained the full use of her legs and went on to be a high school basketball star. Her college track career led her to the Olympics, where despite a swollen ankle, she won two individual events and a team relay race. Pictures of her African-American family and community show the support Rudolph had while she overcame her incredible obstacles. A powerful story beautifully conveyed.

Livingston, Myra Cohn. *Keep on Singing: A Ballad of Marian Anderson.* **Illustrated by Samuel Byrd. 1994. Hard: Holiday. Ages 6–9.**

Poet Myra Cohn Livingston has woven some of Marian Anderson's own words into this poem about her life and accomplishments. The simple verses follow her singing from childhood through her enormous success, when she became the first black woman to sing at the Metropolitan Opera House in 1955. It notes incidents of racism, including rejection at a music school and the famous refusal to let Anderson sing at Constitution Hall. Notes at the end supply information about events that most children will need to understand the ballad. Warm watercolors help make this an accessible introduction for young readers to the life of a distinguished singer.

McCully, Emily Arnold. *The Pirate Queen.* **1995. Hard: Putnam. Ages 5–9.**

According to the book jacket, Emily McCully "loved to draw 'rip-roaring action pictures' " as a child. This tale of Irish pirate queen Grania O'Malley gave her the perfect opportunity for action-filled paintings. In one picture, dark-haired Grania leaps into a crowd of fighting pirates to save her father from being killed. In others, she is commanding a fleet of ships, fighting along with her crew. She ruled over part of the waters off the coast of Ireland and extracted money from ships that sailed those waters. At the height of her power, Grania O'Malley held five castles and married into a sixth. The stirring pictures of the pirate queen and the ocean she sailed dominate the book, leaving a powerful impression of a strong and memorable woman.

McGovern, Ann. *The Secret Soldier: The Story of Deborah Sampson.* **Illustrated by Ann Grifalconi. 1987. Hard: Four Winds. Pbk: Scholastic. Ages 7–10.**

This presents a fictionalized account of the life of Deborah Sampson, a Revolutionary War soldier. Separated from her parents, Sampson had a hard childhood, spent mostly working for other families. She did housework, cared for younger children, helped with the plowing, and learned how to make household items like stools and baskets. She became a teacher, and deliberately taught her female students more academic subjects than most girls studied then. Although old enough to settle down and marry, Sampson wanted to travel before she entered the restrictive life of marriage, and she decided to enlist in the army as a means of adventure and travel. She disguised herself as a man and served for one and a half years. She once pried a bullet from her own leg to avoid detection, but during another illness a doctor discovered her secret. After leaving the army, Sampson married and had children but still had an urge to travel. She became the first woman in the United States to go on the lecture circuit, where she talked about her experiences in the army. Later she received a pension like other wounded soldiers did, and after her death a warship was named for her. This lively story, with its apt illustrations, portrays a brave and adventurous woman who made her own fate.

McGovern, Ann. *Swimming with Sea Lions and Other Adventures in the Galapagos Islands.* **1992. Hard: Scholastic. Ages 5–9.**

This book about the Galapagos Islands takes the form of a girl's diary, illustrated on each page with small color photographs. She is accompanying her grandmother on a thirteen-day boat trip to explore the islands. The two of them snorkel together and go hiking, encountering such animals as penguins, frigate birds, and giant tortoises. Her grandmother goes scuba diving, and is shown in the photographs with two other women in wet suits. The text packs in a lot of natural history about the islands, and an appendix adds even more. The narrator is shown in one photograph, but otherwise no mention is made of her sex. An enjoyable travel adventure.

McKissack, Patricia and Fred. *Mary McLeod Bethune.* **1992. Hard: Children's Press. Pbk: Children's Press. Ages 7–10.**

This is an attractive short biography of an amazing woman. The well-written text covers a lot of ground, from Bethune's childhood through her achievements as an educator, public servant, and African-American leader. Incidents from her life are used to illustrate Bethune's determination and her generosity. Although some of the photographs are not of high quality, they convey Bethune's spirit and sense of dignity. An accessible introductory biography of a woman all children should know about.

Medearis, Angela Shelf. *Dare to Dream: Coretta Scott King and the Civil Rights Movement.* **Illustrated by Anna Rich. 1994. Hard: Lodestar. Ages 7–10.**

Coretta Scott King aided her husband Martin Luther King, Jr., in leading the civil rights movement in the fifties and sixties. After his death in 1968, she continued to work toward racial equality. In her own childhood, described briefly in this short biography, she felt the cruelty of discrimination. After her father succeeded in building a business and then a house, they were burned to the ground, presumably by hostile whites. Coretta excelled at school, then began to pursue her dream to become a professional singer. But she chose instead to marry King and have a family. She put her musical talents to use in their cause, though, giving a series of successful Freedom Concerts all over the country to raise money. It was she who suggested the famous March on Washington in 1963. After King's assassination, she carried on their work and also raised funds and support for the Martin Luther King, Jr., Center for Nonviolent Social Change in Atlanta. This book discusses both her own accomplishments and those with her husband. It also briefly describes the civil rights movement.

Miller, Robert H. *The Story of "Stagecoach" Mary Fields.* **Illustrated by Cheryl Hanna. 1995. Hard: Silver Press. Pbk: Silver Press. Ages 4–8.**

"Stagecoach" Mary Fields was a truly unusual woman. Born a slave in Tennessee around 1832, she was uncommonly strong even as a child and rode horses with the master's daughter. She grew up to be tall and large, learned to read and write, and sometimes smoked cigars. Some time after the Civil War, which gave Mary Fields her freedom, she moved to Montana and got a job delivering the U.S. mail, becoming only the second woman ever to do so. Driving a stagecoach, she sometimes had to rely on her six-shooter to keep the mail safe from bandits, while at other times she fought off wolves to protect her deliveries. After eight years on the mail route, Fields opened a laundry, using force when necessary to collect the money owed her. Large colored-pencil drawings on each page show Fields in action and give a sense of her times.

Miller, William. *Zora Hurston and the Chinaberry Tree*. Illustrated by Cornelius Van Wright and Ying-Hwa Hu. 1994. Hard: Lee & Low. Pbk: Lee & Low. Ages 5–8.

This picture-story book biography of the eminent black writer and folklorist emphasizes how as a child Zora Hurston rebelled against the limitations put on girls. She dreamed of fishing and traveling, activities for males only. She climbed trees, learned to play checkers, and listened to the stories told by men to boys around the campfire. Although her father discouraged her from dreaming, her mother taught her to keep climbing and reaching for the sky. Lovely, expansive watercolors show a determined African-American girl clad in overalls at home in a lush southern countryside. A note at the end gives more details about the life and career of this talented woman.

Patterson, Francine. *Koko's Story*. Photographs by Dr. Ronald H. Cohn. 1987. Hard: Scholastic, o.p. Pbk: Scholastic. Ages 7–10.

This is a fascinating true account of a female scientist teaching a female gorilla sign language. Dr. Patterson began to work with Koko in 1972, when the gorilla was one year old.

From the start, she taught her American Sign Language (ASL). Anecdotes and colorful photographs tell how Koko has learned to sign and show her making friends and interacting with her pet kittens. Koko can joke and even tell lies in sign language. Many photographs show the scientist and the gorilla working and playing together, and depict a typical day in Koko's life, including her nightly ritual of brushing her teeth. This amazing endeavor is an inspiration to future scientists and an enjoyable story for any reader. Another fascinating book is *Koko's Kitten*.

Quackenbush, Robert. *Clara Barton and Her Victory Over Fear*. 1995. Hard: Simon & Schuster. Pbk: Aladdin. Ages 7–9.

As the youngest of five children, Clara Barton stretched her mind and her physical skills to keep up with the others. She learned to ride horseback when she was three, thanks to her older brother. She studied American history and military rankings with her father and mathematics with an older brother. Barton was painfully shy but fought against it and forced herself to become a teacher, turning down offers of marriage to "be more useful to the world." She found it difficult to advance and be paid fairly because she was a woman, so she left teaching. Clara Barton found her real calling in the battlefields of the Civil War, where she served as a nurse. After the war, she went on the lecture circuit to raise money for finding missing soldiers, then went to Europe, where she helped in another war relief effort. Back in the United States, Barton established the first American branch of the Red Cross in 1900, which quickly began offering relief during disasters such as fires and floods. She served the Red Cross for more than twenty-five years without pay, drawing on her own personal funds. Black-and-white illustrations fill every other page of this introduction to the life of a dedicated woman who left an important legacy to her country.

Quackenbush, Robert. *Clear the Cow Pasture, I'm Coming in for a Landing!: A Story of Amelia Earhart.* 1990. Hard: Simon & Schuster. Pbk: Simon & Schuster. Ages 7–10.

The endpapers of this short biography show a map of Earhart's world travels and pictures of such airplane stunts as a barrel roll and a spiral. The succinct text covers the key events and dates in the life of this extraordinary pilot. The pictures, some of which are based on photographs, are unattractive but add some useful details. Each double-page spread also includes a little conversation among some birds about flying, a touch that children may enjoy. An approachable introduction to a female pioneer in aviation.

Quackenbush, Robert. *Stop the Presses, Nellie's Got a Scoop! A Story of Nellie Bly.* 1992. Hard: Simon & Schuster. Pbk: Simon & Schuster. Ages 7–10.

This simple biography makes the impressive story of journalist Nellie Bly, born in 1864, accessible to younger children. While Blos's *Nellie Bly's Monkey*, listed previously, focuses on only one episode in Bly's life, Quackenbush covers more ground. He uses humorous drawings and a running device of two modern children asking each other questions to liven up an already interesting topic. Bly fearlessly went undercover to dig out important news stories, many of them concerning injustices to women. She spent time in a prison and an insane asylum to get her scoops. After her trip around the world in less than eighty days, she ran a manufacturing business, paying male and female workers the same. Bly was ahead of her time in her ideas about women and in her adventurous approach to life.

Ringgold, Faith. *Aunt Harriet's Underground Railroad in the Sky.* **1993. Hard: Crown. Pbk: Crown. Ages 5–8.**

Artist Ringgold has created a dreamlike account of a modern girl and boy who meet Harriet Tubman and travel the Underground Railroad. Powerful paintings, reminiscent of folk art, show the girl's strenuous imaginary trip from slavery to freedom. At each dangerous stop on the Underground Railroad, bounty hunters lurk in the background ready to pounce on her. But a variety of stouthearted railroad conductors help her through. Finally she flies over Niagara Falls and is reunited with her little brother. In a surrealistic ending, the children and Harriet Tubman are surrounded by freed slaves and a huge circle of women dressed in white. Two pages at the end give facts about Harriet Tubman and the Underground Railroad. This is an effective introduction to Harriet Tubman and the evils of slavery, although young children may find it frightening.

Ringgold, Faith. *Dinner at Aunt Connie's House.* **1993. Hard: Hyperion. Pbk: Hyperion. Ages 7–10.**

This is a lesson in the history of African-American women, disguised as a picture book. A girl and her newly adopted male cousin discover a series of twelve paintings, each a portrait of an important woman, and the paintings speak to them. Mary McLeod Bethune, Augusta Savage, Bessie Smith, and nine others give a few sentences about their accomplishments, and the children are inspired to aim high. Ringgold's bright folkloric paintings are based on a quilt she painted, shown at the end. An odd exchange between the two children, who have just met, about how they plan to marry someday weakens the book's conclusion. Ringgold's strengths are her art and her message, not her writing, in this unusual offering.

Sakurai, Gail. *Mae Jemison: Space Scientist*. 1995. Hard: Children's Press. Ages 6–9.

In September of 1992, Mae Jemison became the first African-American woman to enter outer space—but that is just one of the remarkable facts about her. This simple biography describes her childhood, education, and career as an astronaut. Informative photographs show her training to be an astronaut, conducting experiments, and working with her colleagues in the space shuttle Endeavor. An early lover of science, Jemison majored in Afro-American studies and chemical engineering at Stanford, then attended Cornell Medical School to become a doctor. She did some of her medical training abroad and served in the Peace Corps in Africa. She now runs her own consulting firm and pursues projects that will help children fulfill their dreams as she has hers. A readable biography about a truly impressive woman.

San Souci, Robert D. *Kate Shelley: Bound for Legend*. Illustrated by Max Ginsburg. 1995. Hard: Dial. Ages 6–9.

Dramatic oil paintings depict the true story of Kate Shelley, a valiant girl of fifteen who risked her life to save others. In 1881 a fierce rainstorm caused a train wreck near the Shelleys' farm in Iowa. Knowing the wreck would endanger an oncoming passenger train, Kate dragged herself on hands and knees through the howling storm across a 700-foot railroad bridge over the flooded Des Moines River. She reached the Moingona station with her warning, and insisted on leading the men there back to the wreck to rescue two railroad workers. It took Kate three months to recover from illness caused by the ordeal, after which she found herself proclaimed a hero statewide. Fittingly, after college she became the station agent at the Moingona station. Today a museum and a railroad bridge named after her honor her bravery.

Schroeder, Alan. *Minty: A Story of Young Harriet Tubman*. Illustrated by Jerry Pinkney. 1996. Hard: Dial. Ages 6–9.

This large, handsome book tells a fictionalized story about the childhood of Harriet Tubman, whose nickname was Minty. It portrays her as a young slave eager for her rights and understandably resentful of her servitude. Her mistress and the overseer are particularly cruel, as they destroy her only doll and whip her for freeing a trapped animal. Her father encourages her to learn about nature in ways that will help her run away, something she dreams about doing. He teaches her swimming and such outdoor survival skills as how to recognize the north star. In the outstanding watercolor-and-pencil illustrations, Minty's red bandanna provides a bright spot against a muted background, like a beacon of hope. The back cover shows a much older Harriet Tubman, with a walking stick and a red bandanna under a shawl. The author's note at the end gives more details about this courageous woman. A beautiful blend of text and picture.

Schroeder, Alan. *Ragtime Tumpie*. Illustrated by Bernie Fuchs. 1989. Hard: Little, Brown. Pbk: Little, Brown. Ages 6–9.

Extraordinary golden paintings send the reader into the past to St. Louis in the 1910s, where dancer Josephine Baker grew up. This fictionalized story about her tells of a girl named Ragtime Tumpie who loved to dance to ragtime music. Pretending she was a famous dancer, she would practice wherever she went. When a traveling salesman comes to town and proposes a dancing contest, Tumpie competes against adults and wins a shiny silver dollar. At that moment she truly believes in her dream of making a living from dancing. A final page offers a photograph and facts about Josephine Baker, for whom the dream came true.

Spinner, Stephanie. *Little Sure Shot: The Story of Annie Oakley*. Illustrated by José Miralles. 1993. Hard: Random House. Pbk: Random House. Ages 6–9.

This biography introduces the fascinating character known as Annie Oakley. The short chapters, with their bright illustrations, follow her through her childhood, when she learned to shoot and sold game to support her family. Sent to live with her older sister in Cincinnati, she frequented shooting galleries and one day competed against a sharpshooter named Frank Butler for a hundred dollars. Although he was older and more experienced, she won. She ended up marrying him. They traveled around the country and later to Europe giving exhibitions of trick shooting. Annie Oakley, as she called herself onstage, would shoot a coin out of her husband's hand and the end off a cigarette in his mouth. She was extraordinarily talented and she perfected her talent with practice. Annie Oakley was unique in an era when women rarely competed with men in public, especially not for money. A simple biography with well-chosen anecdotes about a remarkable woman.

Stanley, Diane, and Peter Vennema. *Cleopatra*. Illustrated by Diane Stanley. 1994. Hard: Morrow. Ages 7–10.

Cleopatra was far more than a beautiful woman, as this slim biography makes clear. She ruled Egypt for twenty-one years, beginning when she was eighteen. When driven out two years later, she raised an army to fight for her throne. Her two well-known relationships, one with Julius Caesar and the other with Mark Antony, were political alliances as well as romantic ones. According to the historian Plutarch, the men were drawn to her not by her beauty, but by her great intelligence and force of character. This attractive "storybook biography" emphasizes Cleopatra's struggles for power and her ability to recover from defeats. In a time when women rarely wielded direct power, Cleopatra was a fascinating exception. The beautiful ornate paintings reflect Egyptian artwork.

Stanley, Diane, and Peter Vennema. *Good Queen Bess: The Story of Elizabeth I of England*. Illustrated by Diane Stanley. 1990. Hard: Four Winds. Ages 6–9.

This beautifully illustrated short biography introduces one of the most important queens in history. Elizabeth I ruled England for more than forty-four years and presided over the cultural flowering in which Shakespeare wrote and performed. She became queen at age twenty-five and quickly learned to deal shrewdly with her own advisers and with foreign powers. She never married or shared the power of her throne. When Spain sent the Spanish Armada to try to conquer England and convert it to Catholicism, Elizabeth thrilled her defending soldiers by riding through their ranks in steel armor; ultimately England prevailed over Spain. One of the exquisite gouache illustrations shows Elizabeth on horseback brandishing a sword among her troops. The jewellike tones and intricate details of the pictures convey a sense of Elizabeth's glamorous court and the times in general.

Venezia, Mike. *Georgia O'Keeffe*. 1993. Hard: Children's Press. Pbk: Children's Press. Ages 6–9.

This heavily illustrated, short biography in the Getting to Know the World's Greatest Artists series introduces Georgia O'Keeffe in a way that appeals to young readers. The large print makes it easy to read, and the humorous drawings include funny conversation in cartoon balloons. The text itself is straightforward, combining details from the artist's childhood and life with observations about her art. Seventeen paintings from throughout her career appear, along with three photographs of O'Keeffe herself and small reproductions of a few works that influenced her.

Venezia, Mike. *Mary Cassatt*. 1989. Hard: Children's Press. Pbk: Children's Press. Ages 6–9.

Another book in the Getting to Know the World's Greatest Artists series, this slim biography of American artist Mary Cassatt emphasizes her role as a pioneer. She became a painter in the late 1800s, when it was unusual for women to be artists. As a painter, she chose to paint scenes from everyday life rather than the grand subjects most artists painted. She joined the Impressionists, who were using some revolutionary new techniques. Her intimate paintings of mothers and children were another innovation. The brief, simple text describes Cassatt's life and career, using many examples of her paintings. Several colorful cartoons add humor that will attract some children who don't usually choose to read about art. An approachable way to begin appreciating art and an important artist.

Wallner, Alexandra. *Beatrix Potter*. 1995. Hard: Holiday. Ages 5–9.

Ornate illustrations full of intriguing details are a fitting complement to this short biography of Beatrix Potter, well known for her small children's books. The story explains how she escaped from the loneliness of her strict upbringing through art and her love of animals. At thirty-five she turned her energies to writing and illustrating a book for children, and had it printed herself when several publishers rejected it. The result was the very successful book *The Tale of Peter*

Rabbit. With her earnings, Potter bought a farm, which she filled with animals. She died in 1943, the author of more than twenty-five books, many of them known to children throughout the world.

Yolen, Jane. *The Ballad of the Pirate Queens.* Illustrated by David Shannon. 1995. Hard: Harcourt. Ages 5–9.
The distinguishing feature of this book is that it is about two female pirates, a topic of interest to many children. Told in verse, the fictionalized biography is based on sketchy facts about Anne Bonney and Mary Reade, who sailed on the *Calico Jack* and were tried for piracy. Anne and Mary avoided a death sentence because they were pregnant. Melodramatic paintings accompany the uninspired verse. A note at the end gives further factual information about the two pirates.

4

Books for Middle Readers

At this stage, most readers really come into their own. Many wonderful books are written for this general age group (around ages nine to eleven), making it an exciting time for children who like to read. At this point, certain children become voracious readers and consume books by the dozens. Others tend to be interested in only one genre or series. It is not unusual for children to reread favorite books over and over again for pleasure and security.

I have divided the books in this chapter into two main categories, Fiction and Biographies. Fiction is divided further into six genres: adventure and survival stories; contemporary life; sports stories; mysteries; historical fiction; and fantasy and science fiction. The fantasy and science fiction section contains noticeably more books than the other sections, while mystery and sports stories contain the least.

Biographies are divided into seven smaller groups: leaders and activists; professionals and educators; scientists and inventors; women in the arts; sports biographies; women in history; and a miscellaneous group of dynamic girls and women. The women in history section contains a good assortment of books that focus on women's roles in the past with an emphasis on the women's suffrage movement. A very brief section covers poetry and magazines. There is little in either of these categories, a situation I hope will change.

As always, do not limit your choices to this one chapter. Novels and biographies in the preceding and following chapters will suit some middle readers, depending on their reading skill and interests. Like many adults, children this age still enjoy heavily illustrated books. Check the first and second chapters for picture-story books and folktales that sound appealing. Note that the folktale collections at the end of chapter 2 are particularly suited to middle readers.

Fiction

Adventure and Survival Stories

Aiken, Joan. *Is Underground*. 1993. Hard: Delacorte. Pbk: Dell. Ages 10–13.

Is Twite proves to be as brave and quick-witted as her older sister Dido from *Nightbirds on Nantucket*. Having made a promise to her dying uncle to find his son, Is first goes to London, where she learns that her cousin Arn is one of hundreds of missing children. She consciously walks into danger by boarding a train full of children going to "Playland." By coincidence, she finds her great-grandfather and her great-aunt, and realizes that another one of her uncles is enslaving the lost children. For a while, she works as a doctor's assistant, a job that calls for strong nerves. Later, she works with the other children in the foundries and in the mines. Because of a prophecy, the other children believe she will save them from their terrible fate, a prediction Is is determined to fulfill. Unlikely coincidences, melodramatic turns, and crisp dialogue characterize this tale by an outstanding writer. In the fast-paced sequel *Cold Shoulder Road*, Is Twite battles evil again.

Aiken, Joan. *Nightbirds on Nantucket*. Illustrated by Robin Jacques. 1996. Hard: Doubleday, o.p. Pbk: Dell. Ages 10–13.

Dido Twite, who first appeared in the book *Black Hearts in Battersea*, comes into her own in this tale of intrigue laced with humor. She has been picked up at sea, after escaping from a sinking ship, by a whaler from Nantucket. The strange, brooding Captain Casket asks her to befriend his shy daughter, Dutiful Penitence, who is scared of just about everything, including the ocean. When the two of them are deposited on Nantucket to live with Pen's nasty Aunt Tribulation, Dido refuses to be ordered around by the "ungrateful old cuss." Mysteries abound: Is Aunt Trib really who she seems to be? Why is a bird-watcher building a giant gun in the woods? With the help of a boy named Nate and an ever braver Pen, Dido thwarts a dangerous plot and exposes the criminals. She exudes confidence and is always ready with a quick retort or colorful phrase. Pen progresses from complete passivity to having the strength to stand up to the intimidating Aunt Trib; a "real bang-up hero," Dido calls her. A delight to read from beginning to end. In the sequel *The Stolen Lake*, now out of print, Dido visits a mysterious country when her ship from Nantucket to England goes off course.

Cohen, Barbara, and Bahija Lovejoy. *Seven Daughters and Seven Sons*. 1982. Hard: Atheneum, o.p. Pbk: Beech Tree. Ages 10–14.

Set in the Middle East long in the past, this story tells of Buran, the fourth daughter of a poor man who has seven daughters. Whereas sons can help earn money, daughters cost money, to the family's despair. Their uncle, in contrast, is a rich man with seven sons who disdain Buran's family. Buran, whom her father has educated like a son, decides to disguise herself as a man and try her hand at trade. She travels by caravan from Baghdad to Tyre and uses her wits and hard work to try to make a fortune. Buran befriends and then falls in love with Mahmoud, son of Tyre's ruler. In their hours of talk, Mahmoud professes the common wisdom that women are inferior to men. He realizes his mistake only after Buran has left Tyre to seek revenge on her disdainful cousins. A delightful tale about a smart, ambitious woman who succeeds against all odds.

Cottonwood, Joe. *Quake!* 1995. Hard: Scholastic. Ages 10–12.

This realistic novel is based on a powerful earthquake that shook Northern California in 1989. The narrator, fourteen-year-old Franny, and her friend Jennie are baby-sitting her brother while their parents go to the World Series. Their rickety home in the mountains near Santa Cruz is hard hit by the 5:00 P.M. quake. Franny finds courage she didn't know she had as she risks turning off dangerous gas mains in her house and others nearby. The three children roll a Volkswagen off an injured neighbor and find a nurse to help take him to the emergency center. Franny, who wants to be a geologist, meets a female geologist who is analyzing the effects of the quake and who encourages Franny in her ambition. The aftershocks, uncertainty about the fate of their parents, and the continuing dangers provide constant suspense.

George, Jean Craighead. *The Talking Earth*. 1983. Hard: Harper. Pbk: Harper Trophy. Ages 10–12.

Because thirteen-year-old Seminole Billie Wind doubts the legends of her tribe, her uncle sends her off for a night in the Everglades. But the night turns into many weeks, starting when a fire sweeps over the island she is on and Billie must hide in a cave for days. When she emerges, she builds herself a new dugout canoe, but decides not to return home immediately. With a young otter she has saved, she journeys through the Everglades, learning more about the world around her and about herself. She draws on her knowledge of nature to survive by fishing, hunting, and harvesting plants. She turns her dugout into a houseboat and makes her way away from home toward the ocean. Near the end of the journey, her life is endangered by a hurricane, and she must rely again on her ingenuity and good sense to survive. She is a brave, thoughtful, self-reliant girl on a serious quest. Her mother is head of the Wind Clan, and Billie shows the leadership qualities she needs to follow in her mother's footsteps. Although the message about the relationship between humans and their environment gets heavy-handed at times, all in all, this is a good adventure with a serious theme.

Langton, Jane. *The Fragile Flag*. 1984. Hard: Harper, o.p. Pbk: Harper Trophy. Ages 9–12.

Fourth grader Georgie finds herself leading a Children's Crusade when she resolves to walk from Massachusetts to Washington, D.C., to talk with the president. Like many other children and adults, she is worried about his plan to launch a nuclear missile into space. A quietly determined child with an iron will, Georgie inspires other children to join her, first just a few, then thousands. Her best friend Frieda, a born leader, takes over the organization of the pilgrimage, formulating rules and issuing orders. She serves as spokesperson when the media gets interested. Georgie's older stepcousin Eleanor also helps run things, but everyone understands that Georgie is the heart of the march. The children walk along busy streets, sleep outside many nights, and endure nasty weather. As their number swells, so do their spirits. Meanwhile, children around the world respond by marching to their own capitols to protest the nuclear missile. The slightly magical, totally satisfying ending rewards Georgie and her friends for their endurance and faith. An unusual, inspiring story about a girl who is willing to walk more than four hundred miles for her convictions.

Lindgren, Astrid. Translated by Patricia Crompton. *Ronia, the Robber's Daughter*. 1983. Hard: Peter Smith. Pbk: Puffin. Ages 10–12.

In this unusual story translated from Swedish, Ronia lives in a fortress with her father, Matt, her mother, Lovis, and her father's gang of robbers. One day in the woods she meets Birk, son of Matt's greatest rival, Borka, and they forge such a close friendship they feel as though they are sister and brother. Her father disowns Ronia when he hears about the friendship, and she runs away to live in a cave with Birk. Lyrical descriptions capture the joy they take in living outdoors, where they are equals in energy and courage. Both tame wild horses after many tumbles and revel in swimming dangerously near a waterfall. Lovis, a strong and levelheaded mother, supplies them with bread and, though she would like Ronia back, understands her anger at Matt. In the end Ronia and Birk are reconciled with their parents but assert their independence by vowing never to be robbers themselves. Lindgren, author of *Pippi Longstocking*, which is described in the fantasy and science fiction section, has created another indomitable girl who leads a free, exciting life.

Myers, Edward. *Climb or Die*. 1994. Hard: Hyperion. Pbk: Hyperion. Ages 10–13.

Fourteen-year-old Danielle and her family are driving through a snowstorm in the Rockies when they have an accident on a deserted mining road. Danielle's parents are both hurt, so it is up to her and her thirteen-year-old brother Jake to go for help. Danielle's strengths are her fine athletic ability—Jake calls her a jock—and the skills she learned at a mountaineering school. Jake, on the other hand, excels at problem solving but is weak on athletic ability. At first his skills dominate, as he insists they try to climb a mountain to a weather station he believes is at the top. He has brought tools from the car and rigs up a compass. Soon Danielle's strengths come into play as they get higher and she has to teach Jake mountaineering skills. Each of them develops new abilities along the way: Jake challenges himself physically, while Danielle improvises with tools to make climbing equipment. The climb is perilous and the end uncertain, adding to the suspense. A gripping story of physical challenge in which a girl tests her limits.

O'Dell, Scott. *Island of the Blue Dolphins*. 1960. Hard: Houghton. Pbk: Dell. Ages 9–12.

Set on a small island off the coast of California, this survival story concerns a twelve-year-old Native American named Karana. When her tribe is leaving the island for more prosperous lands, Karana jumps off the ship and swims back to her island to get her brother, who was accidentally left behind. She expects the ship will return for them soon, but her brother dies immediately, and many years pass before a ship arrives. The mesmerizing story details her survival tactics as she builds shelters and gathers food. Going against the laws of her tribe for women, she learns to fashion spears and a bow and arrows. She kills wild dogs who endanger her, but befriends a dog left behind by Aleut hunters. Excitement enters her everyday life as she restores a canoe, hoping to leave the island on her own, and when she fights to survive a tsunami and an earthquake. The exquisite writing conveys the beauty of her surroundings and draws readers into her daily life. A modern classic based on a true story, this Newbery Medal winner has been a popular book for more than thirty years. The sequel, *Zia*, recounts the story of Karana's niece.

Roberts, Willo Davis. *Baby-Sitting Is a Dangerous Job*. 1985. Hard: Atheneum. Pbk: Aladdin. Ages 10–12.

Thirteen-year-old Darcy wants to earn enough money to buy her own tape deck, so she takes on a baby-sitting job for the wealthy Foster family. She finds spending afternoons with the three children a challenge, but she persists. Meanwhile, she and her friend Irene are helping out a classmate who has run away from a father who beats her. Darcy finds herself in serious trouble, too, when she and the Foster children are kidnapped. Darcy tries to reassure the children while figuring out a way to outwit the kidnappers. Her courage and cleverness convincingly save Darcy and her charges in this suspenseful story.

Root, Phyllis. *The Listening Silence*. Illustrated by Dennis McDermott. 1992. Hard: Harper. Ages 9–11.

Based on various Native American traditions, this lyrical novel tells the story of Kiri, a girl with the power to become a healer. She has been in the care of the healer and singer Mali since her parents died when she was five. Now Mali is growing older and Kiri must confront her fears about the healers' mystical task of going "within" others to cure them. In a tribe where women are hunters, potters, and leaders, Kiri's need to find her own calling is respected. So she embarks on a wilderness journey in a small boat to seek her own vision and learn her fate. When a winter storm ruins the boat, Kiri must draw on all her outdoor skills to survive: building a shelter, starting a fire, trapping wild animals, and harvesting wild food. In the end, she not only finds her own way but helps an older boy from the tribe survive. A quiet, powerful novel about a girl who takes her vision and her future seriously.

Contemporary Life

Bawden, Nina. *Granny the Pag.* **1996. Hard: Clarion. Ages 9–12.**

Catriona's grandmother defies all stereotypes. She is an eminent retired psychiatrist who still gives lectures and treats a few sad patients. She wears jeans or, when she rides her motorcycle, leather clothes. And to Cat's chagrin, she smokes cigarettes. Granny the Pag, as Cat calls her, has taken care of her granddaughter since Cat was young and her actor parents could no longer take her on the road. Their life together has been eccentric but loving. Now that Cat is eleven, her life has become more complicated. A bully in her class is giving her a bad time because she refuses to be picked on. Worse still, her parents have bought a house in London and want her to live with them. But Cat is unwilling to let her life be decided by others, and she draws on all she has learned from Granny the Pag to prevail. Two strong females, one young and one old, make a formidable team in this engaging British novel.

Chocolate, Debbi. *NEATE to the Rescue.* **1992. Pbk: Just Us Books. Ages 9–11.**

Naimah Gordon's mother is struggling to keep her seat on the city council after a nasty, bigoted opponent has succeeded in having electoral districts redrawn. Thirteen-year-old Naimah and four of her friends resolve to help Ms. Gordon win. These five personable and responsible African-American adolescents know how to succeed when they put their minds to it. They print up flyers and distribute them. Naimah wins the election to be student council president at her junior high. Then the five friends organize a rally of junior and senior high students, during which Naimah urges them to get their parents to vote. A happy ending ensues. The five friends, elated by their victories, decide to call themselves NEATE from the initial letters of their first names.

Clymer, Eleanor. *My Mother Is the Smartest Woman in the World.* **Illustrated by Nancy Kincade. 1982. Hard: Atheneum. Ages 8–12.**

Thirteen-year-old Kathleen Rowan never expects her mother to take her seriously when Kathleen urges her to run for mayor. But her mother does, and the family and all their friends get involved in the campaign. Kathleen misses the attention of a stay-at-home mother, but she is also excited and proud. She is thrilled when her mother takes Kathleen's advice on how to present herself and be more effective. Painlessly, the reader learns about aspects of the political process on a local level, such as citizens lobbying for change and ordinary people running for office. Kathleen's mother encounters sexist reactions from voters and her male opponent, who suggest mothers should stay home rather than run for office. But her mother is persistent and savvy, a great role model for Kathleen and her friends. An enjoyable story that continues to be timely and instructive.

Ephron, Delia. *The Girl Who Changed the World.* **1993. Hard: Ticknor & Fields. Ages 9–12.**

Have you ever had an older sister or brother pick on you? Have you dreamed of revenge? Violet reaches the end of her rope when her older brother hits her with a flyswatter during her piano recital. Her hair is full of dead fly and her heart is filled with rebellion. She starts thinking like a general and organizes the "youngers" in the neighborhood into an army. She trains them in such tools of revenge as smiling when an "older" teases and mimicking everything the older says. The youngers plant lizards in the olders' beds, a trick Violet's older brother has played on her. Violet grows in confidence as she shows herself to be an effective leader. In the end the olders gain some understanding of how mean they have been and the youngers gain some much-needed power. Adults may wince at the animosity between siblings, but many children will recognize it from their own lives. Younger siblings in particular will revel in this exciting, exaggerated tale.

Fenner, Carol. *Yolonda's Genius*. 1995. Hard: McElderry. Pbk: Aladdin. Ages 10–13.

Yolonda is a big, strong African-American fifth grader who has just moved from Chicago to a smaller city in Michigan with her mother and her younger brother Andrew. She knows her own power and in one gripping scene uses it to punish some drug-pushing bullies who have ruined Andrew's harmonica. Yolonda believes her brother, who is slow learning to read, is a musical genius. She uses her own genius at thinking, planning, and asserting herself to convince others of Andrew's abilities. Andrew returns her love and admiration by playing music that conveys how large and powerful Yolonda is, "great like a queen." This is just one of the times that Yolonda's size is viewed as an asset. She takes after her aunt Tiny, a huge woman who owns several immensely successful hairdressing salons. Yolonda's mother, a paralegal, wants her to do well in school and to become a doctor or lawyer. But Yolonda, who takes after her dead father, a police officer, aspires to become Chicago's chief of police someday, which seems possible for a girl of her abilities. This Newbery Honor Book is a gem: a beautifully written story of a queen-sized girl who is cherished by her family and justly confident of herself.

Fitzhugh, Louise. *Harriet the Spy*. 1964. Hard: Harper. Pbk: Harper Trophy. Ages 10–13.

This nearly 300-page novel, a modern classic, follows the ups and downs of sixth grader Harriet Welsch. Harriet, who attends a private school in Manhattan, practices to be a writer by keeping extensive notes in a series of notebooks. She follows a route to observe and write about her neighbors, even hiding in a dumbwaiter to spy on one wealthy woman. She also comments on her friends, who eventually find the book and ostracize her for her brutally honest criticisms. Harriet especially misses her friends Janie, who loves science, and Sport, a gentle boy who takes care of his father. With her parents' help and a bright idea of her own, Harriet restores her two important friendships. Harriet and Janie, who are dedicated to their hobbies, are not interested in being popular. Unlike many fictional girls in contemporary novels, they are unconventional and will likely stay that way.

Greene, Constance C. *Isabelle the Itch*. Illustrated by Emily A. McCully. 1973. Hard: Viking, o.p. Pbk: Puffin. Ages 8–11.

" 'Let's fight at my house today,' Isabelle said to Herbie." So opens this humorous book about a likeable, highly energetic girl. Isabelle and her quieter friend Herbie practice fighting every day and spend time carrying out Isabelle's schemes. She has a flair for causing trouble and usually enjoys the commotions that result. She also tends to say what she thinks, which is funny but causes even more trouble. Determined to buy a new pair of track shoes for an upcoming race, Isabelle earns money by taking over her brother's paper route and in the process makes friends with Mrs. Stern, one of the few adults who doesn't find her irritating. Generally Isabelle gets along better with males than females, but she shows signs that that may change. A realistic, funny portrayal that doesn't feel dated despite its age.

Konigsburg, E. L. *From the Mixed-up Files of Mrs. Basil E. Frankweiler.* **1967. Hard: Atheneum. Pbk: Dell. Ages 10–12.**

This charming story of two children running away to the Metropolitan Museum of Art won the Newbery Medal for its excellent writing. Eleven-year-old Claudia finds life in her suburban Connecticut home unfair because as the oldest child and the only girl she has more than her share of responsibilities. When she decides to run away, her originality and ability to plan come to the fore. She chooses the museum because it will be comfortable and elegant, and she enlists one of her brothers, Jamie, because he is rich for his age and knows how to keep quiet. They pull off the escapade without a hitch, thanks to Claudia's leadership and Jamie's funds. Living secretly in the museum, they become fascinated with a statue of an angel that might have been created by Michelangelo, and they try to solve the mystery of its origin. This leads them to Mrs. Basil E. Frankweiler, the narrator of the story, who is a self-confident, opinionated, and very wealthy old woman who presents them with a further challenge and a wonderful reward. This book has remained popular for many years thanks to its humor, suspense, and fast-moving plot.

Lindgren, Astrid. Translated by Gerry Bothmer. *Mischievous Meg.* **Illustrated by Janina Domanska. 1962. Hard: Viking, o.p. Pbk: Puffin. Ages 8–11.**

Meg's impulsive, adventurous nature gets her into endless scrapes. At nine, there is "nothing soft and sweet about Meg." She jumps off the shed with an umbrella, hoping it will act like a parachute. She climbs out her window at night to help her neighbor trap a ghost. She misbehaves at school, losing things and staining her clothes, then blames it on an imaginary schoolmate named Richard. When her schemes go awry, Meg does not get discouraged or subdued, for something in her "pushed her toward adventure, and she thrived on excitement." The episodic novel has a distinctly Scandinavian and old-fashioned flavor, and includes an odd subplot about the poor family next door. Meg is a good-hearted heroine full of new ideas for fun, one who will appeal to many readers.

Lisle, Janet Taylor. *The Dancing Cats of Applesap*. Illustrated by Joelle Shefts. 1984. Hard: Bradbury, o.p. Pbk: Aladdin. Ages 9–11.

In this funny story, ten-year-old Melba Morri saves Jiggs' Drug Store from going out of business and expands her own horizons at the same time. Melba starts out painfully shy, unpopular with her schoolmates and outshone by her older brother Victor. Her only refuge is the drugstore run by Miss Toonie and inhabited by numerous cats. When the store seems to be going out of business and Miss Toonie turns to Melba for help, Melba learns that having someone rely on her makes her start to believe in herself. A major setback discourages Melba, but she and Miss Toonie regroup and finally succeed. An offbeat, charming novel about a girl who transforms herself and finds a strong voice in the process.

McKay, Hilary. *The Exiles*. 1992. Hard: McElderry. Pbk: Aladdin. Ages 9–12.

The exiles are the four Conroy sisters, ages six, eight, eleven, and thirteen, strong-willed girls who try any outrageous thing they want without worrying about the consequences. This gets them into a lot of trouble but keeps their lives exciting. Under protest, they are sent by their long-suffering parents to spend the summer with their grandmother. Since she is just as insistent on having her way as the exiles are, the visit is a funny series of conflicts that mellows eventually into affectionate exasperation on both sides. The only male character, a practical boy from a nearby farm, is torn between admiration for the girls' daring and shock at their recklessness. Certain readers will laugh out loud at the funny, understated dialogue and the unexpected approach that the exiles take to life. Highly recommended. In the entertaining sequel, *The Exiles at Home*, the two older girls secretly pledge money to pay for an African child's schooling, then struggle to earn it.

Miles, Betty. *The Real Me*. 1974. Hard: Knopf, o.p. Pbk: Avon. Ages 9–12.

Barbara Fisher's first day in junior high goes well until she reaches physical education. Due to her schedule, her only option is slimnastics. She asks to enroll in tennis, but is told it is only for boys. Much as she prefers to be inconspicuous, Barbara is so indignant she and her friends start a petition to change the sexism in PE offerings. At home, her brother Richard offers her his paper route when he makes the basketball team, but the newspaper has a policy against hiring girls. When Barbara asks customers on the route to protest the policy, she gets some positive responses but also finds customers who think girls aren't up to the job. Barbara's congenial family and her friend Oliver support her attempts to change things. In the process, Barbara learns how to speak effectively for what she believes in, without expecting everyone to agree with her. A contemporary feel characterizes this story, which is told in Barbara's witty voice.

Peck, Richard. *Bel-Air Bambi and the Mall Rats*. 1993. Hard: Delacorte. Pbk: Dell. Ages 10–12.

This is a very funny book about a Hollywood family that

moves to a small town somewhere in Middle America. The twelve-year-old narrator Buffie and her slightly older sister Bambi, who attended the Stars for Tomorrow School in Bel-Air, are stunned to find their new school dominated by a gang of destructive bullies, male and female. Furthermore, the gang has closed down the local mall through vandalism, so they can use it as a clubhouse. The adults in town have responded by ignoring the Mall Rats and buying expensive locks. Stylish, smart Bambi decides someone has to take on these juvenile delinquents or life will be unbearable for her and her family. She enlists another former Californian as an ally, then gets her whole family involved. They use their experience creating sitcom pilots to stage a hoax that they hope will scare the gang out of the mall. Told in Buffie's Hollywood voice, the story has an air of wild exaggeration. While few heroines come with designer clothes and as much hair gel as Bambi, she, Buffie, their clever mother, and their gun-toting grandmother are all strong characters who take things into their own hands. Great fun.

Pfeffer, Susan Beth. *Kid Power*. Illustrated by Leigh Grant. 1977. Hard: Watts, o.p. Pbk: Scholastic. Ages 10–12.
This bouncy story about a young entrepreneur feels up-to-date even after twenty years. Eleven-year-old Janie Golden must make her own money if she wants a bicycle, now that her mother has been laid off from her social-work job. The enterprising Janie posts a sign in the grocery store offering to do odd jobs for a dollar an hour. Success follows quickly and she finds herself minding children at a yard sale, running errands for an elderly neighbor, tending a garden, and trying to walk a huge dog. She quickly absorbs financial concepts like gross and net profit and interest-earning savings accounts. She enjoys keeping her financial records, and when business booms,

creating a work schedule. Eventually she has to branch out and add her sister and friends as workers, taking 10 percent as their "agent." Janie excels at solving problems, working hard, and persisting even when the going gets tough. She encounters obstacles, of course, which keep her hopping. But she works these out and even inspires her unemployed mother to try something new. A fast-moving novel about a girl who discovers a talent for management and making money—a topic rarely discussed in children's fiction.

Taylor, Theodore. *The Trouble with Tuck*. 1981. Hard: Doubleday. Pbk: Avon. Ages 8–11.

When Helen's parents give her a dog for her birthday, they hope to teach her responsibility and give her something special in her life. The younger sister of two handsome, athletic brothers, Helen is shy and awkward. But she loves Tuck and works hard to train him, gaining confidence as she does. When Helen turns thirteen, Tuck starts to lose his eyesight. Unwilling to tie him up all day, Helen schemes to get a Seeing Eye dog for Tuck. When her persistence finally pays off, Helen takes on the daunting responsibility of making her two dogs into a team. Despite discouraging setbacks, she succeeds through sheer grit and extraordinary love. Based on a true story, this short novel will have readers cheering for Helen and her dogs.

Thureen, Faythe Dyrud. *Jenna's Big Jump*. Illustrated by Elaine Sandeen. 1993. Hard: Atheneum. Ages 8–10.

New in town, Jenna finds the fourth-grade class unfriendly, particularly a bully named Buzz. Her mother's stories of her daring feats as a child inspire Jenna to fight back against Buzz. She joins forces with a self-confident newcomer named Kate and defeats the bully. Next, she conquers a rope swing in Kate's barn, jumping from higher and higher ledges each time, even though she is scared. Surprisingly, her impetuous mother has trouble with Jenna's newfound willingness to take a risk. As the plot develops, Jenna has several chances to test her courage and change her mother's protective attitude. A gentle story about a girl growing stronger thanks to a girlfriend.

Williams, Vera B. *Scooter*. 1993. Hard: Greenwillow. Ages 8–11.

Artist Vera Williams has created a unique novel by incorporating artwork into the text. Elana and her mother have just moved to a housing project far from their last home. Elana, who loves to perform tricks on her scooter, quickly makes new friends. The children she meets band together into a team to enter a field day in a local park. Acrostics decorated with pictures describe some of her teammates: Beryl is the team captain, Adrienne is strong, and her visiting cousin Nanette is an "especially fast runner." Elana's mother, a working woman who cares about politics and women's rights, encourages Elana's independence. The field day, illustrated with pictures and a wonderful chart, highlights Elana's energy and persistence. An unusually lively book, this is a good read-aloud for younger children, too.

Yarbrough, Camille. *The Shimmershine Queens*. 1989. Hard: Putnam. Pbk: Random House. Ages 9–12.

Angie's father has left and her mother is suffering from mild depression, leaving the ten-year-old girl in need of support and comfort. She gets these from her ninety-year-old cousin Seatta, who doesn't seem to be afraid of anything. Seatta teaches Angie about "shimmershine," the warm, glowing feeling of doing your best and having your efforts succeed. Seatta also tells Angie that her dark skin, inherited from African ancestors, is beautiful. Angie's attempts to share Seatta's wisdom about African-American history in school get her into a fistfight with several other black girls who tease Angie about her dark skin. However, the new dance and drama teacher, Ms. Collier, unites the children in the process of putting on a play about Africa and slavery. Angie finds her voice and learns to speak up for herself, encouraged by the strong female role models in her life. A heartwarming, sometimes sad story that will have readers looking for their own shimmershine feeling.

Sports Stories

Alvord, Douglas. *Sarah's Boat: A Young Girl Learns the Art of Sailing.* 1994. Hard: Tilbury House. Ages 9–12.
This small book combines instruction about sailing with the fictional story of twelve-year-old Sarah Miller. Shy Sarah overcomes more of her nervousness about sailing every time she masters an aspect of it. Black-and-white drawings supply details about boats and how to maneuver them, as do diagrams about tacking, jibbing, and navigating. After practicing and getting tips from her grandfather, Sarah enters a race and skillfully defeats a boy who has poked fun at her boat. A glossary at the back lists parts of boats as well as sailing terms. This is one of the few books available about a girl and her boat; sailors and future sailors won't want to miss it.

Herzig, Alison Cragin. *The Boonsville Bombers.* Illustrated by Dan Andreasen. 1991. Hard: Viking. Pbk: Puffin. Ages 8–10.
Ten-year-old Emma loves baseball, but none of her friends

are interested in it. Her older brother Michael plays with four of his friends, who call themselves the Boonsville Bombers. Michael refuses to let Emma join them until she gives him a coveted baseball card. But his friend Joe is so hostile to girls that when Emma catches his fly ball, he quits and takes the bat with him. When Emma, Michael, and Joe attend a professional ball game together, Emma combines luck with a strong will in a way that leads to a happy ending for her. Emma's baseball-loving aunt, who sends her a baseball cap and baseball cards, lends moral support to Emma, while her mother, though not athletic, is also encouraging. Joe's negative attitude toward girls is annoying, but in the end, the other boys side with Emma rather than him. A light story for baseball lovers.

Jackson, Alison. *Blowing Bubbles with the Enemy.* **1993. Hard: Dutton. Ages 9–11.**

The girls at Jefferson Middle School pull together in a wonderful way for a worthy cause: supporting the girls' basketball team. When talented basketball player Bobby tries out for the boys' team, the coach cheats her of a fair chance and none of the boys object. Her friend Charlotte, editor of the school newspaper, is outraged and lets her readers know it. Her letter, which suggests the boys were cowards and Bobby was braver than all of them, inspires many girls to try out for the girls' team. With the support of their coach, the girls decide to challenge the boys' team, knowing they are likely to lose but resolved to try their hardest. As the best player, Bobby finds herself planning plays and suggesting drills in practice. Meanwhile, other girls in the school show their support and stage a pep rally. Unfortunately, Bobby's first-person voice can be grating. She berates herself frequently for her "big mouth," usually after she has said what she thinks. She also spends too much time mooning over one of the boys on the basketball team, who does not seem to merit her interest. Nevertheless, it is refreshing to read about so many girls uniting to protest unfair treatment and getting excited about a girls' team sport.

Levy, Elizabeth. *The Gymnasts #18: The New Coach?* 1991. Pbk: Scholastic. Ages 9–11.

Eleven-year-old Lauren and her friends on the Pinecones gymnastics team take their sport seriously but not too seriously, an approach that their coach Patrick reinforces. When a high-powered Hungarian coach joins Patrick and starts pushing the girls to work harder, Lauren is upset and uncooperative. But eventually she realizes that she is improving from the tedious repetition and greater risks, and begins to appreciate the new coach. Her mother, a Denver city council member, and her father, a high school principal, value her work in school above her gymnastics activities, which helps Lauren keep her sport in perspective. This book is written in first person, and the conversational tone is appealing and realistic. Certain to please gymnastics fans.

Lord, Bette Bao. *In the Year of the Boar and Jackie Robinson*. Illustrated by Marc Simont. 1984. Hard: Harper. Pbk: Harper Trophy. Ages 9–12.

It is 1947, and Shirley Temple Wong has just moved to New York from China. Everything is strange and worrisome, from the language to the food, from school to the stickball game that other children play. Shirley flounders until the day she walks proudly through the school yard "like an emperor" and interrupts a stickball game. She emerges with two black eyes and one good friend, Mabel, the strongest, scariest girl in the fifth grade. Mabel teaches Shirley how to play stickball and how to appreciate baseball, especially the Brooklyn Dodgers. During summer vacation, Shirley helps her father fix things in their apartment building and becomes adept with tools and repair jobs. One of her dreams for the future is to be an engineer, like her father; another is to be a surgeon. For Shirley, these dreams are connected to her admiration for Jackie Robinson, the first black to play in the major leagues and a symbol of opportunity in America. Shirley's dedication to the Dodgers reflects the rarely depicted devotion many girls feel to a sports team. Marc Simont's sprightly black-and-white illustrations perfectly suit this optimistic story.

Moore, Elaine. *Who Let Girls in the Boys' Locker Room?* 1994. Pbk: Troll. Ages 10–13.

The best thing about this sports novel is how much Michelle, the main character, loves basketball. She has a Michael Jordan poster in her room, she plays on a community center team, and she plans to play on the junior high girls' team. But when school starts, budget cuts have forced the boys' and girls' teams to merge into a co-ed team. The coach is willing to accept the arrangement, but some of the boys are disgusted. Even though she's only four feet ten, Michelle makes the team, along with her tall friend Skye and the awesome Keisha, an eighth-grade girl. When the boys treat their three female players as if they're fragile—and lose a game with this hands-off attitude—Michelle helps the coach solve the problem. The friendship of the girls on the team grows, although a stereotypical antagonism develops between Michelle and a cheerleader. Another cliché is Michelle's misguided romantic interest in a selfish boy. In spite of the flaws, sports fiction about girls and team sports is rare enough to make this worth reading.

Nelson, Vaunda Micheaux. *Mayfield Crossing*. Illustrated by Leonard Jenkins. 1993. Hard: Putnam. Pbk: Avon. Ages 8–10.

In the small town of Mayfield Crossing, four black children and four white children have been friends for years, sharing baseball games and attending the same small school. Now they must switch to Parkview, a new, larger school in a nearby town, where they find the other students unfriendly and in some cases racist. Narrator Meg, who is entering fourth grade, feels the pain of racism, which she had barely encountered before. She also comes to appreciate the strength of her friendships. The friends decide to use baseball to establish their place in the unfriendly school, knowing that they risk public rejection. The main girls in this thoughtful novel—Meg; Mo, hot-tempered Alice, who is known for stealing bases; and one brave Parkview girl—are at home on the baseball field, which becomes a metaphor for bigger issues they must face.

Sullivan, Ann. *Molly Maguire: Wide Receiver*. 1992. Pbk: Avon. Ages 9–11.

Molly Maguire is a fifth grader who loves to climb trees and build forts and rafts. She'd rather be throwing a football around with her neighbor Mr. Brewer than going to the mall with her best friend. The thorn in her happy life is Jason, the boy who sits behind her in class and teases her endlessly. He belabors the idea that, according to his father, girls should concentrate on housekeeping, not science or sports. Infuriated, Molly joins the local parks and recreation football team disguised as a boy. An excellent runner and receiver, she wins the respect of the other players, including Jason. In their first big game, Molly gets two touchdowns. It is troubling that Molly focuses so much on Jason's attitude toward her and that football proves to be dangerous for her. On the positive side, she sticks with her plan even when the going gets hard, and she plays an impressive game of football. A light, sometimes amusing sports novel.

Mysteries

Byars, Betsy. *The Dark Stairs: A Herculeah Jones Mystery.* **1994. Hard: Viking. Ages 10–13.**

Herculeah Jones's mother is a private detective and her father is a police officer, so solving mysteries comes naturally to her. She is as big and strong as her name suggests, and has an iron will. Sure of herself, she plans to be a lawyer who helps children when she grows up. She and her male friend Meat, who is big but not as brave as Herculeah, get involved in a mystery concerning an old house and a strange client of her mother's. When she breaks into the house, she gets locked in but forces her way out. During her second trip to the house, Herculeah stumbles upon a long-lost body and helps her mother solve an old mystery. Although the conclusion is not as scary as the beginning promises, the story has plenty of action and a truly strong heroine. Meat's mother, who arms herself with a frying pan to rescue Herculeah, and Herculeah's mother are strong characters as well. Herculeah continues her detecting in *Tarot Says Beware* and *Dead Letter*.

Elmore, Patricia. *Susannah and the Purple Mongoose Mystery.* **Illustrated by Bob Marshall. 1992. Hard: Dutton. Ages 9–11.**

Susannah is the smartest sixth grader in Oakland, California, according to the narrator Lucy. The two of them and their friend Knievel join forces to solve a mystery about a series of fires suffered by Miss Quigley, a friend of Susannah's grandmother. The suspects include Miss Quigley's next-door neighbor, her foster daughter Theresa, a local real-estate developer, and others. Susannah, who is African-American, is the brains of the bunch, with Lucy on her skateboard and Knievel on his bike always ready for action. Susannah's careful reasoning leads to the unexpected culprit. A lively mystery featuring strong girls and women. Two earlier, recommended mysteries are *Susannah and the Blue House Mystery* (out of print) and *Susannah and the Poison Green Halloween.*

Emerson, Kathy Lynn. *The Mystery of the Missing Bagpipes*. 1991. Pbk: Avon. Ages 8–11.

When an expensive set of ancient bagpipes is stolen from a wealthy man named Ben Orseck, Kim sets out to prove that her friend Woody wasn't the thief. Twelve-year-old Kim and her family are vacationing in Maine so her father, a police officer, can attend bagpiping school at Mr. Orseck's mansion. Kim not only detects the thief, she also uses her pitching skills to save a friend from danger. Kim is the kind of girl who resents bias against women, which abounds in the bagpiping world, so she is pleased to meet a talented female bagpiper. Her mother is a computer expert, and Kim is starting to pursue an interest in photography. Besides solving the mystery, she has to deal with some changes in her family, but finds to her own surprise that she is up to facing new challenges.

George, Jean Craighead. *The Missing 'Gator of Gumbo Limbo: An Ecological Mystery*. 1992. Hard: Harper. Pbk: Harper Trophy. Ages 10–12.

Lisa K. lives outdoors with her mother in Gumbo Limbo Hammock, an undisturbed spot in the Everglades. She fishes expertly, climbs trees, and studies the wildlife around her. One day a hunter hired by the Pest Control Department comes to try to shoot one of her favorite creatures, an alligator she calls Dajun, that the department considers dangerous. Dajun seems to have disappeared, which saves him from the official, but puzzles Lisa K. She proceeds to solve the mystery of his disappearance while also scheming with her friends to thwart the official. Lisa K.'s mother, who has taken Lisa away from an abusive father, is working at a diner and studying for a business degree in order to support the two of them better. Readers will learn a lot of information about ecology as they unravel the mystery.

Keene, Carolyn. *Flying Too High: The Nancy Drew Files 106*. 1995. Pbk: Pocket. Ages 9–12.

This installment in the Nancy Drew Files series, first published in 1991, shows several improvements over the original series. The prose is better, the negative cultural stereotypes are gone, and the settings and topics are updated. However, the case concerns the murder of a young woman, a more violent subject than those of the earlier books. The famous Nancy Drew still encounters far more excitement in one book than most teenage girls go through in a lifetime. In this mystery, she goes undercover in a naval fighter pilot program, in which she performs remarkable feats in the air. She is looking for the killer of the top trainee, a woman who suspected that important computer equipment was being sabotaged. Nancy narrowly escapes danger after danger before she finally figures out the puzzle. A feminist theme emerges as she sees the bias against women in the program; on the other hand, she is strongly attracted to a handsome, macho trainee. An improbable but exciting mystery.

Kehret, Peg. *Screaming Eagles*. 1996. Pbk: Pocket. Ages 9–11.

Two twelve-year-old friends have formed a Care Club

dedicated to caring for animals. When they take a hike in a remote area and see a man taking a baby eaglet from a nest, Rosie and Kayo follow him. They get lost in the woods and even encounter a grizzly bear, which they frighten off. Then they succeed in finding his cabin, where they discover he is a taxidermist who specializes in birds, including endangered species. When the strange man spies them, the two realize their lives might be in danger. The tension mounts as they escape once but are almost caught again, then find them-selves fighting a fire. The athletic Kayo, who loves baseball and lifts weights, and the studious Rosie, who is full of useful facts, make a good team. Although this book is part of a series called Frightmares, the plot is more exciting than frightening. A quick read full of cliff-hangers, this is the kind of adventure book usually written about boys.

Raskin, Ellen. *The Westing Game*. 1978. Hard: Dutton. Pbk: Puffin. Ages 9–12.

This intricate mystery abounds in increasingly strong females. All the characters have just moved into an apartment complex called Sunset Towers and find themselves potential heirs to millions of dollars. Millionaire Sam Westing's will leaves his fortune to whoever can figure out who killed him. The will designates pairs who must work together, and Westing's lawyer doles out clues. The central character is Turtle, a strong-willed, smart ten-year-old who follows the stock market and bets that she can stay in the haunted Westing mansion, at two dollars per minute. Another resi-dent, J. J. Ford, is the first black and first woman elected as a judge in the state, and an intelligent and generous neighbor. Turtle's sister Angela starts out too compliant, but changes as she tries to solve the mystery. Turtle's mother, a pushy social climber, also changes as she finds an outlet for her energy in a business venture. The alert reader gets all the clues she needs as the players collect information about each other in this intriguing mystery. A Newbery Medal winner.

Stevenson, Drew. *Toying with Danger: A Sarah Capshaw Mystery.* **Illustrated by Marcy Dunn Ramsey. 1993. Hard: Cobblehill. Ages 9–11.**

Narrator Clark and his friend Frog find their lives far more exciting when Sarah Capshaw comes to town to visit her grandfather and solve mysteries. When Sarah persuades them to join her in adventures, she is the leader, the first to risk danger, and the one to figure out the puzzle. In this case, something strange is happening at the old Harley farm. An old toy inventor, who is working on a Frankenstein-like robot, may be stealing toy ideas from a company. Or maybe someone is stealing ideas from him. Sarah leads her friends on spooky treks through the Misty Woods, where they encounter mysterious strangers and familiar bullies. Sarah, who doesn't hesitate to fight back when attacked, is a model detective: brave, smart, and persistent. A sketch of Sarah in a fedora, looking like "a detective in an old movie," opens each chapter in this suspenseful mystery. An outstanding girl detective. Other Sarah Capshaw mysteries are *One Ghost Too Many*, now out of print, and *Terror on Cemetery Hill*.

Historical Fiction

Beatty, Patricia. *Eight Mules from Monterey.* **1992. Hard: Morrow. Pbk: Beech Tree. Ages 10–12.**

"Not any one of us Ashmores—Eubie, Mother, or I, Fayette—will ever forget that summer we got mixed up with all those mules, the wild mountain man, and the moonshiners who were shooting at us." So opens this fast-moving novel set in 1916. Fayette's mother has just graduated from library school, and her first assignment is to ride by mule into the mountains and deliver books. So she and her daughter don men's clothing and set off with son Eubie and a shifty-looking mule skinner into the untamed mountains of California. Among the people they meet on their journey are some feisty mountain women who shoot straight and brook no nonsense. By the end of their unlikely adventures, Fayette's mother has gained confidence and chooses work over marriage to a man she doesn't love. Fayette herself is stronger and wiser, and has plenty of stories to tell the folks back home.

Brady, Esther Wood. *Toliver's Secret*. 1976. Hard: Crown, o.p. Pbk: Random House. Ages 9–11.

Before Ellen Toliver's dangerous journey to deliver a secret message to George Washington, her grandfather tells her, "We get over fear by doing things we think we cannot do." From the start, Ellen fears the adventure in which she must disguise herself as a boy, beg a boat ride across a wide bay, and deliver a loaf of bread with the secret message baked into it. Every step along the way she encounters trouble: boys who take the bread, a boat ride to the wrong city, a ten-mile journey through dark woods. Each time she finds the courage to proceed. She whacks the boys with a broom handed to her by a feisty old woman, defies the soldier who wants her bread, fights a pig, and completes her journey in the dark. Proud of her accomplishments, Ellen feels like a new person, ready to face the bully who has scared her for weeks. A good adventure with an important message about taking risks and overcoming fear.

Brink, Carol Ryrie. *Caddie Woodlawn*. 1935. Hard: Macmillan. Pbk: Aladdin. Ages 9–12.

"In 1864 Caddie Woodlawn was eleven, and as wild a little

tomboy as ever ran the woods of western Wisconsin." To the despair of her mother, Caddie spends as much time as she can with her brothers, climbing trees, canoeing, and visiting neighboring Indians. Her courage and friendship send her out on a dark, cold night to warn those Indians of an imminent attack. As the book nears its end, Caddie's parents appear intent on reining her in. Yet at the same time her sedate mother confirms her own allegiance to frontier life, choosing it over England. Caddie, it is clear, will become not a passive lady, but a strong pioneer woman. An enduring American story that won the Newbery Medal. The sequel is *Magical Melons: More Stories About Caddie Woodlawn*.

Climo, Shirley. *A Month of Seven Days*. 1987. Hard: Crowell. Pbk: Troll. Ages 9–12.

When Yankees commandeer the Snyders' home in Georgia during the Civil War, twelve-year-old Zoe is determined to get them to leave. Knowing how superstitious the main officer is, she plants signs that the house is haunted. She also puts herself in danger when she hears some useful information about Yankee plans, which she carries to a neighbor's house. There she learns that Letty, a seemingly spoiled girl, has also been spying on the enemy. Both girls are inspired by the story of Emma Sanson, a Confederate girl whose courage led to the capture of fourteen hundred Yankees. A fast-moving story, this gives a rare picture of strong Confederate females doing their best in dangerous circumstances.

Fisher, Dorothy Canfield. *Understood Betsy*. 1917. Hard: Buccaneer Books; Harmony Raine. Pbk: Dell; Scholastic. Ages 8–11.

Nine-year-old Betsy has been raised by her timid, over-protective Aunt Frances, who has taught her to be afraid of dogs and dirt and hard work. When Aunt Frances must devote herself to her sick mother, Betsy is sent from the city to the country to stay with the Putneys, relatives she has never met. The Putneys—Aunt Abigail, Uncle Henry, and Cousin Ann—believe that children can be helpful and enjoy learning new things. Although doubtful of her abilities, Betsy quickly learns household tasks and overcomes her fear of dogs. Every time she accomplishes something new, she feels a glow of pride. The test of her new competence comes when she and a younger friend are stranded at a county fair, and Betsy earns enough money to get them home. Written in 1917, the story does show boys enjoying more vigorous recess activities than girls, and it has some overly sentimental moments. But overall this warm novel advocates the philosophy of many modern educators: Children learn by doing and feel good about themselves when they conquer a challenge.

Hahn, Mary Downing. *The Gentleman Outlaw and Me— Eli: A Story of the Old West.* 1996. Hard: Clarion. Ages 9–12.

When Eliza Yates's uncle takes his belt to her once again, she takes her dog Caesar and heads west to Tinville, Colorado, to find her father. Eliza quickly discovers she is safer disguised as a boy, and adopts the name Elijah Bates. After she rescues a wounded young man named Calvin Featherstone, a self-proclaimed "gentleman outlaw" who is also on his way to Tinville, the two join forces. Eliza finds life as a boy considerably more enjoyable than her previous life, even when it means pulling Calvin out of dangerous situations. Tinville holds several surprises for Eliza, including a new friend, Miss Jenny Hausmann, a photographer who believes girls have more options than catching a husband. Being a girl doesn't look so bad when Miss Jenny offers to teach Eliza about photography. In Tinville, Eliza also rescues Calvin one last time, an act of defiance and bravery for which she is willing to take the consequences. An action-packed, quick-moving story about a gutsy girl who shapes her own fate.

Hesse, Karen. *Letters from Rifka*. 1992. Hard: Holt. Pbk: Puffin. Ages 9–12.

After Rifka's family flees Russia in 1919 and endures a grueling journey to Warsaw, they find that Rifka cannot board the steamship to America. The twelve-year-old has a case of ringworm, which causes her hair to fall out, so she cannot leave Europe until it is cured. Rifka musters all her courage to stay behind when her parents and two brothers depart. Far from her family on her thirteenth birthday, she makes herself a Star of David and recites Hebrew prayers to celebrate becoming a woman. Even when the ringworm disappears, her troubles are far from over. Her compassion, her ability to learn quickly, especially languages, and her articulate voice save Rifka from having to return to Russia. Told in the form of letters to a beloved cousin, this novel will touch the reader's heart and also make her cheer.

Hyatt, Patricia Rusch. *Coast to Coast with Alice*. 1995. Hard: Carolrhoda. Ages 9–11.

In 1909, sixteen-year-old Hermine Jahns accompanied Alice Ramsey on the first coast-to-coast automobile trip by a female driver. Ramsey, twenty-one years old, had already established herself in contests as a skillful driver when a car manufacturer offered to sponsor her in a cross-country trip. Hermine and two older women went along, although Ramsey did all the driving. This is a fictionalized account of that fifty-nine-day trip, faster than the only two previous cross-country trips, both by men. The book, which takes the form of Hermine's journal, describes the places they passed and the hazards the women faced along the way. In the 3,800 miles, Ramsey had to change eleven flat tires and have the axle replaced three times, due to mud, potholes, and generally poor roads. One well-chosen photograph shows her changing a tire, a skill she taught to male journalists unfamiliar with cars. In another episode, Ramsey temporarily wires the broken axle together with baling wire and extra hairpins. The photographs of the four women on the road are a wonderful addition, although the other illustrations add little. This is a fascinating slice of history about a pioneer doing something we now take for granted.

Karr, Kathleen. *Go West, Young Women.* 1996. Hard: Harper. Ages 10–12.

In this farcical novel, twelve-year-old Phoebe, her older sister Amelia, and their parents set out for the Oregon Territory with a wagon train. In an outrageous plot device, the author engineers a buffalo stampede that eliminates most of the men, leaving a few temporarily immobile, including Phoebe's father. This means the women are in charge of their own fates, a change they thrive on. One of the two well-educated "maiden ladies" in the party takes charge, while the other one scrutinizes the guidebook for useful information. The women bury the men, butcher the buffalo, and forge ahead toward Fort Laramie, four hundred miles west. Narrator Phoebe has a keen eye and a wry tongue. From Amelia, who plans to be a writer, to Happy Hawkins, who persuaded her husband to go west, this is a group of resourceful women who have a chance to conquer the West without taking direction from men. Not all readers will appreciate the broad humor with which men, Indians, and some of the girls are drawn, but some will laugh all through this first book in The Petticoat Party series. In the next book, *Phoebe's Folly*, the women continue their wild journey to Oregon Territory.

Lowry, Lois. *Number the Stars*. 1989. Hard: Houghton. Pbk: Dell. Ages 9–12.

During World War II, the small country of Denmark protected its Jewish citizens and helped smuggle nearly all seven thousand of them to Sweden. Based on a true story, this novel tells of ten-year-old Annemarie Johansen and her family, who help her Jewish friend Ellen Rosen in such an escape. Annemarie and Ellen do not understand the danger the Nazis in Copenhagen pose until one night when Nazi soldiers come searching for Jews and find Ellen sleeping over at Annemarie's. Thanks to the bravery of both girls, Ellen escapes detection. With Annemarie's mother and her younger sister, the girls travel to the Danish coast across from Sweden. Again, Annemarie encounters soldiers and faces the dangerous challenge of convincing them she is innocent, even though she is carrying a valuable package to help Ellen and her family escape. Told from a child's point of view, this novel alludes to the atrocities of the war but focuses more on the courage of the Danish people, both Jewish and Christian. A moving story of friendship and strength that won the Newbery Medal.

Lunn, Janet. *The Root Cellar*. 1983. Hard: Scribner. Pbk: Puffin. Ages 10–13.

Twelve-year-old orphan Rose, lonely in her new home with her aunt's family in Canada, travels through time in an old root cellar. She finds herself back in the Civil War and embarks with a girl from the past named Susan on a dangerous journey to Washington, D.C., where they hope to find Susan's friend Will. Rose disguises herself as a boy and takes charge of their travels, a role she finds she enjoys. She does strenuous work for a blacksmith when they need money and gets them through the confusion of New York City. Although the girls do find Will, who has been fighting for the North, his painful descriptions of war and death temper their joy. Rose's developing sense of leadership comes into play again on the journey back to Canada. An outstanding time travel story, this novel won the Canadian award for best children's book of 1982.

Nixon, Joan Lowery. A *Family Apart*. 1987. Hard: Bantam, o.p. Pbk: Bantam. Ages 10–12.

In this first book in the Orphan Train Quartet, Frances Mary Kelly and her five younger siblings are living with their widowed mother in New York City in 1860. Although Mrs. Kelly and Frances clean buildings and sew piecework, poverty forces Mrs. Kelly to send her children west on the Orphan Train to find other families to live with. The Children's Aid Society takes them to Missouri, where the children are chosen by different families. Frances, determined to stay with six-year-old Petey, disguises herself as a boy so she'll be more likely to attract a farm family. Strong from her work scrubbing floors, she performs as well as a boy could at farmwork for the kind Cummings family, who chose them. Frankie, as she calls herself, takes pride in her work but worries about her disguise being discovered. Everything she does, including her aid to escaped slaves, she approaches with courage, strength, and hard work in this gripping story.

Ross, Rhea Beth. *The Bet's On, Lizzie Bingham!* 1988. Hard: Houghton, o.p. Pbk: Houghton. Ages 10–13.

Lizzie Bingham's blood boiled (as will the reader's) listening to her sixteen-year-old brother Jack's speech against giving women the right to vote. "Suffrage," he says, "would put undue stress on the system of the delicate, emotional female." Lizzie, two years younger than Jack, is anything but delicate, and she spends the summer proving it. When she bets Jack she won't ask for his help all summer, he immediately begins a campaign to win. The book is set in a small Missouri town in 1914, and Lizzie's adventures do have a Tom Sawyer–like quality: She witnesses a murder and gets threatened with death herself. She gets into one fascinating mess after another and proves herself equal to most of them. At the summer's end, Jack has revised his opinion and so has Lizzie's very proper mother. A rip-roaring story.

Smucker, Barbara. *Runaway to Freedom: A Story of the Underground Railroad.* **Illustrated by Charles Lilly. 1978. Hard: Harper. Pbk: Harper Trophy. Ages 10–12.**

Before Julilly is sold away from the only home she's ever had, her mother tells her about following the north star to Canada. On her new, much harsher plantation, the twelve-year-old befriends a girl named Liza and they resolve to escape together. With help from two male slaves, an abolitionist, and the Underground Railroad, the girls disguise themselves as boys and head north. "You have foresight and great courage," the abolitionist tells them before they leave, and they prove their courage again and again. Separated from the men, the girls battle pain, fatigue, and fear as they make their way toward Canada. Suspense builds as they elude the men and hounds following them from the plantation. Can Liza survive the ordeal despite her ill-health? Can they really trust the members of the Underground Railroad? Even if they make it to Canada, will Julilly ever see her mother again? An exciting but sad story that will grip the reader from start to finish.

Stolz, Mary. *Bartholomew Fair*. 1990. Hard: Greenwillow. Pbk: Beech Tree. Ages 10–13.

Queen Elizabeth I loved to mingle with her people during her long reign as ruler of England. This novel describes such an occasion in 1597, when Elizabeth visited the Bartholomew Fair, a raucous event that took place in London. Five other people, one of them a young girl called Merrycat who works in the palace kitchen, also make their way to the fair that day. Although the focus is as much on the three boys and one man who attend the fair as on Elizabeth and the irrepressible Merrycat, the importance of the queen to her country comes through. This well-crafted novel conveys the popularity and spirit of Elizabeth, perhaps the greatest female ruler of all time.

Strasser, Todd. *The Diving Bell*. 1992. Hard: Scholastic. Pbk: Scholastic. Ages 9–12.

Set in Mexico several hundred years ago, this adventure pits a native girl named Culca against greedy Spanish invaders. Culca, to her mother's dismay, wants to dive for shells like her brother does. She gets a chance at it, but has to quit to study Spanish, religion, and mathematics with the local friar. When Spaniards take away all the village divers, including her brother, to dive for sunken treasure, everyone believes the divers will never return. But Culca devises a rescue plan involving her clever design for a diving bell. With the help of the friar, Culca must convince officials that her idea will work. Plot plays a greater role than character development in this adventure, and some may find Culca's unschooled genius implausible. But exciting books about boys have similar faults, while few books about girls portray such an ingenious, forceful main character.

Streatfeild, Noel. *Ballet Shoes*. 1937. Hard: Random House, o.p. Pbk: Random House. Ages 9–12.

This wonderful, timeless story follows the fortunes of three adopted sisters—Pauline, Petrova, and Posy Fossil. A fossil hunter they call Great-Uncle Matthew, or GUM, has adopted them, then left them with his niece Sylvia and her old nanny. When GUM doesn't return after five years abroad, money starts to run out in their large London house. So Sylvia takes in boarders, including a dance teacher who encourages the girls to attend a special dance and acting school. There Pauline shows great acting talent and Posy an equally great dancing ability. Petrova, in contrast, spends her spare time learning about cars, reading airplane magazines, and mending things. All three, especially Pauline, concern themselves with family finances and take their own interests very seriously. The girls are resolute and talented, but they suffer the everyday problems of all children. For nearly fifty years, readers have shared the worries and dreams of these three sympathetic characters who have never lost their charm. Related books include *Theatre Shoes*, *Dancing Shoes*, and more.

Whitmore, Arvella. *The Bread Winner*. 1990. Hard: Houghton. Ages 9–11.

After moving from a farm to a shanty in town, sixth grader Sarah Puckett realizes just how poor she and her parents are. It is the Depression, and a fourth of the men in the country are out of work. Her father tries desperately to find a job while her mother earns a pittance taking in laundry. After Sarah's father teaches her how to defend herself from neighborhood bullies, Sarah wins a few key fights and makes a good friend after one skirmish. She also uses her bread-baking skills—her bread was awarded a blue ribbon at the county fair—to earn a little money. She gets interested in how money works as she buys the ingredients to make more bread and barters with the neighborhood grocer. Her skills at baking and business prove vital to her family as she truly becomes a "breadwinner." She learns to stand up for herself and try out her ideas, even if it means risking failure. A heartwarming story about an enterprising girl.

Fantasy and Science Fiction

Avi. *Poppy*. **Illustrated by Brian Floca. 1995. Hard: Orchard. Ages 9–12.**

The striking dust jacket will draw readers into this fantasy in which a large family of mice live under the rule of Mr. Oxac, a most unpleasant owl. The clan's leader, Lungwort, believes that Mr. Oxac protects the mice despite the fact that the owl occasionally eats one of them. Lungwort's daughter Poppy begins to question her father's beliefs and defies Mr. Oxac by traveling to New House, a possible new home for the mice. One of the few female leads in an animal fantasy, Poppy gains courage and resourcefulness as she pursues her goal and becomes a leader herself. Several of the engaging black-and-white illustrations show Poppy brandishing a porcupine quill as if it were a sword, a weapon that figures in the downfall of the owl. Ereth, a helpful porcupine, adds comic relief to this exciting tale of an increasingly bold female mouse. An outstanding animal fantasy.

Babbitt, Natalie. *Tuck Everlasting*. **1975. Hard: FSG. Pbk: FSG. Ages 9–12.**

In this beautifully written novel, ten-year-old Winnie Foster moves toward independence, away from a loving but restrictive family. At first she just ventures out of the yard and into the woods. But that step leads her into an unexpected adventure when she meets the Tucks, a family who will live forever after drinking from a nearby spring. Winnie grows to love the earthy, disheveled Tuck family. When Mae Tuck attacks a man to defend Winnie, Winnie does her best to help Mae, even though it means breaking the law and disappointing her proud family. This is a magical novel that draws the reader into the world of Winnie and the Tucks, and raises the perplexing question that Winnie will have to answer someday: Do you want to live forever? Don't miss this book.

Banks, Lynne Reid. *The Farthest-Away Mountain*. Illustrated by Dave Henderson. 1977. Hard: Doubleday, o.p. Pbk: Avon. Ages 9–11.

In this fairy-tale novel, fourteen-year-old Dakin refuses to get married and settle down, the usual fate in her village for a girl her age. Instead, she makes three resolutions: to visit the farthest-away mountain that she can see from her window, to meet a gargoyle, and to marry a prince. In her journey to the mountain she meets a troll and a talking frog, hides from a giant, and speaks to three lonely gargoyles. She is frightened several times but refuses to give up. She finally faces the evil spirit who rules the mountain, knowing that only one of them can survive the encounter. Every chapter holds a new danger for Dakin, which requires all her courage and ingenuity. A surprising twist near the end leads to a satisfying conclusion.

Bond, Michael. *The Tales of Olga da Polga*. Illustrated by Hans Helweg. 1971. Hard: Macmillan. Ages 9–11.

Olga da Polga is "the sort of guinea pig who would go places." In this cheerful account of her adventures, she goes from a pet shop to live with Karen and her parents—the Sawdust family, as Olga calls them. There she revels in their attention and her own beautiful home. In Olga's first encounter with the family cat, she sinks her teeth into his tail just out of curiosity, but later becomes friends with him, a neighboring hedgehog, and a turtle, all male. She regales them with stories, some about how fierce and brave she has been. Unfortunately, too many of her escapades make her look silly or teach her to be less daring. Still, she remains irrepressible, as the many black-and-white illustrations show. Olga da Polga, another of the few female leads in an animal fantasy, certainly knows how to enjoy herself.

Chetwin, Grace. *Out of the Dark World*. 1985. Hard: Lothrop. Ages 10–13.

This eerie modern fantasy combines Celtic mythology, parapsychology, and computer technology. When Meg has nightmares about a boy who is trapped in a Dark World, her sister Sue suggests trying a technique she has read about in a parapsychology book. Meg agrees and starts manipulating her dreams, bringing two helpers into them: the powerful Celtic witch, Morgan le Fay, and a man named Peter Saltifer. Meanwhile Sue, who likes computers, and Meg realize that the boy in the nightmare has his mind trapped in a computer loop. Meg must try to rescue him, knowing she too could end up trapped. But Meg fashions a sleek vehicle like a hovercraft to carry her into the Dark World and uses all her strengths to carry out the mission. A suspenseful and original story.

Coville, Bruce. *The Dragonslayers*. Illustrated by Katherine Coville. 1994. Hard: Pocket. Pbk: Minstrel. Ages 8–10.

Princess Wilhelmina, known as Willie, objects to her

parents' plans to marry her off. She wants to be free to make her own choices and plan her own life. So when the king promises half his kingdom and Willie's hand in marriage to whoever can kill a troublesome dragon, she sees it as a way to win her own freedom. She disguises herself as a boy and uses her tracking skills to follow the official dragonslayers, an old squire named Elizar and a page named Brian, into the forest. Just in the nick of time, she swoops in on a vine to confront the dragon, which is about to devour young Brian. But will she be able to overcome the beast, by force or cunning? The final scene relies heavily on coincidence to tie the ends together, which is characteristic of Coville's pedestrian writing. Nevertheless, his fans will enjoy this story about a feisty princess and her exploits.

Furlong, Monica. *Juniper.* **1991. Hard: Knopf. Pbk: Random House. Ages 10–13.**

Juniper is used to a luxurious life as a medieval princess, but she gives it up to study magic with her godmother Euny. The girl adjusts to cold and hunger but chafes at not learning more magic. Only when she returns to her family home and finds it in danger from her aunt's black magic does Juniper realize the powers Euny has helped her acquire. Laced with magic and herb lore, the story reaches its climax with a fight between good and evil. Sure to appeal to fantasy fans.

Furlong, Monica. *Wise Child.* **1987. Hard: Knopf. Pbk: Random House. Ages 11–14.**

This fantasy's main character, nicknamed Wise Child, has no parents at home and lives with her aged grandmother. Her mother deserted her and her father is at sea. When the grandmother dies, only Juniper, a local woman said to practice magic, will take the girl. But to Wise Child's surprise, living with Juniper is a pleasure despite the hard work she must do. Juniper teaches her about herbs and their uses as well as how to keep house, milk a cow, and eventually practice magic. Despite her happy new home, Wise Child is tempted when her evil mother appears and promises her riches and a life of leisure. Wise Child grows in knowledge and courage, a courage that is put to a serious test. An entrancing fantasy about two memorable females.

Hoover, H. M. *Away Is a Strange Place to Be.* **1990. Hard: Dutton. Ages 10–13.**

In this adventure set in the future, Abby Tabor is reluctantly visiting an amusement park with Bryan, a spoiled guest at her uncle's inn. They are kidnapped from the park and transported to another planet, where they and other children labor to prepare the planet for future settlers. Living conditions are harsh and the work taxing, a bewildering change for both children. Abby employs all her wit and courage in trying to figure out a way for the two of them to escape. Although Abby is twelve, she has already studied management because she will inherit the inn, and she puts these skills to use in planning their escape—a nice touch.

Jacques, Brian. *Mariel of Redwall.* **1992. Hard: Philomel. Pbk: Avon. Ages 9–13.**

Mariel is a warrior at heart. In this entry in the popular Redwall series, the young mousemaid seeks revenge on the cruel pirate Gabool the Wild. When the story opens, Mariel has lost her memory but retained her spirit. She fashions herself a weapon and makes her way to the Abbey Redwall, a delightful refuge of comfort, food, and kind souls. A piece of poetry sends her on her way again, this time with three animal companions. As she sets off, Mariel is "filled with a sense of freedom and adventure," for she is an adventurer at heart. She leads the group on their quest, which culminates in a large battle against Gabool. Although most of the characters are male, the hare Rosie shows unparalleled courage, and the badger Mother Mellus takes up bow and arrows when necessary. Among the array of animals that makes up the friends and residents of Redwall, males and females respect each other and share authority far more than usual in fiction. For readers who enjoy long, exciting fantasies, this is highly recommended.

Kaye, M. M. *The Ordinary Princess*. 1984. Hard: Doubleday, o.p. Pbk: Dell. Ages 8–11.

At her christening, Princess Amethyst receives charm, wit, grace, and courage from visiting fairies, until one disgruntled fairy, named Crustacea, announces, "You shall be Ordinary." To the dismay of her parents and her six exquisitely beautiful older sisters, as she grows up, Princess Amy is ordinary in looks and feminine accomplishments. Unlike her sisters, she loves to escape to the nearby Forest of Faraway to climb trees and swim. Her parents' schemes to marry her off cause Amy to run away to the forest and eventually to take a job as a kitchen maid in another castle. In the end, her determination to go her own way and defy conventions wins her a happiness good looks alone would never provide. She is hardworking and takes pleasure in all aspects of life. Full of puns and other lighthearted humor, this is an enchanting and unusual tale of a princess.

Keller, Beverly. *A Small, Elderly Dragon*. Illustrated by Nola Langner Malone. 1984. Hard: Lothrop. Ages 8–10.

"Dorma's eyes were gray and nearsighted—from reading, some whispered. Her brown hair had been chopped off just above her shoulders when she got it tangled in her tiara." Even though her own father King Wincealot ignores her and her handmaidens laugh at her, Princess Dorma slowly starts to assert herself. She pickets and protests, and writes up lists of demands. She climbs down a castle wall and swims a moat to save the small, elderly dragon that the king wants to kill. In the end, she must confront an evil sorcerer to wrest her kingdom from him. Magical elements abound in this convoluted, funny story in which nothing turns out as predicted.

King-Smith, Dick. *The School Mouse*. Illustrated by Cynthia Fisher. 1995. Hard: Hyperion. Ages 8–11.

Flora is the only mouse in the school who cares about learning to read. Born in the kindergarten room, she follows the teacher's lessons and masters the alphabet. She then moves to the first-grade room and progresses in her studies. Her new skills save her and her parents from being poisoned when she reads the label on an exterminator's packets. For a time, Flora is alone in the school after her parents and their newest brood move outdoors. But a student brings a pet mouse named Buck to school and he and Flora become friends. When life outdoors turns dangerous, Flora bravely brings her mother and little sister back to school. She becomes the first mouse schoolteacher ever, instructing Buck and her family, and she ultimately decides to combine a career with raising a family of her own. Flora, her mother, and her sister are more assertive and independent than the pleasant but muddled males, an unusual twist in an animal fantasy. An amusing tale with apt, funny illustrations.

Klause, Annette Curtis. *Alien Secrets*. 1993. Hard: Delacorte. Pbk: Dell. Ages 10–12.

Even before Puck boards the spaceship to journey to the

planet Aurora, she witnesses what seems to be a murder. Early in the trip, which she is making because she was expelled from school, Puck befriends an alien nicknamed Hush who has enemies aboard the ship. But Puck and Hush cannot tell whom they can trust among the passengers and the crew; even the female captain of the ship may be in league with criminals. In one exciting scene Puck risks her life climbing between the inner and outer hulls of the ship to recover a sacred treasure belonging to Hush. While gaining confidence as well as testing her courage, Puck learns to overcome her prejudices in dealing with aliens. In a final heartwarming scene all she has learned comes together to reward her in the best way possible. The gripping adventure also has touches of humor, such as the futuristic slang Puck uses. A quick-moving, highly enjoyable story.

L'Engle, Madeleine. *A Wrinkle in Time*. 1962. Hard: FSG. Pbk: Dell. Ages 10–13.

This modern classic describes the suspenseful quest of Meg Murry, her younger brother Charles Wallace, and their friend Calvin to rescue Meg's father from forces of evil. They travel to another planet through a "wrinkle in time" with the help of three wise and powerful women. Meg, a misfit at her high school, gains confidence and learns to rely on herself rather than on the males around her. The three wise women encourage her to draw on her "faults"—anger, impatience, and stubbornness. Though not usually encouraged in girls, these traits prove a source of strength for Meg, who plays the central role in completing their mission. Meg is unusually good at math, better than Calvin, and her mother is a dedicated scientist who combines work and family. This exciting adventure, beautifully written, was well ahead of its time in its vision of the role females can play. Winner of the Newbery Medal. Not to be missed.

Lindgren, Astrid. Translated by Florence Lamborn. *Pippi Longstocking.* **Illustrated by Louis S. Glanzman. 1950. Hard: Viking. Pbk: Puffin. Ages 8–11.**

Pippi Longstocking is unique. She lives with her horse and her pet monkey Mr. Nilsson in an old house, supported by bags of gold from her missing seafaring father. To the astonishment of her sedate neighbors Tommy and Annika, Pippi does what she likes when she likes. She is so strong that she can lift two policemen and defeat the strong man at the circus. She can climb any tree, a skill she uses to rescue two children from the top of a burning building. After the rescue, the crowd watching gives her three cheers while Pippi characteristically gives herself four. Pippi gives school a try, in order to get vacations, but she finds it too confining. No adult intimidates her; she chastises the teacher for asking too many questions about arithmetic, calling her "my dear little woman." She is quite happy with herself and her life, and with living alone. It's too bad Annika tends to be easily scared, but Tommy is not much braver. They both overcome their prim upbringing to join Pippi in her adventures, as any child would want to. A most remarkable girl.

Lisle, Janet Taylor. *Forest.* **1993. Hard: Orchard. Pbk: Scholastic. Ages 9–12.**

Angry at her father, twelve-year-old Amber has climbed a tree to spend the night. There she discovers mink-tailed squirrels living in the Upper Forest, who have a sophisticated civilization, complete with language and social structure. Most of the squirrels view her as an invader, certain to cause trouble. Only Woodbine, a young male squirrel, sees her differently. When her father comes to the forest the next day to shoot squirrels, almost hitting Amber by mistake, war begins between the humans and the squirrels. Amber is determined to halt the war. Her brother Wendell believes she may succeed because she is, as he sees her, "a master of detail, a maestro of design, a thinker of dazzling cleverness." She and eight-year-old Wendell enlist the help of Professor Spark, a dynamic older woman who studies woodland animals and gives Amber a role model she desperately needs. On the squirrels' side, Woodbine, his sister, and her friend Laurel also take risks to avert the war. Packed with action and ideas, this is a unique novel about strong human—and squirrel—females.

Mahy, Margaret. *The Blood-and-Thunder Adventure on Hurricane Peak*. Illustrated by Wendy Smith. 1989. Hard: McElderry. Pbk: Dell. Ages 8–11.

This short, snappy book is a lark. Full of puns and other jokes, the story centers around the Unexpected School on Hurricane Peak, a school run by a magician for only six pupils. The two new students are Huxley Hammond and his sister Zaza, who is "even more blood-and-thundery than Hammond." A dastardly villain who wants to shut down the school in order to mine the mountain also plans to kidnap and marry ace inventor Belladonna Doppler, an atomic scientist. Belladonna, meanwhile, has set off to visit the Unexpected School. The villain's adopted aunt, a talented mechanic, can remember only the last forty years of her life, exactly the amount of time the headmistress of the Unexpected School has been missing. All the females, including the talking cat, are smart and adventurous; even the briefly mentioned police constables are brother and sister. "Always expect the unexpected" is the school motto and the theme of this madcap adventure. Short chapters and many comical drawings add to the book's strong appeal.

Service, Pamela F. *Being of Two Minds*. **1991. Hard: Atheneum. Pbk: Juniper. Ages 10–12.**

Ever since her birth, fourteen-year-old Connie has been having fainting spells. But what her parents and schoolmates don't know is that during her unconscious periods, she is in the mind of a boy born the same day. The boy Rudolph, prince of the small Central European kingdom Thulgaria, also experiences spells and enters her mind. They enjoy the exchanges, although regret having to worry their parents. Their unusual link becomes a matter of life or death when Rudolph is kidnapped and Connie has to convince skeptical adults to pay attention to her information about it. She flies to Thulgaria, where she finds her own life at risk as she tries to find the castle where Rudolph is being held. With the help of their psychic link, the two overpower a guard and escape—only to be captured again. Connie, whose parents have been over-protective because of her spells, has to face physical challenges, scrambling over rocks and down cliffs. She draws on all her powers of quick thinking and bravery for the final push to safety in this appealing story.

Smith, Sherwood. *Wren to the Rescue*. **1990. Hard: Harcourt. Pbk: Dell. Ages 10–13.**

Wren is stunned to learn that her best friend at the orphanage, Tess, is a princess, who invites Wren to accompany her to her parents' castle. Tess's real identity has been kept secret to protect her from enemies. When an evil sorcerer kidnaps Tess, Wren sets off to rescue her, joining forces with two boys. She proves herself as brave as the boys and more knowledgeable in some ways as they journey past hazards to the sorcerer's stronghold. They get help from a female magician and, relying on Wren's cleverness, try to rescue Tess.

Toughened by her upbringing as an orphan, Wren is a loyal, courageous friend. An exciting fantasy with many strong female characters. Wren has more dangerous magical adventures in *Wren's Quest* and *Wren's War*.

Sreenivasan, Jyotsna. *The Moon Over Crete*. Illustrated by Sim Gellman. 1994. Pbk: Holy Cow! Press. Ages 9–11.

This time-travel adventure, which was excerpted in *New Moon* magazine, follows eleven-year-old Lily back in time to the island of Crete. Lily has been harassed recently by boys at school, and she has noticed how obsessed her best friend is getting with looks. She longs for a place where women are equal to men, and she finds it in ancient Crete. This worthy theme dominates the book, which is stronger on message than plot. The dramatic tension comes from Lily's desire to tell the Queen of Crete about a disaster that will overtake her people, which Lily knows about from studying history. But her music teacher, Mrs. Zinn, who has brought Lily to ancient times, forbids her to alter history. Lily's struggle with her conscience and her observations about a more equal culture and its rituals comprise most of the book. Noteworthy for its unusual setting.

White, E. B. *Charlotte's Web*. Illustrated by Garth Williams. 1952. Hard: Harper. Pbk: Harper Trophy. Ages 8–11.

When the pig Wilbur first meets the spider Charlotte A. Cavatica, he likes her but finds her fierce and bloodthirsty. Little does he know that she will do her best to save his life. Charlotte is smart and articulate, a talented weaver like her mother before her, and a loyal friend. Like the old female sheep in the barn where they live, Charlotte knows more than Wilbur does and gives him good advice. When Charlotte weaves the words "Some Pig" into her web, to make Wilbur more precious to his owners, the Zuckermans, Mrs. Zuckerman observes that it's the spider who's extraordinary, not the pig. Although Fern, the girl who raised Wilbur, grows more stereotypically girlish, and her mother and aunt are traditional farmer's wives, Charlotte and the other spiders she describes are strong females. Written in flawless prose and illustrated with memorable pictures, this modern classic is a joy to read aloud. A Newbery Honor Book.

Wrede, Patricia C. *Dealing with Dragons*. 1990. Hard: Harcourt. Pbk: Scholastic. Ages 10–13.

Cimorene finds being a princess boring. Every time she tries to study something interesting such as swordplay and politics, her father stops her. When her parents decide she must marry a dull prince, Cimorene runs away and lands a job as princess to a female dragon named Kazul. Although constantly having to discourage princes who try to rescue her, Cimorene is happy with her duties of cooking and putting the dragon's treasures and books in order. Her routine is interrupted when wizards try to poison Kazul, and Cimorene must lead a fight to outwit these enemies. Her allies are a businesslike witch named Morwen, a prince, and another dragon's princess. Cimorene is strong-willed, brave, and smart, as are Kazul and Morwen: definitely an unusual trio of females. Full of humor, this fantasy series has quickly become a popular one. The equally appealing sequels are *Searching for Dragons*, *Calling on Dragons*, and *Talking to Dragons*, although the final book focuses on a male relative of Cimorene.

Yep, Laurence. *Dragon of the Lost Sea*. 1982. Hard: Harper, o.p. Pbk: Harper Trophy. Ages 10–13.

The young dragon princess Shimmer is determined to recover a magic pebble in order to restore the ocean—which has been magically removed by Civet, a powerful witch—to her people. In her pursuit of Civet, Shimmer befriends a human boy named Thorn. At first he seems like a burden but instead proves to be an unexpected help as well as a rare friend. They swoop through the sky on their journey, encountering various magical creatures and dangers that they can overcome only as a team. The dragon Shimmer is a strong and headstrong heroine, more interested in adventure than in caution. The sequels are *Dragon Steel*, *Dragon Cauldron*, and *Dragon War*.

Biographies

Leaders and Activists

Colman, Penny. *Fannie Lou Hamer and the Fight for the Vote*. 1993. Hard: Millbrook. Pbk: Millbrook. Ages 8–10.

Fannie Lou Hamer was a true heroine. This attractive, brief biography opens with Hamer's experience at the 1964 Democratic Convention, where she and her fellow delegates were told to take a backseat to another, all-white delegation from Mississippi. Unwilling to accept a role as a token, Hamer protested publicly and then left. In 1968, she was seated at the Democratic Convention with a standing ovation. None of Hamer's political victories came easily. Determined to vote, she and her husband both lost their jobs and put their lives in danger. She was beaten cruelly by police, receiving injuries she never fully recovered from. She not only continued her quest, but she organized and inspired other blacks to join her. After the 1968 convention, she started the Freedom Farm Cooperative in Mississippi to form a community where poor people had work and housing.

Colman, Penny. *Mother Jones and the March of the Mill Children*. 1994. Hard: Millbrook. Ages 8–11.

Mary Harris Jones fought for better working conditions for poor workers and an end to child labor. She helped organize unions, strikes, and publicity to aid her causes. A "hell-raiser," as she called herself, Mother Jones went to jail many times for her beliefs. She was outraged and distressed at the prevalence of child labor, popular because children could be paid less, were easy to control, and wouldn't form unions. In 1903, as part of a textile workers' strike that included sixteen thousand child workers, Jones planned a march from Philadelphia to Long Island, where President Teddy Roosevelt was at his summer home. The march, which began with nearly three hundred people, dwindled as the days went on, until Mother Jones arrived at Roosevelt's summer place with only a handful of adults and children. Although the president refused to see her, the march was not in vain, for it garnered the publicity Mother Jones sought and helped bring about labor reform. Photographs show Mother Jones at her work and the underfed children she was fighting for. A moving introduction to a determined, effective activist.

Freedman, Suzanne. *Ida B. Wells-Barnett and the Anti-lynching Crusade*. 1994. Hard: Millbrook. Pbk: Millbrook. Ages 8–10.

In 1892, when three black men were unfairly arrested and then killed by a mob in Memphis, journalist Ida Bell Wells wrote an article in protest in the black newspaper *Free Speech*. Three months later, her newspaper office was wrecked and her life threatened. But she moved to New York and continued her career as a journalist, as well as becoming a crusader against lynching, which was a common practice in the United States, especially the South. Incidents like this one fill this brief biography and underscore what a remarkable woman she was. Born into slavery, she heeded her parents' emphasis on education and became a teacher. When she was twenty-two she successfully sued a railroad whose conductor threw her off the train when she insisted on sitting in the ladies' car rather than the smoking car for blacks. Her forceful personality served her well in many ways: fighting lynching, promoting suffrage for women, organizing blacks for political power, and raising a family of four children. Amply illustrated with photographs and drawings from the time, this is a well-written, absorbing biography of an outstanding woman.

Gherman, Beverly. *Sandra Day O'Connor.* **Illustrated by Robert Masheris. 1991. Hard: Viking. Pbk: Puffin. Ages 9–11.**

In 1981, Sandra Day O'Connor became the first woman to serve on the U.S. Supreme Court, an incomparable honor. This short biography traces her personal and professional lifes from childhood through the appointment, with several pages about her performance on the bench. Even for a future Supreme Court justice who graduated third in her class, finding a good job was much more difficult because she was a woman. She married a fellow law student and gave up law practice after having their third child, but became active in volunteer work. This led to involvement in local politics and eventually election to the Arizona state senate, where she was chosen the first female majority leader in the country. She ran successfully for trial judge and later was appointed to the Arizona Court of Appeals, then the U.S. Supreme Court, where the one hundred and one Supreme Court justices chosen before her had all been male. A readable introduction to an eminent modern woman.

Karnes, Frances A., and Suzanne M. Bean. *Girls and Young Women Leading the Way: 20 True Stories about Leadership.* **1993. Pbk: Free Spirit Press. Ages 10–14.**

These girls and young women have tapped their leadership abilities to make a difference in their communities and schools. Each describes her achievement and gives her views on how to lead. The first ten girls focused on needs in their communities: hunger and homelessness, environmental problems, literacy, and more. Often they coordinated efforts with other children, such as putting on a play to save an arts program. In school, several of the projects concerned recycling or other ecological issues. One particularly impressive achievement was a booklet expressing the views and feelings of the disabled children at the school to enlighten other students and teachers. At the end of each essay are a short list of questions to prompt ideas in the reader, and the names of relevant organizations. The final section of the book, a "Leadership Handbook," gives suggestions, inspiration, and information, including a bibliography about women leaders. The messages, that girls can be leaders and that a few people can make a big difference, come across effectively through the many exciting examples.

Lazo, Caroline. *Rigoberta Menchu.* **1994. Hard: Dillon. Ages 10–13.**

Rigoberta Menchu, a Mayan Indian, was awarded the Nobel Peace Prize in 1992 for her work in her native country of Guatemala. After her parents were tortured and killed by Guatemalan soldiers when Menchu was a teenager, she took up their cause of human rights for Guatemalan Indians. Because of her role as leader of the Peasant Unity Committee (PUC), a nonviolent group that seeks peace, Menchu had to flee to Mexico in 1981 to protect her own life and to speak out freely about atrocities at home. Only thirty-three years old when she won the Nobel Prize, Menchu is a remarkable woman who has dedicated her life to her people. This readable biography discusses her life, her tragedies, and her achievements, including enough history of Guatemala to set the story in context. The black-and-white photographs, although not of high quality, convey a sense of Rigoberta Menchu through her expressive face.

Levin, Pamela. *Susan B. Anthony: Fighter for Women's Rights*. **1993. Hard: Chelsea House. Pbk: Chelsea House. Ages 9–12.**

The name "Susan B. Anthony" is synonymous with the fight for women's right to vote. Raised in a liberal Quaker family, Anthony grew up with strong beliefs. Her first political cause was the temperance movement because she saw the harm done to families by alcohol, and she came to believe that women needed the vote before they could affect this and other issues. She was a powerful speaker and successful fund-raiser who made great strides in obtaining more rights for women. Although women didn't secure the vote until 1920, in 1906, at age eighty-six, Anthony characteristically told her fellow suffragists, "Failure is impossible!" This eighty-page biography succinctly sums up the career and accomplishments of this inspiring woman.

McPherson, Stephanie Sammartino. *I Speak for the Women: A Story about Lucy Stone*. **Illustrated by Brian Liedahl. 1992. Hard: Carolrhoda. Ages 8–11.**

Lucy Stone broke through an enormous barrier to women's progress by becoming a public speaker. Amazing as it seems now, the idea of a woman speaking in public was shocking, even scandalous, in the mid-nineteenth century. When, in 1843, Lucy Stone attended the liberal Oberlin College, one of the few colleges open to women, the curriculum offered public speaking courses to men but not to women. She and her female friends formed a secret debating society to hone their skills. Stone's ambition was to speak out against slavery and for women's rights. Through practice she became a skilled speaker and gave many public lectures, facing hostile opposition and mockery. This introduction to her life highlights her speaking career, her role in the women's movement, and her unusually egalitarian marriage, in which she used her own last name. The unattractive black-and-white drawings detract from the text, but the story of Lucy Stone's life is a compelling and important one.

Siegel, Beatrice. *Marian Wright Edelman: The Making of a Crusader*. 1995. Hard: Simon & Schuster. Ages 10–13.

No one could be more focused than Marian Wright Edelman, perhaps the country's most prominent advocate for children. Edelman, who started and runs the Children's Defense Fund, lobbies tirelessly for better laws and policies for children. This elegant biography, illustrated with photographs, describes her childhood in a strong family and her education through law school. She was the first black woman admitted to the bar in Mississippi, where she worked for the NAACP, a dangerous job at the time. Her experiences there led her to try to improve conditions for the poor. Although her personal life is discussed, the biography concentrates on her career as an advocate for children, in which she has used her leadership skills to make a significant difference.

Sobol, Richard. *Governor: In the Company of Ann W. Richards, Governor of Texas*. 1994. Hard: Cobblehill. Ages 8–12.

This photo-essay follows former governor Ann Richards through ten days of work when she held office as the governor of Texas. Working sixteen hours a day, she appears to be on the go constantly from office to meetings to speeches. The many clear photographs show the brightly clad Richards to be an unusually vital person, energetic throughout her long days of meeting with constituents, politicians, and her staff. The text combines descriptions of her activities with Richards's own words as she reflects on her job. She notes that raising a family and running a household gave her skills she has employed as a politician, and points out that when she was young, "Politics was a male province. Women made the coffee and men made the decisions." As an important executive, she had many men who worked for her, and she dealt with male legislators, as the pictures show. Richards's party affiliation is irrelevant to the essay, which stresses her daily work rather than her political views. She offers a rare role model of a powerful woman leading a large state.

Professionals and Educators

Brown, Drollene P. *Belva Lockwood Wins Her Case*. Illustrated by James Watling. 1987. Hard: Albert Whitman. Ages 8–11.

A remarkable nineteenth-century American, Belva Lockwood was the first woman admitted to practice law before the U.S. Supreme Court. Her life was a series of accomplishments. In the successful schools she started and ran, girls learned public speaking and practiced sports, both innovations. She put herself through college and law school despite opposition from within the schools, then ran a lucrative law office. Lockwood was the first woman to run for president; she won more than four thousand votes, all from men, although she lost the election. She was a noted and popular public lecturer and an active suffragist, working for the vote and fair laws for women. This interesting biography interlaces facts with catchy anecdotes, such as her habit of riding a three-wheel bicycle when it was not yet an accepted practice for women.

Ferris, Jeri. *Native American Doctor: The Story of Susan LaFlesche Picotte.* **1991. Hard: Carolrhoda. Pbk: Carolrhoda. Ages 9–11.**

Any woman who wanted to become a doctor in 1886 faced many obstacles, but Susan LaFlesche had the additional challenge of being an American Indian (as she referred to herself) in a hostile world. After graduating from the Hampton Institute in Virginia, where she was inspired by the school's woman doctor, she moved to Philadelphia to attend the Women's Medical College. She and her classmates studied medical sciences (such as anatomy and histology), dissected human bodies, and watched operations, to the astonishment of those who believed women too delicate for such work. She returned to the reservation permanently after getting her M.D. and served as its doctor. Despite her ill-health, she became an important advocate for her Omaha tribe, once traveling to Washington, D.C., to secure the tribe's control over their own finances, a striking accomplishment. This serviceable biography relates how Susan LaFlesche Picotte attained nearly impossible goals and went on to benefit her tribe for many years.

Lauber, Patricia. *Lost Star: The Story of Amelia Earhart.* **1988. Hard: Scholastic. Pbk: Scholastic. Ages 9–13.**

When Amelia Earhart was in her late teens, she kept a scrapbook of magazine and newspaper clippings about women who did jobs usually reserved for men, including a bank president, a brick layer, and a fire watcher. This is the sort of interesting detail Lauber uses to convey the spirit of Amelia Earhart. Earhart aspired to break barriers for women and encouraged others to do so, too. As an aviator, she was the first person to fly from Hawaii to California and the first woman to fly solo over the Atlantic ocean. She was not interested in security and comfort but instead was intent on achievement and showing that women could do what men did. Her life, though it had many problems and ended tragically, offers a truly unique example of a woman who risked everything to reach her goals. Black-and-white photographs give a glimpse of the aviator and her planes.

Meltzer, Milton. *Mary McLeod Bethune: Voice of Black Hope*. Illustrated by Stephen Marchesi. 1987. Hard: Viking, o.p. Pbk: Puffin. Ages 9–12.

Mary McLeod Bethune, an educator of great note, was founder and president of the school that became Bethune-Cookman College in Florida. At a time when education for African-Americans was poorly funded and often unavailable, Bethune dedicated herself to offering education at all levels to blacks. She also became an influential national leader and an adviser to President Franklin Delano Roosevelt. Bethune organized the Federal Council on Negro Affairs, a group of blacks in federal government, and created the National Council of Negro Women. This biography effectively conveys the spirit of this tireless, effective crusader, one of the most important women of this century.

Rowan, N. R. *Women in the Marines: The Boot Camp Challenge*. 1994. Hard: Lerner. Ages 10–13.

Every year approximately two thousand women join the U.S. Marine Corps, the branch of the military some consider most challenging. This book is about the boot camp they attend for thirteen weeks. Ample quotations from the recruits explore their varied reactions to the difficulties of boot camp, but also stress how the hard work builds self-confidence. A platoon of forty female recruits stays together for training, which includes physical conditioning, learning to use weapons, and basic warrior training. Black-and-white photographs show the female recruits rappelling down a tower, shinnying across a rope over a muddy pond, crawling under barbed wire, and throwing live grenades. The last two chapters describe possible careers in the Marines, and the growing opportunities for women thanks to changes in laws and regulations. Even readers with no interest in the military may enjoy this picture of women holding their own in a traditionally male world.

Siegel, Beatrice. *Faithful Friend: The Story of Florence Nightingale*. 1991. Pbk: Scholastic. Ages 8–11.

To read about Florence Nightingale's world and background is to understand how great her accomplishments were. She revolutionized nursing in England, shocking her aristocratic family by working in a field considered unfit for "nice" women. A woman of tremendous ability, Nightingale, knowing a conventional life would stifle her, pursued her interest in public health issues despite her family's objections, helped by strong women relatives and friends. She opened the first British school of nursing in 1860 and influenced health policies in other ways. While acknowledging negative aspects of her personality, this informative biography concentrates on the success of this powerful woman in improving the world around her.

Scientists and Inventors

Conley, Andrea. *Window on the Deep: The Adventures of Underwater Explorer Sylvia Earle.* **1991. Hard: Franklin Watts/A New England Aquarium Book. Ages 8–11.**

Sparkling color photographs, many of them taken underwater, are the highlight of this biography of a record-breaking deep-sea diver. In 1979, Sylvia Earle descended to 1,250 feet below the ocean's surface and walked unconnected to surface support, a deep-ocean record. Five years later, she went down to 3,000 feet, breaking her own record for deep solo diving. For that dive, Earle helped design the submersible, the clear-domed vehicle that provided her air and protection from the ocean's cold. A marine biologist, she became the chief scientist for the National Oceanic and Atmospheric Administration in 1991. She is also active in the fight against pollution, particularly that of the ocean. Although the writing could be better, the many photographs convey the beauty and excitement of the underwater world Earle explores.

Dewey, Jennifer Owings. *Wildlife Rescue: The Work of Dr. Kathleen Ramsay.* **Photographs by Don MacCarter. 1994. Hard: Boyds Mills. Ages 8–11.**

The dust jacket shows a laughing woman dressed in work clothes holding a large beaver, the perfect introduction to Dr. Kathleen Ramsay, a veterinarian who founded a wildlife center in New Mexico in 1985. She loves the injured or sick animals she tries to save, a pursuit into which she pours endless time and energy. Vibrant color photographs follow her through her hectic days full of quick decision-making, difficult surgery, and too many interruptions. She grieves for the animals hurt by humans and most of all for those who die despite her care. But she also has reasons to rejoice, as illustrated in a series of photographs showing her releasing healed birds back into the air. Her husband and young son have accompanied her on this day, both clearly pleased to share in her important work. The combination of lively text and photographs captures the intensity of this veterinarian and her dedication to a cause.

Gallardo, Evelyn. *Among the Orangutans: The Biruté Galdikas Story.* **1993. Hard: Chronicle. Pbk: Chronicle. Ages 8–11.**

Biruté Galdikas has been studying orangutans in Borneo since 1971. A pioneer in her field, Galdikas set up camp in an unpopulated area of Borneo, where she tracked orangutans, learned to identify individuals, and rescued orphaned young to be raised at the camp. The text describes the problems her work has caused in Galdikas's personal life, but it focuses on her impressive strides in the study of orangutans. Galdikas has also concentrated on helping orangutans survive despite the threats of poachers and declining rain forests. Color photographs on every page, many of orangutans, add interest to this short biography of a dedicated scientist.

Goodall, Jane. *My Life with the Chimpanzees.* **1996 revised edition. Pbk: Pocket. Ages 9–11.**

Using a conversational style, prominent ethologist Jane Goodall tells her own story from childhood through her twenty-five years of studying chimpanzees. Her groundbreaking work in the study of animal behavior stems from her strong interest in animals as a child. She credits a supportive family as well as her own initiative and good luck for her start in the field. She and her mother are so close that Goodall invited her mother to live with her for several months at her first research site in the Gombe Stream Game Reserve in what is now Tanzania; her mother started a medical clinic while Goodall observed chimps. Despite encounters with dangerous buffalo and leopards, and the knowledge that scorpions and poisonous centipedes infested the camp in damp weather, nothing stopped her from her work. Goodall gives fascinating details about the chimps she watched and learned to love, and about life in the wilderness. The small black-and-white photographs have the feel of a family album, which suits the autobiography's informal tone.

Heiligman, Deborah. *Barbara McClintock: Alone in Her Field*. Illustrated by Janet Hamlin. 1994. Hard: Scientific American Books for Young Readers, o.p. Pbk: Scientific American Books for Young Readers. Ages 8–10.

One of the founders of modern genetics, Barbara McClintock is a brilliant and influential scientist. She was the first woman to win an unshared Nobel Prize in Physiology or Medicine, and the third woman ever to win an unshared Nobel Prize in Science. Hers is a remarkable story of stubborn dedication to the research she believed in even when it was discounted by her colleagues. This short biography reflects on her unconventional childhood, during which her spirit of independence and her pleasure in solving problems emerged. As a female researcher she faced the sort of bias that made it difficult at first to secure the kind of research position she wanted. But the biography also stresses her great success in eventually finding her place and being recognized. She once said to an interviewer, "I've had such a great time. I can't imagine having a better life." A stirring message to girls to follow their dreams.

Karnes, Frances A., and Suzanne M. Bean. *Girls and Young Women Inventing: Twenty True Stories about Inventors plus How You Can Be One Yourself.* **1995. Pbk: Free Spirit Press. Ages 9–14.**

The impressive stories about girl inventors in the first part of this book make inventing look like fun. The second section gives practical advice on how to go about it. Essays by each of the twenty inventors, who range in age from elementary school to college, describe the process of thinking up an invention and making it. They make inventing seem not just possible but enjoyable and satisfying. In many cases, the girls improved on something they used themselves for chores, like a mop, or for entertainment, like a board game for girls. Some of the young inventors have applied for patents and explored ways to sell their products. All of them agree that the challenge and rewards of inventing are an end in themselves. The directions on how to set about inventing reduce an intimidating concept to manageable steps. Information at the back includes useful addresses, a list of books about inventors, and inspiring quotations. Read this valuable book and you will look at inventing in a new way.

McGovern, Ann. *Shark Lady: True Adventures of Eugenie Clark.* **1978. Hard: Four Winds. Pbk: Scholastic. Ages 8–10.**

When Eugenie Clark was nine, she began to visit an aquarium most Saturdays and decided that she wanted to study fish. Unusually determined, she eventually became a world-famous expert on sharks and the director of a marine laboratory. She learned to deep-sea dive before divers wore oxygen tanks, when it was more dangerous and difficult than today. But danger didn't stop this scientist. She traveled and wrote books, meanwhile raising four children. McGovern has chosen intriguing anecdotes from Clark's life, from the time that she boiled a rat in order to study its skeleton to her experience teaching the crown prince of Japan how to dive. A woman well ahead of her time, this "shark lady," as she's known, is another fine example of a woman who succeeded in a man's world and greatly enjoyed her success. The book ends with a letter from Eugenie Clark encouraging children to pursue their dreams as she did.

McPherson, Stephanie Sammartino. *Rooftop Astronomer: A Story about Maria Mitchell*. Illustrated by Hetty Mitchell. 1990. Hard: Carolrhoda. Ages 8–11.

Maria Mitchell deserves to be far better known than she is. A Nantucket native, she was the first woman to discover a comet. As a result of her discovery, Mitchell was voted the first female member of the American Academy of Arts and Sciences and of the Association for the Advancement of Science. Trained in math and science mainly by her father, she had no college education. In 1865, Vassar, one of the first women's colleges, hired her to teach, a job into which she poured her energy. Despite her accomplishments, Vassar paid her less than male professors received, and her formal protest resulted in only a small raise. Increasingly involved in the movement for women's rights, Mitchell served as president of the American Association for the Advancement of Women. The first woman astronomer in the United States, Mitchell will be an inspiration to anyone who reads about her.

Parker, Steve. *Marie Curie and Radium.* **1992. Hard: Harper. Pbk: Harper Trophy. Ages 9–11.**

Marie Curie won two Nobel Prizes for her pioneering scientific work: one in physics, which she shared with two male scientists, and one alone in chemistry. This attractive short biography, abundantly illustrated with photographs and other pictures, discusses her life and work. Polish by birth, she attended the Sorbonne, then continued to live in Paris with her husband and fellow scientist Pierre Curie. Except for time spent bicycling and with their two children, the Curies devoted themselves to their research. Marie Curie spent years purifying radium, helped by male assistants, and working on other research with male peers. Her husband's father moved in with the family to care for their two children. After her husband's early death, Curie became the first female professor at the Sorbonne. This inviting biography provides a useful page of information on atoms and radioactivity, and sidebars on well-chosen topics such as Curie's daughter's work as a scientist.

Pringle, Laurence. *Jackal Woman: Exploring the World of Jackals.* **Photographs by Patricia D. Moehlman. 1993. Hard: Scribner. Ages 8–11.**

For more than twenty years, Patricia Moehlman has studied jackals on the Serengeti Plain in Tanzania. This short book, amply illustrated with Moehlman's photographs, combines biographical information about this behavioral ecologist with facts about jackals. Moehlman, who first went to Africa to work with Jane Goodall, has spent countless hours observing certain jackals from her Land Rover. Living alone in her camp overlooking Lake Lagarja, she enjoys her solitude and has developed the skills she needs to live in harsh conditions, including the mechanical knowledge to fix her Land Rover. This is an exciting book about a female scientist working today who is having an impact in her field and in wildlife conservation—a superb role model.

Ride, Sally, with Susan Okie. *To Space & Back*. 1986. Hard: Lothrop. Pbk: Beech Tree. Ages 8–11.

In this book about life on the space shuttle, Sally Ride writes in first person, giving just the kind of details children want to hear. Many large color photographs add to the information in the text, showing astronauts eating, floating around, working in space outside the shuttle, sleeping, and even playing with a Slinky. A number of the pictures show women besides Sally Ride, including Rhea Seddon, Anna Fisher, and Kathy Sullivan. No particular point is made of the fact that they are women; Ride writes as if it were simply the norm. She serves as an excellent guide to the experience of riding in the shuttle, making it sound like a fine adventure. The attractive design, the fascinating photographs, and Sally Ride's engaging voice result in an outstanding book.

Scott, Elaine. *Adventure in Space: The Flight to Fix the Hubble*. Photographs by Margaret Miller, photographer. 1995. Hard: Hyperion. Ages 8–11.

After the $1.6 billion Hubble space telescope was launched in 1990, scientists realized it didn't work properly. A group of seven astronauts traveled 4.4 million miles and eleven days to fix it in space. This photo-essay describes that mission, with a slight emphasis on the role of Kathy Thornton, the most experienced woman astronaut in the world. Physicist Thornton was one of the four astronauts who donned space suits and went outside to fix the telescope. The mother of three daughters, Thornton advises girls to study the hard sciences, and to take calculated risks, just as she risks the dangers of space flight to gain the benefits of being an astronaut. Photographs show Thornton and the other astronauts planning, practicing, and accomplishing their goal in space. An attractive book about an important space mission.

Vare, Ethlie Ann. *Adventurous Spirit: A Story about Ellen Swallow Richards.* **Illustrated by Jennifer Hagerman. 1992. Hard: Carolrhoda. Ages 8–11.**

Notable nineteenth-century scientist Ellen Swallow Richards was the first woman to attend and get a degree from the Massachusetts Institute of Technology (MIT). As the first professional female chemist in the United States, she overcame many obstacles her male peers did not have to face. Through her efforts, MIT opened its doors to many more female students, although the Chemistry Department refused to award Richards the doctorate she had earned. Richards went on to make a name for herself as a pioneer in studying water pollution and promoting good nutrition. She founded the American home economics movement, introducing scientific principles into women's work in the home, a revolutionary idea in a time when women were thought incapable of understanding science. "Keep thinking," she wrote at the end of all her letters, a maxim she followed herself throughout her hardworking and illustrious life.

Women in the Arts

Gherman, Beverly. *Georgia O'Keeffe: The "Wideness and Wonder" of Her World.* **1986. Hard: Atheneum. Pbk: Aladdin. Ages 10–13.**

Using apt quotations and anecdotes, this competent biography stresses Georgia O'Keeffe's individuality as an artist. While others expected her to become an art teacher because she was a woman, she herself planned to be a full-time artist as soon as possible. Once she had reached that goal, she pursued her own artistic vision regardless of criticism or current trends. "All the male artists I knew, of course, made it very plain that as a woman I couldn't hope to make it," she once observed. But, in fact, her career brought her fame and financial security. Her marriage to photographer and gallery owner Alfred Stieglitz, who helped launch her success, was unconventional. O'Keeffe kept her name and eventually spent part of the year in New Mexico while Stieglitz stayed in New York. Unfortunately, the reproductions of her paintings are in black and white, but otherwise this is a good midlevel biography of a fascinating woman.

Hurwitz, Johanna. *Astrid Lindgren: Storyteller to the World.* **Illustrated by Michael Dooling. 1989. Hard: Viking, o.p. Pbk: Puffin. Ages 8–11.**

Readers may be surprised to find out that *Pippi Longstocking* is one of the twelve most translated books in the world. Clearly Astrid Lindgren has made her mark through her original characters and stories. Born in Sweden in 1907, Lindgren spent her childhood romping outdoors, climbing trees, and swimming. When she created her most famous character in 1945, she drew on her own experiences and feelings. The reaction to the book about such a loud, strong, independent girl was mixed: Some adults were disturbed by Pippi's behavior, but most children were thrilled. The worldwide success of this and others of Lindgren's books have brought her many honors as well as financial rewards. She has also been influential as a children's book editor and translator in Sweden. Pippi fans will enjoy reading about her creator, a strong woman in her own right.

Kamen, Gloria. *Hidden Music: The Life of Fanny Mendelssohn.* **1996. Hard: Atheneum. Ages 10–13.**

Fanny Mendelssohn, sister of the famous musician Felix Mendelssohn, provides a historical example of how women have been held back in music. From a well-to-do family, Fanny was a talented and skillful pianist whose domineering father restricted her to performing only for friends and family. In a letter to Fanny about music, he wrote: "For you it can and must only be an ornament," not a profession. Although she published a small number of the four hundred compositions she wrote in her lifetime, Fanny received little encouragement from her successful brother. A stark contrast emerges between the lives of Fanny, who married and lived on her parents' estate, and Felix, who traveled widely and was renowned for his musical accomplishments. An epilogue discusses other female musicians in the last two centuries and the obstacles they faced. A bibliography suggests further reading. One of the few children's books on a female musician, this is accessible and interesting.

Lyons, Mary E. *Stitching Stars: The Story Quilts of Harriet Powers.* **1993. Hard: Scribner. Ages 8–11.**

This beautifully designed book explores two story quilts sewn by Harriet Powers, an African-American born into slavery and freed by the Civil War. Although little is known about her early life, the book discusses typical conditions of the times and region where she lived, including the importance of quilting bees. Despite poverty and a hard life, Powers created two remarkable story quilts. The first, based on biblical stories, she made for herself but had to sell during hard times. When that quilt went on display at an exposition, a second quilt was commissioned. This one incorporated religious stories and historic natural events such as an enormous meteorite shower. The text and captions explain and analyze many of the individual quilt panels, in which graceful textile figures tell stories and express religious feelings. With no art training, Powers took everyday materials and an everyday craft and turned them into enduring art.

Martinez, Elizabeth Coonrod. *Sor Juana: A Trailblazing Thinker*. 1994. Hard: Millbrook. Ages 8–11.

Juana Ines de Asbaje y Ramirez, who lived in Mexico in the 1600s, was determined to become educated even though higher education was reserved for males. She was exceedingly intelligent, learned to read at age three, and mastered Latin and other ancient languages as a teenager. She so impressed the royal court that the officials decided to have her tested by experts when she was fifteen; she answered all their questions perfectly. Because nuns were the only women who could pursue studies, Juana joined a convent and became Sor Juana. She wrote plays and poetry, studied sciences, and played music. Only when the church officials forbade her to continue writing because she was female was this brilliant woman silenced, four years before her death at age forty-seven. Her writings expressed her belief that women should be allowed to think and study, goals she herself attained against all odds.

Mühlberger, Richard. *What Makes a Cassatt a Cassatt?* 1994. Pbk: Metropolitan Museum of Art/Viking. Ages 8–11.

The main thrust of this excellent book is to acquaint the reader with Mary Cassatt's artwork, but it also outlines the basics of her life. One in a series mostly about male painters, it looks closely at paintings and prints, analyzing influences and innovations. Cassatt's main subjects were women and children, often a mother and her child, an area in which she went far beyond other painters. Unlike other Impressionists, Cassatt focused on the relationships between people in her paintings. This attractive book teaches the reader how to see more in artwork and introduces the work of a distinguished female artist.

Pettit, Jayne. *Maya Angelou: Journey of the Heart*. 1996. Hard: Lodestar. Ages 9–11.

This seventy-page biography describes both the difficulties and the notable accomplishments in the life of writer Maya Angelou. In her childhood she was often separated from her parents, living with her grandmother in Arkansas and later her grandmother in St. Louis. The book briefly discusses that she was raped at age eight by a friend of her mother's, who was murdered before he could be imprisoned. Although she has also encountered many troubles as an adult, Angelou has succeeded as an actress, an activist, and a writer of striking prose and poetry. She has been honored in several fields, nominated for an Emmy for her acting role in the television series *Roots* and nominated for a Pulitzer Prize for poetry. Her inaugural poem for President Clinton moved listeners throughout the country. The rich life of this distinguished woman reads like a dramatic novel.

Turner, Robyn Montana. *Rosa Bonheur*. 1991. Hard: Little, Brown, o.p. Pbk: Little, Brown. Ages 7–10.

Like the other entries in the Portraits of Women Artists for Children series, this biography has an elegant open design, good reproductions of paintings, and a noteworthy subject. Though the writing tends to be awkward, it does supply the important facts about the artist. Born in 1822 in France, Rosa Bonheur was supported in her career as a painter by her mother, who encouraged her to draw on the walls of their house, and by her father, an artist who eventually took his daughter into his studio to study. Bonheur's stunning talent combined with her determination led to early recognition, even in a period when there was much prejudice against female artists. When she was twenty-three, she won third prize in the Salon, the annual art show in Paris. Three years later she won the Salon's gold medal. She began to earn large sums for her paintings, and spent the rest of her long life as a successful artist, mostly painting animals. Her earnings allowed her to buy a chateau, whose grounds she stocked with animals, including a yak and a lion. In 1865, Bonheur became the first woman to be awarded the medal of the French Legion of Honor, a powerful recognition of her accomplishments. A notable example of a nineteenth-century woman who achieved great success critically and financially in her chosen field.

Wadsworth, Ginger. *Julia Morgan: Architect of Dreams*. 1990. Hard: Lerner. Ages 10–13.

At a time when few women were architects, Julia Morgan ran her own architectural office in San Francisco and designed more than seven hundred buildings. She graduated from the University of California in engineering in 1894 and proceeded to Paris, where she was the first woman to receive a certificate from the Ecole des Beaux-Arts, an eminent architectural school. Morgan was also the first woman to be licensed as an architect in California. Her largest project was at the Hearst estate in San Simeon, where she designed and supervised the construction of several large, ornate buildings, including the well-known "Hearst Castle." Wadsworth's fluent text, amply illustrated with photographs and sketches, focuses on Morgan's work, the all-consuming center of her life. Her success was partly thanks to the patronage of women, including the millionaire Phoebe Hearst, who gave her many commissions. A pioneer in a man's world, Morgan offers inspiration to future architects and engineers. An appendix lists a large selection of her buildings with their addresses.

Sports Biographies

Breitenbucher, Cathy. *Bonnie Blair: Golden Streak.* **1994. Hard: Lerner. Pbk: Lerner. Ages 9–12.**

As of the 1994 Winter Olympics, speed skater Bonnie Blair had won more medals—five gold and one bronze—than any other U.S. athlete in the Winter Olympics. She has participated in four Olympic games and numerous other speed-skating events. Only great athletic ability combined with intense dedication could produce such a record, and Bonnie Blair has both. This upbeat biography with its admiring tone focuses mainly on her career with details of her race history and her many successes.

Donohue, Shiobhan. *Kristi Yamaguchi: Artist on Ice.* **1994. Hard: Lerner. Pbk: Lerner. Ages 8–11.**

Kristi Yamaguchi started skating at age six, entered her first local competition when she was seven, and progressed rapidly in singles skating and pairs skating. Her technical prowess and artistic performances have won her many medals and honors, including an Olympic gold medal and the "triple crown" of winning the national, world, and Olympic figure skating championships in a single year. This straightforward biography, illustrated with adequate black-and-white photographs, concentrates on Yamaguchi's skating achievements rather than her personal life.

Goldstein, Margaret J., and Jennifer Larson. *Jackie Joyner-Kersee: Superwoman.* **1994. Hard: Lerner. Pbk: Lerner. Ages 8–10.**

From an early age, Jackie Joyner was an amazing athlete. At twelve she could jump farther than most high school athletes and was faster than most boys, including her fourteen-year-old brother Al. She has gone on to a stunningly impressive college and Olympic career, not yet finished. This six-chapter biography describes her childhood and athletic achievements. It discusses setbacks, talks briefly about her marriage to her coach Bob Kersee, and touches on her philanthropic work. The authors shy away from the negative, and some readers will question the credit given to Bob Kersee, who, one patronizing caption says, "makes sure that Jackie stays healthy and in top condition." The text amply describes Joyner-Kersee's talent, hard work, and athletic accomplishments, including back-to-back Olympic gold medals in the heptathalon. The mediocre black-and-white photographs capture exciting moments in the career of this superb athlete.

Harrington, Denis J. *Top Ten Women Tennis Players.* **1995. Hard: Enslow. Ages 9–12.**

Ten tennis legends past and present—Maureen Connolly, Margaret Court, Chris Evert, Zina Garrison-Jackson, Althea Gibson, Steffi Graf, Billie Jean King, Martina Navratilova, Gabriela Sabatini, and Monica Seles—are profiled in this slim sports book. Each sketch describes highlights of the athlete's career with anecdotes and details from important matches. Color and black-and-white photographs capture the players in action. Fact boxes, career statistics, and an index are other features of this utilitarian volume. Geared specifically toward reluctant readers, this collective biography is more up-to-date than the few other children's books on women's tennis.

Knudson, R. R. *Babe Didrikson: Athlete of the Century.*
1985. Hard: Viking, o.p. Pbk: Puffin. Ages 9–12.

Although not well known today, Babe Didrikson was one
of the most talented athletes ever. Born and raised in Texas,
she excelled at sports from childhood. She left high school to
play basketball with the Golden Cyclones, a women's team
sponsored by an insurance company. Although she technically earned her salary as a secretary, in fact the company
encouraged her athletic growth and sponsored her in track
events, too. When she was twenty-one she gave a stunning
performance at the Amateur Athletic Union national track
meet, where she took first place in six women's events and
fourth place in another. Shortly after that, she took two
gold medals and one silver at the Olympics. Because she
needed the money, she worked relentlessly at golf until
she made herself into a star and even a millionaire. Before
her death at forty-three, she worked to establish the Ladies'
Professional Golf Association. This short biography gives a
balanced picture of an immensely talented and determined
woman who liked to brag about her own prowess in a way
usually reserved for male athletes. Nicknamed "Babe" after
Babe Ruth, she deserves to be as well known as that more
famous Babe.

McGovern, Ann. *Down Under, Down Under: Diving
Adventures on the Great Barrier Reef.* **Photographs by Jim
and Martin Scheiner and the author. 1989. Hard:
Macmillan. Ages 8–10.**

Told in first person, this is a photo-essay about a twelve-
year-old girl diving in the Great Barrier Reef with her marine
biologist mother. A junior certified diver, the girl spends ten
days on a boat, diving up to three times each day. She gets
advice and help from her mother and the female dive master.

Amazing underwater color photographs show the girl and the many beautiful creatures she sees in her dives. Although she is initially afraid of sharks and sea snakes, her enthusiasm and her mother's reassurances always overcome her doubts about going in. She feeds sharks from a platform, gets up the courage to handle a sea snake, and explores a ghostly shipwreck. The final chapter gives information about diving equipment and techniques, with a photograph of the narrator fully suited up for diving. This will undoubtedly make many readers eager to try scuba diving.

McMane, Fred, and Cathrine Wolf. *Winning Women: Eight Great Athletes and Their Unbeatable Stories*. 1995. Pbk: Bantam/Sports Illustrated for Kids. Ages 9–11.

This breezy collective biography acquaints the reader with eight illustrious athletes in different sports. Each chapter focuses on one woman, giving a bit of biographical information, then detailing her athletic accomplishments. The athletes, many of them Olympic medalists, are runner Gail Deavers, skater Oksana Baiul, Hispanic-American pro golfer Nancy Lopez, jockey Julie Krone, tennis star Steffi Graf, gymnast Shannon Miller, speed skater Bonnie Blair, and basketball star Teresa Edwards. An inset of color photographs shows each of the winning women at her sport.

Sanford, William R., and Carl R. Green. *Billie Jean King*. 1993. Hard: Crestwood House. Ages 9–12.

Billie Jean King not only made a name for herself as one of the best women tennis players of all times, but also changed the sport for the women after her. In 1970, King, angry at the large disparity between men's and women's prize money at tournaments, joined eight other women to start a separate women's tennis association. Her leadership and hard work made women's tennis more prestigious and more lucrative. She also defeated self-proclaimed male chauvinist Bobby Riggs, who bragged that no woman could beat a top male pro. King's list of major victories on the court is extensive, making her one of the best women players of all times. Brief chapters, frequent black-and-white photographs, and boxed trivia questions give a cluttered look to this brief biography, which touches on problems in King's personal life but focuses primarily on her accomplishments and her contributions to tennis.

Wadsworth, Ginger. *Susan Butcher: Sled Dog Racer*. 1994. Hard: Lerner. Ages 8–10.

The strength of this short biography is its subject. Susan Butcher is a remarkable woman who became dominant in dogsled racing, a sport previously led by men. She has won the 1,049-mile Iditarod Trail Sled Dog Race four times, an amazing feat. It is a grueling, dangerous trial through snow and ice that takes all year to train for. Butcher's life is centered around her dogs and racing, and she thrives on the physical and mental challenges of her sport. The straightforward text touches on Butcher's background, then details the ups and downs of each Iditarod she has entered. Although the colorful cover is attractive, the black-and-white photographs in the text are disappointing. Still, this is a readable introduction to a daring athlete.

Women in History

Colman, Penny. *Spies! Women in the Civil War*. 1992. Pbk: Shoe Tree Press. Ages 10–14.

This slim paperback offers fascinating reading about women spies during the Civil War. Four spies, two for the

North and two for the South, each merit a whole chapter. Elizabeth Van Lew, a northern sympathizer living in Confederate Virginia, risked her life and spent her family fortune spying for the Yankees. Harriet Tubman, known for her role in the Underground Railroad, organized a network of spies to aid the North. Rose O'Neal Greenhow, widow and mother of four, hosted brilliant social events in Washington, D.C., and used her contacts and sharp powers of observation to obtain information for the Confederates. The other southern spy, seventeen-year-old Belle Boyd, is known for her role as a courier. Greenhow and Boyd both spent time in prison, which did nothing to lessen their commitment to the South. A final chapter gives short descriptions of other female spies in the Civil War, followed by a chronology, a list of historic places to visit, and a list of further reading. A well-balanced history of some little-known, courageous women.

Fleming, Candace. *Women of the Lights*. 1996. Hard: Albert Whitman. Ages 9–12.

From 1768 until 1947, two hundred and fifty women staffed lighthouses in the United States, a dangerous job that took physical strength, mental toughness, and an expert knowledge of weather. This fascinating book describes five such lighthouse keepers, with a final chapter about the exploits of several other women. Ida Lewis, a lighthouse keeper in Newport, Rhode Island, rescued many people from boating accidents and became a national celebrity. Kate Walker of New York, who succeeded her husband as a lighthouse keeper, saved more than fifty people—and one little dog—in her time. Most surprising is Emily Fish, who turned her Monterey peninsula lighthouse into a gracious social center, complete with pedigreed poodles. Her daughter emulated her mother by becoming a lighthouse keeper on an island in San Francisco Bay. All the women described broke traditions and proved the ability of women to do this difficult job.

Fritz, Jean. *You Want Women to Vote, Lizzie Stanton?* Illustrated by DyAnne DiSalvo-Ryan. 1995. Hard: Putnam. Ages 9–12.

Skillful biographer Fritz turns her hand to a key figure in the women's suffrage movement: Elizabeth Cady Stanton. Using apt anecdotes and fascinating details, this short biography explores the factors that turned Stanton into a writer and orator for the cause. Struggling to raise seven children with little help from her husband, she participated when she could in the movement that eventually won women the vote. She was outspoken and unafraid of negative reactions to her views. The book highlights the harsh conditions that affected women at the time: No married woman could own property; men could legally beat their wives; only men had the power to obtain a divorce; and more. The highly readable and entertaining text will open the eyes of readers unfamiliar with the history of women in this country. Occasional black-and-white illustrations add humor and interest. An excellent introduction to a remarkable woman and a vital cause.

Igus, Toyomi, ed. *Book of Black Heroes, Volume II: Great Women in the Struggle*. 1991. Hard: Just Us Books. Pbk: Just Us Books. Ages 9–12.

More than eighty biographical sketches describe the contributions of important black women. Each one-page entry includes a photograph or drawing, a quotation by or about the woman, and a summary of her life and achievements. The volume is organized into eight sections: freedom fighters; educators; writers and fine artists; performing artists; athletes; entrepreneurs; lawyers and policy makers; and scientists and healers.

Each category features women from the past and present. Some, such as Sojourner Truth, Harriet Tubman, Angela Davis, and Oprah Winfrey, will be well known to many readers. Others may not be, such as Queen Nzingha, an African queen who resisted white domination. Maggie Lena Walker was the first female bank president in the United States and also opened an insurance company, and Charlotte E. Ray was the first black woman lawyer. The list goes on, from political activists to judges to cancer researchers to college presidents. The book presents an impressive array of women from many backgrounds who have in common their determination and success. It is troubling that the book describes the Emancipation Proclamation inaccurately twice. However, this collective biography presents a fine array of inspiring black women.

Johnston, Johanna. *They Led the Way: Fourteen American Women.* Illustrated by Deanne Hollinger. 1973. Pbk: Scholastic. Ages 9–11.

This simple introduction to fourteen important women extends from colonial times until women won the vote in 1920. Five to ten pages, with occasional black-and-white illustrations, tell each woman's story, using some fictionalized dialogue. First comes Anne Hutchinson, who argued that women could receive signs from God and had the right to speak out on their religion; she was banished from the Massachusetts Bay Colony for her boldness. Anne Bradstreet was the first American poet published in England, and Phillis Wheatley the first black poet published in the colonies. Lady Deborah Moody, a wealthy widow, started the town of Gravesend, now in Brooklyn, for which she wrote the laws and planned the design. Ernestine Rose, a Polish Jew, defied convention by speaking out publicly against injustice in Europe and the United States in the nineteenth century. Other better known women discussed are Abigail Adams, Elizabeth Blackwell, Clara Barton, and Harriet Beecher Stowe. Victoria Woodhull, one of the first women brokers and a presidential candidate before women could even vote, is described briefly, as is journalist and adventurer Nellie Bly. A good way to spark an interest that may lead children to longer biographies.

Johnston, Norma. *Remember the Ladies: The First Women's Rights Convention*. 1995. Pbk: Scholastic. Ages 10–13.

The Seneca Falls Woman's Rights Convention took place over two long days in 1848 and was the beginning of a revolution that led to women getting the vote. This history of the convention is divided into three parts: the background of the key women, the convention itself, and the aftermath. Of the five women who planned the convention, two are most significant and get the most coverage, Elizabeth Cady Stanton and Lucretia Coffin Mott. The discussion of Mott also briefly covers the role of Quakers in the women's movement and abolitionism, two closely linked causes. The middle section of the book gives a detailed account of the convention, with a chapter for each morning, afternoon, and evening meeting. It includes the entire Declaration of Rights and Sentiments modeled on the nation's Declaration of Independence. The final section describes some of the consequences of the convention historically and for the planners themselves. Back matter includes a list of important dates, end notes, a bibliography and an index. This relatively short book, illustrated with photographs, provides an excellent overview of the birth of the women's movement.

Katz, William Loren. *Black Women of the Old West*. 1995. Hard: Atheneum. Ages 10–14.

This attractive volume, illustrated with black-and-white

photographs and prints, fills a gap in most history books: the role of black women in settling the American West. Full of anecdotes and examples, it describes African-American women suing for their rights and working to form successful communities. It emphasizes the importance of blacks in helping others escape from slavery, in providing homes for the Underground Railroad, and more. The emphasis women put on their children's and their own education comes through again and again. They organized to fight segregated schools in the West, and achieved higher literacy rates than white women on the frontier. To avoid isolation in sparsely populated areas, black women banded together in cultural societies and charitable organizations. Black women owned real estate, ran businesses, worked a wide range of jobs, and sometimes made a lot of money. Profiles of individuals tell their stories, and captions under the numerous photographs add more information. Although some of the photographs are damaged or hazy, there is something powerful and haunting about these faces looking out from the past. An outstanding photo-essay.

Sullivan, George. *The Day the Women Got the Vote: A Photo History of the Women's Rights Movement*. 1994. Pbk: Scholastic. Ages 9–12.

The Nineteenth Amendment to the Constitution, finally recognizing women's right to vote, became official on August 26, 1920. This wide-ranging photo essay details the movement that led up to that historic day as well as what has happened to the movement since. The numerous photographs and etchings give faces to the leaders and participants in the movement from past to present. Besides offering basic facts about the effort to secure the vote, the many short chapters highlight a variety of topics: factory women, dress reform, equal education, women at war, the equal rights amendment. Many famous women, from Susan B.

Anthony to Betty Friedan, are described briefly. In his attempt to cover a huge amount, the author sometimes resorts to over-simplification. In general, however, this provides a valuable pictorial introduction to a neglected aspect of American history.

More Dynamic Girls and Women

Fritz, Jean. *The Double Life of Pocahontas*. Illustrated by Ed Young. 1983. Hard: Putnam. Pbk: Puffin. Ages 9–12.

This biography with its soft, evocative illustrations provides an antidote to the Disney version of Pocahontas. The verified facts about her life are combined with speculation to give the sense of her as a real person. The "double life" of the title refers to her roles in the world of her tribe and in that of the English settlers and later in England. As the daughter of a chief, Pocahontas knew the privileges and responsibilities of a powerful family. When she was sent to negotiate with the settlers for captured Indians, her father admonished her not to beg, but to leave that to her companions. Later, when the English kidnapped her and her father refused to pay the ransom, Pocahontas turned her intelligence and energies to learning English ways. She married Englishman John Rolfe and bore a son, but died on a trip to England in 1617 at the age of twenty-one. Best known for her friendship to John Smith, whose life she saved, her life was a more complex and poignant one than many realize.

Goldin, Barbara Diamond. *Bat Mitzvah: A Jewish Girl's Coming of Age*. Illustrated by Erika Weihs. 1995. Hard: Viking. Ages 10–14.

This is a warm, friendly book about the coming-of-age ceremony for Jewish girls known as bat mitzvah. Goldin discusses

Jewish history, highlighting the role of women in the Bible and more recent history with surprising facts and anecdotes. She explains the different branches of Judaism and the place of women in each. In a conversational tone, she gives details about how girls study for the ceremony and the ways they individualize it, with examples and comments from participants. The text goes through the study process and the ceremony itself, followed by a lighter chapter on the parties that follow the ritual. This is an approachable introduction to bat mitzvah of interest to girls who are preparing for it and others who are simply curious about this important rite of passage.

Green, Carl R., and William R. Sanford. *Belle Starr*. 1992. Hard: Enslow. Ages 8–11.

This brief biography describes the exploits of Belle Starr, who was known as the Bandit Queen of the West. Starr lived from 1848 to 1889, in Missouri, Texas, Arkansas, and the nearby Indian Territory. As a child she learned to ride horseback and became an expert shot. Legend has it that she served as a spy for the Confederates and saved her brother's life by recklessly riding cross-country to warn him of Union plans. She married outlaw Jim Reed, and lived a wild life in Dallas, where she was known for galloping through the streets, firing her pistols in the air. After Reed's death, she married a Cherokee named Sam Starr, and their home in Indian Territory became a hideout for their bandit friends. Belle was found guilty of horse stealing and spent nine months in a prison, after which she decided to mend her ways. Since her death, Belle Starr has become a legend through stories that exaggerate her crimes and adventures. This biography, illustrated with photographs and etchings, sets the story straight about this unusual female outlaw.

Rappaport, Doreen. *Living Dangerously: American Women Who Risked Their Lives for Adventure*. 1991. Hard: Harper. Ages 10–14.

Rappaport describes dangerous episodes from the lives of six women, inventing dialogue to bring the stories to life. The feats include going over Niagara Falls in a barrel, accompanying hunters stalking an elephant, and diving for fossils and bones. One woman was the first licensed African-American pilot and another an accomplished mountain climber. The final story is of a woman amputee who finished a marathon in her wheelchair. Grainy black-and-white photographs give a glimpse of each woman. The stories vary in excitement, but the more impressive ones make the book worth reading.

Seymour, Tryntje Van Ness. *The Gift of Changing Woman*. Paintings by Apache artists. 1993. Hard: Holt. Ages 8–11.

In the culture of the Apache—or the Ndee, as they call themselves—a girl goes through the Changing Woman ceremony when she reaches twelve or thirteen. During the ceremony, which lasts four days, the girl moves from childhood to womanhood with the help and blessing of her people. In Apache mythology, Changing Woman alone survived a terrible flood, and all the Apache descend from her. For this reason, Apaches join their mother's clan, not their father's, a sign of the importance of women in Apache tradition. This slim book, beautifully illustrated with paintings by Apache artists, describes the Changing Woman ceremony. After the long ceremony, which involves hours of dancing, the girl's family and friends treat her as a woman and expect her to act as one. It is fascinating to read of a ceremony in today's world in which a girl and her womanhood are so honored.

Thomson, Peggy. *Katie Henio: Navajo Sheepherder*. Photographs by Paul Conklin. 1995. Hard: Cobblehill. Ages 9–11.

Katie Henio has spent most of her life in New Mexico herding sheep and weaving their wool. Although now a great-grandmother, she sleeps out many nights with her sheep and tends them all day on horseback, sometimes fighting off coyotes. She is skilled with a rope, able to lasso sheep by the head or heel. She has been shooting since she was eight, and driving a truck since she was fifteen. Recently the Smithsonian honored her weaving skills as part of the Smithsonian Folklife Festival. Clear, informative color photographs show her shearing sheep with her daughters, riding horseback with her rifle across her knees, and much more. The tradition of strong women in the Navajo culture molded Katie Henio, from her coming-of-age ceremony to her current role as a community mediator. By her own standards, her life is ordinary, but to those outside her culture, she seems to be an extraordinary woman of great strength.

Van Meter, Vicki, with Dan Gutman. *Taking Flight: My Story*. 1995. Hard: Viking. Ages 10–13.

Readers will sense the flavor of this amazing true story from the dust jacket, which shows a smiling girl wearing a flight suit and headset, with a small plane in the background. She is Vicki Van Meter, who broke a record as the youngest girl to fly across the country. In a breezy style, she describes learning to fly and her preparations to fly coast to coast in 1993, accompanied by her flight instructor. Only her steady determination kept her going during the grueling flight, during which she was plagued by bad weather and sickness. Her accomplishment set three aviation records: youngest girl to fly across the country, youngest pilot to fly east to west, and farthest distance any child had flown. Vicki enjoys her fame, but her focus is on flying. She gives technical information on planning trips and readying the plane, and on the act of piloting. "There's a lot of math involved in flying," she reports. "Fortunately, I like math." She also describes her flight across the Atlantic in 1994, a dangerous, record-setting feat. Four pages of color photographs and numerous black-and-white photographs show Vicki with her family and on her trips.

Poetry & Magazines

Glaser, Isabel Joshlin, selector. *Dreams of Glory: Poems Starring Girls*. Illustrated by Pat Lowery Collins. 1995. Hard: Atheneum. Ages 8–12.

The thirty short poems in this anthology are divided into three sections: Sports, Power, and Dreams of Glory. The Sports poems are especially strong and include skiing, skating, horseback riding, baseball, track, and diving. Among the Power poems, "Abigail" is a particularly wonderful poem about a girl who doesn't fit in but who later writes a book that "would curl your hair," a happy revenge on a stifling life. There is a lack of poems about girls going on adventures or actually accomplishing something exciting. Far more concern hopes, dreams, and frustrations. But since few anthologies exist of poems about girls, readers will find new material here. It is a good start that signals the need for more poems about girls.

***New Moon: The Magazine for Girls and Their Dreams*. New Moon Publishing, P.O. Box 3620, Duluth, MN 55803-9905. 1-218-728-5507.**

Aimed at girls aged eight to fourteen, this offers an alternative to the many magazines for girls that emphasize fashion, movie and TV stars, and dating. It is edited by a group of girls, and encourages readers to submit their own writing. Its six issues per year contain articles, stories, poems, letters, and drawings with a young feminist slant. A related publication is *New Moon Network* for parents.

Sports Illustrated for Kids. P.O. Box 830606, Birmingham, AL 35282-9487. 1-800-323-1422.

Although this glossy magazine, aimed at children aged nine to fourteen, has more information about male athletes than females, it offers the best way for children to keep up on girls and women in sports. It features children who excel in their sport as well as professional athletes, with short articles and lots of color photographs. Unfortunately it contains many more advertisements than most children's magazines.

5

Books for Older Readers

Many fine writers focus on writing for adolescents, so the selection that follows is a rich one. The best of these books are more sophisticated in plot and vocabulary than most books in the previous chapter. Some challenge readers with more complex characters, more layers of meaning, and more ambiguous endings. At their finest they enable readers to stretch their imaginations as they enter the lives of the characters. The annotations and age ranges will indicate which books are appropriate for advanced younger readers and which are best for readers with more emotional maturity. Although the age ranges only go up to fourteen, older teenagers may also enjoy some of these books.

At this age, approximately twelve to fourteen, many readers start reading books written for adults, a few of which are listed here. Fantasy and mystery fans are particularly likely to supplement their reading with adult fiction. But all adolescents should be encouraged to read the "young adult" literature written for them, which speaks directly to their concerns and interests.

The chapter below, as in chapter 4, is divided into two large sections: Fiction and Biographies. Within Fiction are adventure and survival stories; contemporary novels; sports stories; mysteries; historical fiction; and fantasy and science fiction. Biographies are divided into leaders and activists; professionals and educators; scientists and inventors; women in the arts; sports biographies; and women in history.

Be sure to check for more suggestions in chapter 4 and in the collections of folklore in chapter 2. And keep in mind that the picture-story books associated with younger children can offer teenagers excellent examples of writing and art, and a kind of comfort to readers on the verge of growing up.

Fiction

Adventure and Survival Stories

Alexander, Lloyd. *The Illyrian Adventure.* **1986. Hard: Dutton, o.p. Pbk: Dell. Ages 10–14.**

Sixteen-year-old Vesper Holly is a unique heroine, a female Indiana Jones living in the 1870s. She "has the mind of a chess master," knows six languages, and can swear in all of them. She can use a slide ruler but would rather do calculations in her head. Curious about the country Illyria, which her now-dead father had visited, Vesper organizes an expedition to go there with the help of Professor Brinton Garrett, her guardian and the narrator of the story. They find themselves caught up in a rebellion and at odds with an evil power. Vesper, whose life is in danger more than once, plays a key role in the future of the small country, thanks to her intelligence and courage. A lark to read. Others in the series are *The El Dorado Adventure*, *The Drackenberg Adventure*, and more.

Avi. *The True Confessions of Charlotte Doyle.* **1990. Hard: Orchard. Pbk: Avon. Ages 10–14.**

"Not every thirteen-year-old girl is accused of murder, brought to trial, and found guilty" is the opening line of this thrilling tale. When ladylike Charlotte Doyle boards the *Seahawk* in 1832 to sail from England to Rhode Island, she expects to be chaperoned by two families. Instead, she finds herself the only female aboard a ship on which a mutiny is planned. At first disdainful of the scruffy crew, Charlotte comes to realize that they hate the cruel captain for good reason. She herself joins the crew and, though she has never done any manual labor, learns to climb the riggings and shoulder her share of the work. As her spirit and strength grow, the captain's hatred for her increases until it culminates in trying her for a murder she didn't commit. The book's ending is enough to make readers cheer for this heroine who has too much courage and spirit for the conventional life she has left behind. A Newbery Honor Book.

Dickinson, Peter. *A Bone from a Dry Sea*. 1993. Hard: Delacorte. Pbk: Dell. Ages 11–14.

Alternating chapters tell the stories of two girls, one in the present who is visiting a paleontological dig in Africa; and the other, Li, a hominid living four million years earlier in the same area. Vinny, whose father works on the dig, discusses evolution and geology with him, and advocates a theory she has read about how humans may have evolved from hominids who lived partly in water. She holds her own, even when he scoffs at her, and she later defies the leader of the dig when he tries to intimidate her into becoming part of the dig's publicity campaign. Wrangling among the males on the dig is paralleled in Li's time by males vying for dominance, one of the many intriguing similarities between the two times. Li is a genius in the context of her primitive life. She devises innovations to help her tribe, fashioning a net to catch shrimp and swimming with dolphins who drive fish toward shore for Li. Both girls are emotionally strong as well as intelligent. In the satisfying conclusion, they are linked across time by a shark bone, which Li has bored with a primitive awl and which Vinny recognizes as important. A thought-provoking, beautifully written book.

George, Jean Craighead. *Julie of the Wolves.* **Illustrated by John Schoenherr. 1972. Hard: Harper. Pbk: Harper Trophy. Ages 11–14.**

Miyax is an Eskimo girl on a journey across the tundra, running away from a bad situation, who finds herself lost and without food. Remembering her father's teachings, she befriends a small pack of wolves and with their aid tries to survive the light months until the north star becomes visible again. The details of her survival and how she carefully learns the ways of the wolf pack make fascinating reading. She works diligently to make a place in the wilderness, but then must face the question of whether to leave. An extraordinary but convincing adventure of a remarkable girl. Winner of the Newbery Medal. The sequel is *Julie.*

Griffin, Peni R. *Switching Well.* **1993. Hard: McElderry. Pbk: Puffin. Ages 11–14.**

In this outstanding time-travel book set in San Antonio, two girls switch places in time a hundred years apart. Amber is tired of urban life in 1991 and longs for a simpler, cleaner age. Ada finds the role of females in 1891 too constricting and wishes she were living in the future. Each gets her wish but finds the other time to be less wonderful than expected. Amber finds poverty and more restrictions than she's used to. Her forthright ways cause her to clash with the adults she meets and she feels frustrated at every turn. Ada gets by only with the help of Violet, a strong and generous girl at Ada's 1991 foster home. Ada and especially Amber have to draw on reserves of courage and resourcefulness they didn't know they had. Bound to make the reader contrast past and present roles of women and African-Americans, this is an unusually thoughtful and enjoyable story.

Masterson, David. *Get Out of My Face.* **1991. Hard: Atheneum. Ages 11–13.**

Kate is worried when her father remarries and the two of them move in with Pamela and her children, Linda and Joey. Teenagers Kate and Linda start a friendship, but twelve-year-old Joey detests Kate and makes her life miserable. Kate's diary entries alternate with the story of the fateful canoe trip the three of them take. When their canoe crashes on the rocks in the rapids, all Kate's resources are tested. She rescues Joey and then finds Linda, who has a badly broken leg. Kate realizes that their survival depends on getting Joey to cooperate with her. She uses her first-aid experience to splint Linda's leg and ingeniously fashions a stretcher. Carrying her pushes the limits of Kate's physical strength, but her conditioning from being on swimming and basketball teams makes the difference. She and Joey, who is physically weaker, forge an unsteady alliance. Suspense builds as Linda contracts a fever, a storm sets in, and they have to cross both a stream and a rising river. An exciting and plausible survival story.

Mazer, Harry. *The Island Keeper.* **1981. Hard: Delacorte, o.p. Pbk: Dell. Ages 11–14.**

In this quick read, Cleo, an unhappy, overweight sixteen-year-old, could be a character from a soap opera. Her very wealthy family shuffles her from school to school, but money cannot buy what she really wants: her mother and her sister, who are both dead from accidents. Grieving for her sister, Cleo runs away to a Canadian island her father owns to spend the summer. She learns to survive on her own, despite the inner voice that constantly tells her what a failure she is, a message she has received all her life from her grandmother. Although it lacks the detail of some survival novels, the story does show Cleo coming to terms with killing animals in order to eat. When the weather turns cold, Cleo decides to go home—only to have her canoe smashed by a falling tree. How will she make it through the winter? Cleo is up to the challenge, stronger and more resourceful than when she started her saga.

Mikaelsen, Ben. *Stranded.* **1995. Hard: Hyperion. Pbk: Hyperion. Ages 10–13.**

Koby lives on one of the Florida Keys in a boat named the *Dream Chaser.* She spends her happiest time out in her dinghy, where it doesn't matter that half of one of her legs is missing, lost in an accident. On her way home from fishing one evening, she spies a pilot whale in trouble, caught in a net. Koby bravely cuts the net, knowing the whale could hurt her, then rescues the whale's newborn calf. Not too many days later, she finds the whales stranded on the shore and stays with them through the night to keep them wet. A rescue squad, including a female marine veterinarian, takes charge of the whales and tries to rehabilitate them. Koby volunteers to help and, as the only person the whales respond to, ensures their survival. Although she has trouble dealing with her parents' floundering marriage, Koby faces most of her challenges with courage and determination, forging ahead even when she is afraid. An appealing adventure, especially for animal lovers.

Nelson, O. T. *The Girl Who Owned a City.* **1995. Hard: Runestone. Pbk: Dell. Ages 11–14.**

This survival story set in the near future takes as its starting point the unlikely premise that everyone over twelve has died from a virus. Left in a world of children and dwindling supplies, ten-year-old Lisa discovers her extraordinary talent for leadership. She organizes the children on her suburban block, carefully strategizing to convince them to follow her. She fearlessly confronts Tom Logan, leader of a marauding gang. Eventually she moves her hundreds of followers into a well-fortified high school, but their problems continue. The author's philosophy about self-reliance figures blatantly in the writing, but even more disturbing for some readers is the emphasis on fighting and violence. Great enthusiasm goes into forming a militia and fortifying the school. While the focus on violence may be realistic and doesn't come near what appears nightly on television, it is unusual in children's books. However, Lisa shows strong leadership abilities rarely attributed to girls. A gripping, disturbing novel.

O'Brien, Robert C. _Z for Zachariah_. 1975. Hard: Atheneum. Pbk: Aladdin. Ages 11–14.

This futuristic thriller hums with suspense. Fifteen-year-old Ann Burden thinks she may be the last person alive, having survived a nuclear holocaust thanks to the microclimate of the valley she lives in. Although she is coping well alone on her family's farm, she gets excited when a man appears dressed in a radiation-resistant suit. But the man, John Loomis, becomes increasingly dangerous to her, intent on taking control of the farm and of her life, until one night she barely escapes when he comes into her bed. A stalwart heroine, Ann is adept at farming, driving a tractor, doing mechanical tasks, and shooting. But little in her protected childhood has prepared her to face the increasingly disturbed man. Finally she takes the offensive. The book is genuinely hard to put down as the reader waits for the next move in this gripping game of survival.

Pullman, Philip. *The Ruby in the Smoke*. 1987. Hard: Knopf. Pbk: Knopf. Ages 12–14.

An incomparable stolen ruby, a dangerous secret society, mysterious sailors, and evil landladies all come together in this intriguing melodramatic story. Living in London in 1872, Sally Lockhart, a sixteen-year-old orphan, makes a first-class heroine. She always carries a gun and is an excellent shot. Her father has schooled her in bookkeeping and the stock market, and has skipped the traditional female lessons. Her cool head comes in handy as she becomes embroiled in the intrigue surrounding the lost ruby of Agrapur. She makes friends, including an attractive young male photographer who treats her like an equal, and soon all of their lives are in danger. Nonstop action keeps the reader breathless until the very end, when the mysteries of Sally's life are unraveled. A plausible, strong, and smart heroine in an exciting tale. The sequels are *The Tiger in the Well* and *Shadow in the North*.

Pullman, Philip. *The Tin Princess*. 1994. Hard: Knopf. Pbk: Random House. Ages 12–14.

Another romantic thriller set in the nineteenth century, this one focuses on the small imaginary country of Razkavia, coveted for its mineral wealth by Germany and Austria. Through her marriage to unassuming Prince Rudolph, former London street urchin Adelaide finds herself a princess, and soon, the ruling monarch of Razkavia. Her native wit and steely determination make Adelaide an astute ruler. But can her courage and intelligence prevail in the face of treason and encroaching armies? The queen's translator and companion, sixteen-year-old Becky, calls on her own resources to help the queen and herself. Intrigue, love, runaway trains, wintry battles at ruined castles—the action in this melodramatic novel is fast and the atmosphere romantic in every sense of the word. Highly enjoyable.

Thesman, Jean. *Rachel Chance*. 1990. Hard: Houghton. Pbk: Avon. Ages 11–14.

"Nothing ever happens that we don't make happen," declares fifteen-year-old Rachel Chance to her wise neighbor Druid Annie. After Rachel's two-year-old brother Rider is stolen by a traveling revival show, Rachel's already troubled family can barely cope. So Rachel decides to get Rider back. She, her irascible grandfather, Druid Annie, and Hank, the boy who helps at their farm, set forth in an unreliable old truck to a meeting of the revival. They experience so many setbacks that finally Rachel goes off on her own. Although suffering from self-doubt, Rachel does what she has to. Love motivates her, but strength and intelligence keep her going. A subplot about Hank's aunt, an abused wife who shoots her husband, raises questions for Rachel about how women are treated and how they should be. A fine novel of adventure, romance, and courage.

Voigt, Cynthia. *Jackaroo*. 1985. Hard: Atheneum. Pbk: Fawcett. Ages 12–14.

In this adventure set in an imaginary kingdom in the past, Gwyn, an innkeeper's daughter, feels constrained by being lower class and female in a strictly traditional society. She learns to read, even though it is forbidden to her class, and develops her strengths in unconventional ways. Her goal is to help the poor and hungry, who are preyed upon by thieves and thieving soldiers. Yet what can a sixteen-year-old girl do, even if she is strong and smart? When she discovers the clothing of Jackaroo, a legendary hero from the past, she secretly dons the costume, enjoying the freedom of men's clothing, and sets off on horseback to bring help to those who need it. With the help of a man who cherishes her forceful nature, Gwyn ultimately makes a path in life that suits her, boding well for her future. A long but very satisfying adventure.

Voigt, Cynthia. *On Fortune's Wheel*. 1990. Hard: Atheneum. Pbk: Fawcett. Ages 13–14.

Fourteen-year-old Birle, restless with her life at her father's inn, stumbles into adventure one night when she hears someone stealing her father's boat. Following the boat leads her to a journey with Orien, an earl's grandson, to an unknown land. Her ability to fish and live off the land surpasses his, and she keeps them going with her practical nature. Encountering one danger after another, they survive, only to be captured and sold separately as slaves. Birle, whose work is not as brutal, knows it is up to her to save Orien from enslavement, which might kill him. Suspense builds as she pieces together a clever but dangerous plan. In the course of the adventure, Birle becomes strong enough to survive on her own and to enjoy her independence. This is both an adventure and a romantic story about love between two forceful people.

Contemporary Novels

Higginsen, Vy, with Tonya Bolden. *Mama, I Want to Sing*. 1992. Hard: Scholastic. Pbk: Point. Ages 12–14.

When Doris Winter joins the adult gospel choir at her church as an eleven-year-old, her mother is proud and happy. But when Doris becomes interested in "worldly" music, listening to Billie Holiday and Sarah Vaughan on the radio, her mother objects. Doris takes her own voice seriously and wants to be a professional singer, even if it means defying her mother. She and three friends secretly form a group and perform near their homes in Harlem at the Apollo Theater's Amateur Night. Doris knows from her mother's friend Sister Carrie that a singing career is not all glamour and joy, but she still wants to pursue her dream and make it come true. The females in this novel, which is based on a musical, are strong and determined. Sister Carrie and Doris's mother both work and support themselves; Doris and her friends succeed in establishing careers in music, a fact revealed right away. Readers will enjoy following Doris on her way to becoming a star.

Johnson, Angela. *Toning the Sweep*. 1993. Hard: Orchard. Pbk: Scholastic. Ages 11–14.

Wonderful older women inhabit the desert community where fourteen-year-old Emily's grandmother Ola lives. Ola, who has cancer, is packing up her house and saying good-bye to her close friends, with the help of Emily and her mother. Emily makes a videotape for Ola as a memento, learning a lot about her mother and grandmother in the process. As she tapes Ola's friends, Emily sees the strength and love of a community of confident, sometimes boisterous, women. Emily gains an appreciation, rarely seen in children's books, of the support women give each other. Enriched by this community, the intrepid Ola, a fast driver and world traveler, has lived happily by herself for many years, and now must face moving in with Emily's family. The relationship between Emily, a young woman who is growing stronger, and Ola, a wise woman who is facing change and death, is fully realized. A brilliant, beautifully written novel about an African-American family.

Kate, Marilyn. *Lydia*. 1987. Hard: Harcourt. Pbk: Harcourt. Ages 10–13.

Bored with her work on the conservative school newspaper, ninth grader Lydia and three friends start an alternative paper in their junior high. Their proposal that football become a coed sport sparks more controversy than even outspoken Lydia, who likes to take risks and rebel, likes. But

Lydia and her friends decide they have to fight for what they believe in. When Lydia runs a meeting to air the issue, many students begin to support the co-ed team idea. The town's female mayor shows up with Lydia's mother to voice her support. Boys as well as girls let Lydia know they admire her determination. The likeable Lydia comes across as a leader beginning to test and develop her powers. A believable story about a modern girl intent on making a difference.

Mark, Jan. *Handles*. 1985. Hard: Atheneum. Ages 11–14.

Erica wants to be a motorcycle mechanic, an idea her father would consider "almost as unnatural as men having babies," if she told him. When she is sent away to visit dreary relatives, Erica is bored and unhappy until she discovers Elsie Wainwright's motorcycle repair shop. She hangs out there until the eccentric Elsie eventually lets her help him with repairs. Erica has found what so many adolescents look for—a place in which she would like to belong—and she works hard at making her mark there. By the time the three-week visit is over, she knows she has a talent for mechanics, and that when she's ready, there'll be a job waiting for her in Elsie's shop. She heads home ready to face the future. Although her mother and aunt are dully conventional, Erica is a wonderful character with an original mind and nontraditional interests. The author's wit and love of language make this excellent novel a joy to read.

Moore, Yvette. *Freedom Songs*. 1991. Hard: Orchard, o.p. Pbk: Puffin. Ages 12–14.

Fourteen-year-old Sheryl, who aspires to be pretty and popular, changes her mind about what she wants after a visit to the South in 1963. In North Carolina she encounters blatant prejudice and understands why her college-age uncle

Pete has joined the nonviolent protesters known as the Freedom Riders. Knowing he is risking his life for the cause, Sheryl returns to Brooklyn wanting to help. She and her friends band together to raise money for the Freedom Riders by giving a concert. In the process, Sheryl starts to take her artistic talent seriously and struggles with being a leader. Strong female relatives abound in Sheryl's family, such as her aunt whose carpentry business is at risk because of her belief in equality. The family needs all its strength when tragedy strikes close to home. A moving story about the evil of racial prejudice, and the courage of those who fought for freedom in the sixties.

Naidoo, Beverley. *Chain of Fire*. Illustrated by Eric Velasquez. 1990. Hard: Lippincott. Pbk: Harper Trophy. Ages 12–14.

Set in South Africa in the 1980s, this intense novel follows the fate of fifteen-year-old Naledi, her family, and her friends when the government announces plans to move them to a bleak "homeland." Devastated, Naledi and the others slowly start to fight back. She earns the respect of her peers by defying their unfair school principal, and they elect her as one of their leaders. They organize a peaceful march made violent by the police. The resistance brings painful retaliation, but Naledi also feels a growing sense of solidarity. Her own voice gets stronger as she speaks out against the inhumane acts of the government. Courageous older women provide leadership and inspire Naledi to keep strong. No unrealistic happy ending mars the story's dignity. Instead the sense of hope for Naledi and the others comes from their bond as they continue the struggle for what is right. Full of tragedy and injustice, this novel will grip the reader from beginning to end. An earlier book about Naledi is *Journey to Jo'burg*.

Pinkwater, Jill. *Buffalo Brenda*. 1989. Hard: Macmillan. Pbk: Aladdin. Ages 11–14.

Narrator India and her best friend Brenda live in a boring suburb on Long Island. But whenever Brenda is around, things get livelier. When the two friends enter high school, Brenda uses the school newspaper to stir up excitement—too much excitement for the school administration. Ousted from the paper, Brenda and her friends run an underground paper for a while, exposing a scandal in the school cafeteria. When the turmoil from that exposé is over, Brenda has her best scheme of all: their school team, the Buffalos, needs a mascot. Why not a live buffalo? Readers tired of conformity will cheer on these two girls who get stronger from one outrageous scheme to the next.

Staples, Suzanne Fisher. *Shabanu: Daughter of the Wind*. 1989. Hard: Knopf. Pbk: Random House. Ages 12–14.

Growing up in contemporary Pakistan, Shabanu has little in common with American adolescents. She and her family are nomads in the Cholistan desert who rely on camels for their livelihood. Shabanu's thirteen-year-old sister Phulan will be married soon to a man her parents have chosen, and Shabanu knows her turn will be next. Since she has no brothers, she has had more freedom than most girls while helping her father with the camels. But there is no escaping her fate in such a patriarchal society, and Shabanu knows that soon she will have to leave her beloved freedom in the desert. Her aunt Sharma, who built up her own herd and then left her abusive husband, gives Shabanu a sense of hope when the future looks most bleak. The realistic ending suggests that Shabanu's strength of character will see her through future struggles. A beautifully wrought portrait of another culture and a sympathetic young woman. A

Newbery Honor Book. The sequel *Haveli* is about Shabanu's daughter.

Temple, Frances. *Tonight, by Sea*. 1995. Hard: Orchard. Ages 13–14.

This painful novel takes place in Haiti in 1993, when brutal soldiers and other terrorists are making life unbearable for ordinary people. Paulie lives with her uncle and grandmother, barely getting enough to eat. During an American journalist's visit, Paulie's neighbor Jean-Desir speaks out against the government. When the soldiers retaliate, Paulie courageously makes her way to the city to find the journalist again, risking her life. She puts her safety in jeopardy more than once for the cause of freedom and the love of her country. She also risks her life to try to save a neighbor. She keeps on trying, as she has learned from her uncle and grandmother, even after tragic events surround her. An afterword gives more details about the modern history of Haiti.

Voigt, Cynthia. *Bad Girls*. 1996. Hard: Scholastic. Ages 11–13.

Margalo and Mikey, new girls in the fifth-grade class, sit next to each other and quickly become friends. Margalo could be friends with more sedate girls, but she is drawn to Mikey, who is never boring. Mikey, who has no interest in being nice like other girls, objects loudly to boys dominating the soccer field. A talented, aggressive player, she and a few other girls insist on joining the recess games, then join the school's all-boy team. Mikey's main rival and enemy is Louis, but she also offends a self-satisfied girl named Rhonda, who lashes back publicly. When Margalo decides to defend her friend, she pulls some outrageous tricks on Rhonda. Their escapades liven up an already rambunctious class and keep the stern teacher hopping. Both strong personalities, the two girls clash as they work out their friendship in a realistic way. While not Voigt's strongest writing, this novel does offer an unconventional portrayal of girls.

Voigt, Cynthia. *Homecoming*. 1981. Hard: Atheneum. Pbk: Fawcett. Ages 11–14.

Dicey Tillerman is a stubborn, resourceful thirteen-year-old, "a fighter," as she calls herself. When their mentally ill mother deserts Dicey and her three siblings, Dicey struggles valiantly to keep the family together, leading them on an arduous journey to find an unknown aunt. Along the way, Dicey invents solutions to every problem that arises, including their desperate need for money; her ideas don't always work, but she never gives up. Her relationship with her two younger brothers and younger sister is loving but tough. After many hard miles, they find a possible home, but it will take Dicey's ingenuity and more hard work to keep them there. Dicey is a sympathetic modern heroine who is making her way through a difficult world. The excellent sequels include the Newbery Medal winner *Dicey's Song* and *Seventeen Against the Dealer*.

Walter, Mildred Pitts. *Trouble's Child*. 1985. Hard: Lothrop. Ages 12–14.

Martha, whose island community's school goes only through the eighth grade, wants to continue her education in nearby Louisiana. But her indomitable grandmother, the island healer and midwife, insists that Martha stay and learn her trade. At fourteen, Martha is old enough by island standards to get married, and the women in the island's strong African-American community pressure her to do just that. Martha needs all of her moral courage to approach her grandmother about diverging from the traditional expectations for women. She gets some help from a young man from off-island, and from a few longtime friends, but ultimately she must rely on herself. Although the time period is not specified, the conflict that faces Martha is a timeless one: to find and pursue her own dreams or to meet the expectations of her family. The evocative writing paints a vivid picture of a superstitious but caring community.

Wolff, Virginia Euwer. *The Mozart Season*. 1991. Hard: Holt. Pbk: Scholastic. Ages 11–14.

In this well-paced novel, twelve-year-old Allegra spends a watershed summer practicing for a violin competition and growing up. She learns about tenacity, defined by her violin teacher as "holding on when it would be more comfortable to let go," and confronts her fears of performing. Like training for serious softball, which Allegra did in the spring, practicing the violin requires discipline but also the ability to relax. Tension builds as the competition comes closer and Allegra tries to make the Mozart concerto her own. Allegra is surrounded by supportive friends and family and has a rich relationship with her mother, a professional violinist who loves and admires her daughter. Evocative, almost magical, writing about music makes this an exceptionally beautiful novel.

Sports Stories

Baczewski, Paul. *Just for Kicks*. 1990. Hard: Lippincott. Ages 11–14.

Although this amusing book is narrated by a fifteen-year-old boy, its two strong female characters make it noteworthy.

Brandon manages his high school's football team, on which his two older brothers are stars. The only thing the team needs to be really competitive is a kicker, and Brandon knows just the person to do the job: his sister Sarah. The militaristic Coach Knox agrees to let her play, expecting Sarah to crack under the pressure and hard work. But Sarah, the only player brave enough to talk back to the coach, excels and even gives useful tips to her male teammates. When Knox vows to make her life miserable, she replies, "Well, you just give it your best shot, big guy." Meanwhile, Brandon falls for Janice, a talented basketball player who makes him rethink some of his sexist attitudes. He is not yet a feminist, and his interest in cheer-leaders and the swimsuit issue of *Sports Illustrated* will bother some readers. The book's strengths are two athletic females, a hilarious parody of football, and a narrator who learns a lesson in viewing girls as equals. An unusual sports novel.

Duder, Tessa. *In Lane Three, Alex Archer*. **1989. Hard: Houghton, o.p. Pbk: Bantam. Ages 13–14.**
New Zealander Alexandra Archer wants to go to the 1960 Olympics in swimming. To succeed, she has to win a quali-fying race against her rival Maggie Benton. The book opens as fifteen-year-old Alex is standing on the starting block of the final race. After a glimpse into her thoughts, the story reverts to the beginning of her quest. A talented athlete, Alex also has other interests: her studies, acting, piano, ballet, and even-tually a boyfriend. She plans to become a lawyer—after the Olympics. Her confidence and ambition bother some of her peers, although the teachers at her all-girls school are sup-portive. Alex takes risks and pushes herself to her limit, and when tragedy strikes, she suffers but continues training for the big race. An exciting drama about an indomitable girl. Alex pursues her swimming in the sequel *Alex in Rome*.

Dygard, Thomas J. *Forward Pass*. 1989. Hard: Morrow. Pbk: Puffin. Ages 11–14.

Desperate for a football player who can catch long passes, Coach Gardner recruits Jill Winston, a star from the girls' basketball team. The story, narrated by the coach, traces his innovative solution from his first conversations with Jill to the championship game. Jill, a consummate athlete, is a girl of few words but outstanding athletic ability. Obstacles appear, of course—the coach deals with a furious girls' basketball coach and some angry opposition football coaches. Jill faces resistance from her father, although her mother likes the idea, and from her boyfriend, who is also on the football team. As the season ends, Jill has to make a choice between boys' football and girls' basketball. Like most sports fiction, this book describes games in detail, including the plays and strategies. But it also paints a plausible picture of a female athlete excelling on a boys' team.

Levy, Marilyn. *Run for Your Life*. 1996. Hard: Houghton. Ages 13–14.

Based on a true story, this compelling novel follows the fate of a girls' track team at a community center in Oakland, California. Most of the girls on the team, including the narrator Kisha, live in a housing project. Most have serious difficulties in their lives, such as poverty, sexual abuse, and troubled parents, but the team gives them a source of security. Darren, the center's director, understands their situations but requires hard work and good grades. Several of the girls, including Kisha, come close to quitting as they struggle with their personal lives. Dramatic tension builds as the team prepares for a national track meet. A powerful, hopeful novel that shows how important sports can be to young women.

Spinelli, Jerry. *There's a Girl in My Hammerlock*. 1991. Hard: Simon & Schuster. Pbk: Aladdin. Ages 10–13.

Although Maisie tries out for the wrestling team because she has a crush on one of its members, she finds she loves wrestling. She takes grief from the coach, players, and her friends, but sticks with her resolve and makes the team. Maisie is a terrific athlete, but it takes a special show of physical courage before her teammates will accept her. Even then, boys on opposing teams default rather than wrestle a girl. Students and town members vent their hostility at wrestling matches and in the town newspaper. But Maisie persists through it all, and in the end she triumphs in an unpredictable way. A warm, amusing story with a realistic picture of how unwelcome a girl can be in a boys' sport.

Voigt, Cynthia. *Tell Me If Lovers Are Losers*. 1982. Hard: Atheneum. Ages 12–14.

Set at a New England women's college in 1961, this is the story of Ann Gardner, her two freshman roommates, and their volleyball team. One roommate, Niki, is an intensely competitive athlete with a sharp tongue and no patience for lesser players. The other roommate, Hildy, a North Dakota farm girl with an unshakable moral code, brings out the best in her fellow volleyball players. The team gets increasingly serious about defeating the other freshman teams and challenging the sophomores. Ann, who is not athletic, grows in strength and sureness on the volleyball court; the team becomes her main social circle. The sport ultimately takes second place in the plot to friendship issues and a final tragedy. This thought-provoking novel does a fine job of capturing the intensity of female athletes and their bonding through sports.

Wallace, Bill. *Never Say Quit*. **1993. Hard: Holiday. Pbk: Minstrel. Ages 11–13.**

An unusual combination of sports and sentiment characterizes this novel about a soccer team. Three girls and four boys, rejected from the school team for social reasons, decide to start their own team. They must have a coach, but the only candidate is Paul Reiner, an alcoholic school principal. They lure him with beer scrounged from garbage cans until he agrees to stay. The girls on this team do as well as the boys, on the whole. Sixth grader Justine, who tells the story, scores a key play; and tough Terri Jarman is an excellent goalie when she isn't busy fighting. The girls start lifting weights to hold their own against growing boys. Aside from soccer, the plot focuses on personal problems of the coach and players in a heavy-handed way. Some readers will also find the Japanese and Mexican accents hard to take. This is a flawed novel, but one in which girls and boys work well together on a sports team and truly respect each other.

Mysteries

Duffy, James. *The Man in the River*. **1990. Hard: Scribner. Ages 11–13.**

When Kate and Sandy's father dies mysteriously and leaves them $300,000 in life insurance money, the insurance company suggests the death was suicide. The girls' friend, retired police officer Agatha Bates, offers to help them find out the truth about their father, whose alcoholism and violence had driven them and their mother away. When they discover two ivory sculptures at his apartment, a retired female museum curator identifies them as priceless Inuit carvings. Agatha and the girls take several trips to collect information about the father's suspicious new job selling artifacts, putting themselves in danger to solve the mystery. Reality permeates this story in which women face real problems in marriage and work, and children live in imperfect families. A good puzzle with a gritty atmosphere. An earlier mystery with the same characters is *Missing.*

Haddix, Margaret Peterson. *Running Out of Time.* 1995. Hard: Simon & Schuster. Ages 11–13.

In this intriguing thriller, Jessie believes that she lives in 1840 in an Indiana village where her friends and family are dying from diphtheria. Recognizing Jessie's courage, her mother tells the thirteen-year-old the truth: it is really 1996, and they live in a reconstructed village that tourists view through hidden cameras. The forces that run the village have quit giving the villagers medicine or letting them leave. Jessie must escape from the village into the modern world and quietly get help. She gathers her strength and copes with the strange new world, but just as it seems all is well, she realizes that she is about to be killed. She needs to save her own life and figure out a way to save those dying in the village, a seemingly impossible task for someone who has never used a telephone, seen a car, or watched television. How can she come up with a scheme that will work in the dangerous modern world? A well-crafted page-turner about a resourceful girl.

Nixon, Joan Lowery. *The Name of the Game Was Murder.* 1993. Hard: Delacorte. Pbk: Dell. Ages 11–14.

Impetuous fifteen-year-old Samantha invites herself to spend two weeks with her great-aunt and her aunt's husband, the famous writer Augustus Trevor. Little does she know she will be trapped on an inaccessible part of an island off the coast of California with a murderer. Trevor has invited five famous guests for the weekend and threatened to reveal a dark secret about each of them in his forthcoming book. Their only chance to avoid public humiliation is to solve a mystery Trevor has devised. But before the game can continue, the writer is found murdered. The guests are desparate to find Trevor's manuscript and destroy it, while Samantha is determined to find out who the killer is. Unusually good at breaking codes, she pieces together clues to solve the crime, but then must decide what to do with the answer. Initially underconfident and impetuous, Samantha thrives on her ability to outwit the adults around her. A fast-paced mystery with an Agatha Christie–like setting and a group of glamorous characters.

Nixon, Joan Lowery. *Shadowmaker.* **1994. Hard: Delacorte. Pbk: Dell. Ages 11–14.**

The crimes in the small Texas town of Kluney keep getting more and more serious: first shoplifting, then burglary, armed robbery, and finally murder. The sheriff and townspeople blame outsiders passing through town, but newcomer Katie Gillian has other suspicions. She has the same sort of inquiring mind as her mother, Eve, an investigative journalist who is taking time off to write a novel. While Katie is puzzling out the crime wave, her mother gets drawn into an investigation of toxic waste dumping. Both are smart, strong females who persist in looking for the truth despite threats and harassment. Tension mounts as shadowy figures lurk about their isolated house at night, throwing rocks and causing damage. Her mother confronts the waste company, with Katie's help, while Katie comes up with an unwelcome solution to the crimes. A suspenseful thriller about a brave mother-daughter team.

Springer, Nancy. *Looking for Jamie Bridger.* **1995. Hard: Dial. Ages 11–14.**

Who are Jamie Bridger's parents? The fourteen-year-old has been raised by her meek grandmother and domineering grandfather. Neither will tell her anything about her parents, although she knows she's not adopted. When her grandfather dies suddenly and her mentally ill grandmother becomes dependent on her, Jamie resolves to seek her answers soon. She gathers information and takes several trips on her own, including a dangerous one to New York City. Her loyal friend Kate, a female lawyer, and an eccentric turtle-loving old woman help her out along the way until at last Jamie learns the strange secret about her life.

Tate, Eleanor E. *The Secret of Gumbo Grove.* **1987. Hard: Franklin Watts, o.p. Pbk: Bantam. Ages 10–13.**

Living in modern South Carolina, narrator Raisin Stackhouse has a strong interest in history. When a neighbor, Miss Effie, needs help cleaning up an old cemetery, Raisin helps out and becomes fascinated by the history of the local African-American community. But when she starts to pass on the stories she's learning about black ancestors, the adults around Raisin get nervous. They don't want anyone digging up the past, even if it reveals the importance of African-Americans in the town's early history. But once Raisin gets involved in something, she doesn't give up. She slowly unravels a mystery from the past. Raisin is an appealing combination of smart, persistent, impulsive, and a bit rebellious. She is surrounded by women and girls who have strong opinions and speak their minds.

Vigor, John. *Danger, Dolphins, and Ginger Beer.* **1993. Hard: Atheneum. Ages 11–13.**

Twelve-year-old Sarah and her two younger brothers are camping on an island in the Caribbean while their father is away on a trip. The family of avid sailors is sailing around the world on a yacht. When a motorboat wounds a dolphin, Sarah and her brothers save it and nurse it back to health. They also rescue a man and a woman when their boat smashes into a reef, but this good deed puts their lives in danger. It will take all of Sarah's leadership and sailing skills to bring them to safety. A fast-moving mystery full of danger and adventure.

Historical Fiction

Armstrong, Jennifer. *Steal Away.* **1992. Hard: Orchard. Pbk: Scholastic. Ages 11–14.**

What would it be like for two lonely girls, one a white orphan, the other a black slave, to escape to the North together in 1855? Living in the South, Susannah longs to return to her home in Vermont after the death of her parents, while Bethlehem has no hope for happiness as a slave and fears the intentions of her young master. They set off disguised as boys, scarcely knowing each other or the danger they are getting into. Each girl tells the story from her own perspective as they slowly make their way North. Shy Susannah blossoms under the freedom of being disguised as a boy, free from worry about her behavior or threats from men. Bethlehem struggles with her desire to learn to read, knowing it is illegal for a slave, and with the burdens freedom brings. Underlying themes about the powerlessness of girls and blacks give deeper meaning to this exciting adventure. In the book's layered structure, Susannah and Bethlehem are telling their story forty years later to two thirteen-year-old girls, whose reactions add another dimension. A sophisticated novel about freedom, females, and our country's troubled history. Highly recommended.

Carter, Dorothy Sharp. *His Majesty, Queen Hatshepsut.* **Illustrated by Michele Chessare. 1987. Hard: Lippincott. Ages 10–14.**

Hatshepsut ruled for more than twenty years as the king of Upper and Lower Egypt. The daughter of Thutmose I and wife of Thutmose II, she defied her husband's dying wish that his young son become ruler and declared herself Pharaoh. This fictionalized account of her life from age thirteen until her death portrays Hatshepsut as a shrewd and accomplished ruler who strengthened her country internally. Hatshepsut narrates her own story, describing the constant resistance she felt from the powerful priesthood and other men, and the network of spies she created to learn of plots against her. Although she is painfully besotted with one of her advisers, she also believes herself superior to him and everyone else. The few black-and-white illustrations show Hatshepsut, known to her subjects as "His Majesty," dressed both as a man and as a woman. A study in power and intrigue in the ancient world, with a woman at its center, this novel is one of a kind.

Cole, Sheila. *A Dragon in the Cliff: A Novel Based on the Life of Mary Anning.* **Illustrated by T. C. Farrow. 1991. Hard: Lothrop. Ages 11–14.**

Mary Anning was a real British teenager who discovered the first complete skeleton of an ichthyosaur in 1812. This novel, based on information about her life and times, speculates on the effect such a discovery would have had then on a young woman. The daughter of a cabinetmaker who supplemented his income digging fossils, Mary carried on the work after her father died. She apparently never married, and in her lifetime discovered a number of complete skeletons. Her discoveries fueled a debate among scientists about geologic eras and fauna. Yet as a working-class female with little education, Mary was not free to join the debate, and in fact saw her own discoveries credited to men in academic publications. At the same time, her occupation was unorthodox for a woman, and the novel shows her ostracized by her conservative neighbors. The author chooses to explore these effects by having Mary fall in love with an upper-class young man also interested in fossils. Her neighbors disapprove, and Mary comes to realize the class difference makes marriage between them unthinkable. Anning was clearly ahead of her time and experienced the loneliness of a pioneer. Yet despite her troubles, the fictional Mary finds solace in her work and its importance, as one hopes the real Mary Anning did. Interesting notes at the end separate the fictional from the real and add information about the rest of Anning's life. A thoughtful, readable novel about a surprising real person.

Collier, James Lincoln, and Christopher Collier. *War Comes to Willy Freeman*. 1983. Hard: Delacorte, o.p. Pbk: Dell. Ages 10–13.

A free black girl living through the Revolutionary War, Willy Freeman sees the war and the colonies from an unusual perspective. After her father dies fighting for the colonies and the British take her mother, she questions what good either side will do for her people. Willy uses her sailing skills to flee from Connecticut to New York City, where, disguised as a boy, she finds work at a tavern. The freedom the disguise gives her leads Willy to reflect on women's lack of freedom: "When I came to think about it, when you was a woman you was half a slave, anyway." Willy has her eyes wide open as she looks at the world around her, and it is all she can do some days to suppress her anger. Losing her temper gets her involved in an important legal case for blacks, with surprising results. The bittersweet ending promises no easy life for Willy, but her courage and intelligence give the reader hope for her future.

Collier, James Lincoln, and Christopher Collier. *Who Is Carrie?* 1984. Hard: Delacorte, o.p. Pbk: Dell. Ages 11–14.

Carrie is a black girl who lives in New York City just as President Washington is taking office. As far as she knows, she is a slave of Samuel Fraunces, who owns the most popular tavern in the city. But she knows nothing about her parents or other family. When she overhears a conversation that suggests Fraunces may not own her, Carrie resolves to find out about her origins. She narrates the story in an animated, witty voice that endears her to the reader. So it is painful to realize there will be no fairy-tale ending for such a sympathetic character in this entertaining and thought-provoking story. The authors give information at the end about their sources for this fictionalized tale, and explain their choice to include in the dialogue the word "nigger," commonly used during this time period.

Cushman, Karen. *Catherine, Called Birdy.* 1994. Hard: Clarion. Pbk: Harper Trophy. Ages 12–14.

Catherine, daughter of a small-time nobleman in medieval England, is hilarious. In a diary format she records her daily life, the outrages she suffers as a girl, and her often humorous assessment of things. She longs to be outside frolicking instead of inside sewing, and she chafes at her lessons in ladylike behavior. Birdy is the sort of girl who organizes a spitting contest and starts a mud fight. She makes a list of all the things girls cannot do, such as go on a crusade, be a horse trainer, laugh out loud, and "marry whom they will." She battles with her father, who wants to marry her off to the highest bidder, no matter how repulsive. Many of her best sarcastic remarks are reserved for him, and she irritates him whenever possible. She has a bawdy sense of humor and a palpable love of life. Few fictional characters are so vivid and funny—do not miss this one. A Newbery Honor Book.

Cushman, Karen. *The Midwife's Apprentice*. 1995. Hard: Clarion. Ages 11–14.

The heroine of this book starts so low in life she doesn't even have a proper name, but is known as Brat and then Beetle. Taken in by a cranky midwife, Beetle very slowly gains some sense of self and confidence, eventually renaming herself Alyce. By secretly watching the midwife at births, Alyce learns something about delivering babies. On her way to becoming a midwife, Alyce learns that risking and failing is unavoidable, but that giving up is the worst thing she can do. This classic lesson, which boys are taught far more often than girls, makes this book valuable. Alyce makes herself keep trying in the face of discouragement, a real act of courage. Winner of the 1996 Newbery Medal.

Duffy, James. *Radical Red*. 1993. Hard: Scribner. Ages 11–14.

It is 1894 and Susan B. Anthony is in Albany, New York, to tell the legislature why women have a right to vote. Twelve-year-old Connor O'Shea, who has a boy's name because her father wanted a son, knows nothing about women's rights. But she does see her alcoholic father beat her mother, and she sees how hard her mother works as a laundress only to have her father take the money. She also knows she does better in school than many boys who will eventually have the vote when she won't. Connor and her friend

Doreen volunteer to help the suffragists; then so does Connor's mother. When her father finds out, he gets more violent than ever, and mother and daughter have to make a choice about their future. This engrossing novel, in which Susan B. Anthony appears as a character, brings an era and a movement to life in a way that readers can understand. The legislators' argument that women's delicate natures will be harmed by the vote looks ludicrous in view of the kind of life Connor's mother has. Sympathetic characters combine with important history to make this a book well worth reading.

Garden, Nancy. *Dove and Sword: A Novel of Joan of Arc.* 1995. Hard: FSG. Ages 12–14.

In this fictionalized account about Joan of Arc (in French, Jeannette d'Arc), the main character is Gabrielle, another peasant girl from Jeannette's village. Gabrielle, a friend of Jeannette's brother, follows Jeannette on her quest. Disguised as a boy, Gabrielle uses her talents as a healer to help care for those wounded in battle. An observant girl who chafes at the roles assigned to women, Gabrielle aspires to be a great doctor and makes the most of her chance to study with Christine de Pisan, a famous writer of the time and a great proponent of women. Gabrielle serves as an excellent narrator of Jeannette d'Arc's quest to see the true French king crowned. Both these young women are strong and brave. Gabrielle is the dove who heals instead of fights, and Jeannette, the bearer of the sword. Theirs is an exciting tale, full of danger and love.

Gregory, Kristiana. *Earthquake at Dawn.* 1992. Hard: Harcourt. Pbk: Harcourt. Ages 11–14.

This historical novel dexterously blends fact and fiction in its story about the 1906 San Francisco earthquake. Told by a fictional character named Daisy Valentine, a fifteen-year-old servant who grew up in mining country, it follows the adventures of Daisy and her employer, Edith Irvine. Edith, a real person, was a twenty-two-year-old photographer, daughter of a wealthy mine owner. She plans to take Daisy with her on a world tour, but when they reach San Francisco, the earthquake hits. They take refuge with friendly strangers, with whom they flee to Golden Gate Park. There they camp out with thousands of others, experiencing the aftershocks and waiting for fires to abate. Defying the mayor's orders against photography, Edith records the pain and ruin around them in photographs only made public eighty years later. Daisy surprises herself with her own bravery, defending Edith against the attack of a soldier and fighting off rats in the park. An exciting survival story laced with intriguing details about a true historical event.

Hendry, Frances Mary. *Quest for a Maid*. 1988. Hard: FSG, o.p. Pbk: FSG. Ages 10–14.

"When I was nine years old, I hid under a table and heard my sister kill a king." This tantalizing first sentence sets the tone for this exciting adventure novel about a hardy Scottish girl named Meg. The youngest daughter of a shipbuilder, Meg is outspoken and brave. After she rescues a young lad named Davie from danger, and another named Peem from a cruel master, the three of them swim and sail together, often breaking rules and taking the punishment. When Meg goes with a Scottish delegation to fetch a young Norwegian princess for her wedding to an English prince, a storm wrecks their ship on the way back. Once again, Meg's unflagging courage comes into play as she and her friends fight to keep the princess safe. The suspense and excitement rarely slow down in this gripping novel that blends history and magic. All the children have strengths, but Meg is the center of the group, a heroine not to be missed.

Houston, Gloria. *Mountain Valor.* **1994. Hard: Philomel. Pbk: Paper Star. Ages 11–14.**

Valor longs to live up to her name and the medal of valor her father gave her when he left to fight for the Confederacy. In her mountain life, she finds several women to emulate, including an herb gatherer who rides her horse astride in men's clothes, rather than sidesaddle. This old woman introduces Valor to the phrase "sister of the wind," meaning a woman who goes her own way with freedom and courage. Furious at Yankees who have devastated her family, Valor disguises herself as a boy and follows them to retrieve stolen livestock. She faces a series of dangers on the way and gets some unexpected help. Based on a true story, this is an exciting adventure about a girl who grows up to become a "sister of the wind."

Karr, Kathleen. *Oh, Those Harper Girls!* **1992. Hard: FSG. Pbk: FSG. Ages 11–14.**

Lily Harper, her five older sisters, and her parents may lose their Texas ranch if they cannot raise some money soon. Lily's father comes up with a scheme to have the girls, who range in age from thirteen to eighteen, steal their neighbor's cattle. That plan fails, as does the moonshine still they set up. Finally, nothing seems possible except robbing a stagecoach. The robbery attempt brings them fame instead of money, and they capitalize on it in an unlikely, colorful way. Each girl has a well-defined character, and although Lily is the most daring and athletic, the others have talents, and all know their minds. A rollicking story of the Wild West and some of its amusing daughters.

Konigsburg, E. L. *A Proud Taste for Scarlet and Miniver.* 1975. Hard: Atheneum. Pbk: Dell. Ages 11–14.

This novel explores the life of Eleanor of Aquitaine, the most powerful woman in the twelfth century. It opens with four people—an abbot, a knight, Eleanor, and her mother-in-law—sitting around heaven, reminiscing. Each narrates a part of Eleanor's life, with Eleanor herself describing her final years. Although fictionalized, the story is faithful to the facts of her life and times. She was a queen who steeped herself in luxury, music, and art. She loved to travel and even went on one of the Crusades. A political force in her own right, Eleanor became the queen of France through her first marriage and the queen of England through her second. At times she had the authority to collect taxes, administer lands and castles, and sit in judgment in the courts, but more often her influence was indirect, through her husbands and sons. In either case, she was a shrewd politician who reveled in power. This sophisticated novel, punctuated with humorous observations, brings a fascinating woman to life.

O'Dell, Scott. *Carlota.* 1977. Hard: Houghton. Pbk: Dell. Ages 11–14.

Because her brother died as a baby, Carlota has been raised as a boy. Her father has taught her to ride, to wield a lance and a lasso, and to help run their large ranch in Spanish California in the mid-1800s. At sixteen, Carlota dresses in leather pants and jacket, and rides astride instead of sidesaddle, to her grandmother's disgust. The dictatorial old woman rolls her own cigarillos, and argues constantly with her son and grand-daughter. Carlota's love of horses makes it easy to follow her father's unconventional wishes, but as she gets older, she doesn't always agree with him. When she goes off with him to fight the American army, Carlota starts to follow her own conscience and to speak her mind. Combining physical courage and strength, kindness and honesty, Carlota is an original heroine in a captivating setting.

O'Dell, Scott. *My Name Is Not Angelica*. 1989. Hard: Houghton. Pbk: Dell. Ages 11–14.

Sixteen-year-old Raisha is living a full and happy life in Africa when her world is shattered. She and Konje, the chieftain she expects to marry, are kidnapped and sent together to the island of St. John to be slaves. Raisha uses her wits and stamina to make the best of a horrible fate, learning Danish quickly and suppressing her anger. During their first year of slavery, Konje escapes and starts a rebellion. In response, the governor prescribes drastic punishment for escaped slaves. But when the right moment comes to make her move, Raisha does not hesitate despite the danger. She knows how to live off the land if she needs to, and how to bide her time. Her final, unexpected choice in the face of tragedy proves her fierce will has not been broken. The book opens with ten female warriors coming to an African village; Raisha is another kind of warrior, fighting a battle no one should have to fight.

O'Dell, Scott. *Sarah Bishop*. 1980. Hard: Houghton. Pbk: Scholastic. Ages 12–14.

After Sarah Bishop's home and family are destroyed at the beginning of the Revolutionary War, a British officer unfairly accuses her of setting a fire. Lonely and scared, Sarah escapes punishment by fleeing westward, buying a musket on the way and selling her hair to buy supplies. Her musket saves her from an unwanted approach by a man she meets on the road, but the encounter convinces her to get away from people. Within walking distance of a village, she finds a cave and sets about preparing to stay there for the winter. She grows more confident when she finds she can survive on her own, and she learns to love her solitude. Although the ending hints that she may seek the company of others soon, her time apart has made her independent and strong. An outstanding survival story.

Paterson, Katherine. *Lyddie*. 1991. Hard: Dutton. Pbk: Puffin. Ages 11–14.

Lyddie Worthen faces her hard life in the 1840s with unflagging determination, hard work, and unexpected help from other women. Forced to leave her family's farm, she makes her way to Lowell, Massachusetts, to work in the textile mills, one of the few places females could get a relatively well-paying job. The work is dangerous and difficult, but Lyddie masters it while also learning to read well. As the hours and work increase and Lyddie has to ward off the overseer's unwanted advances, she has to decide whether to join other workers in protesting the bad working conditions. A friendship with a new worker leads Lyddie to a painful choice between keeping her integrity or her job, but she emerges from the struggle stronger in spirit, with clear goals for the future. Skillfully crafted by a talented writer, this challenging story portrays a fiercely independent young woman who battles for a place in a harsh world. Highly recommended.

Roberts, Willo Davis. *Jo and the Bandit*. 1992. Hard: Atheneum. Ages 11–13.

In this action-packed Western adventure, twelve-year-old Josephine Whitman, known as Jo, and her younger brother

Andrew go to live with their uncle, a judge in Texas, surviving a stagecoach robbery on the way out. When Jo and Andrew arrive in Muddy Wells, they find that Judge Macklin doesn't much like children, especially girls. He does start to appreciate Jo when he realizes she can help do the accounts and staff the counter at the general store he owns. Jo learned her assertiveness from her grandmother, the judge's mother, who taught her to "learn to like to work, because you're going to have to earn a living." She also told Jo that "a smart woman could outwit a man anytime if she sets her mind to it." Adventures abound when the bandits from the stagecoach robbery show up in town. A little romance, a lot of action, and a feisty heroine make this great fun to read.

Speare, Elizabeth George. *The Witch of Blackbird Pond*. 1958. Hard: Houghton. Pbk: Dell. Ages 10–14.

Kit has been raised to think for herself and to enjoy life. When her grandfather dies and she must leave Barbados for colonial Connecticut, her headstrong nature leads her into friendship and trouble. She chafes under the grim Puritan authority of her uncle but doesn't let him break her spirit. When Kit befriends a neglected little girl and an old Quaker woman who is branded a witch, she risks being accused of witchcraft herself. Despite the patriarchal nature of their lives, the women Kit encounters manage to develop strength and wisdom of their own, although men have more freedom and opportunities. This engaging modern classic received the Newbery Medal.

Taylor, Mildred D. *Roll of Thunder, Hear My Cry*. 1976. Hard: Dial. Pbk: Puffin. Ages 10–14.

Cassie Logan comes from a strong, proud family that struggles against virulent racial prejudice in their rural area in the South. They farm their own land, but are in constant danger of losing it during the Depression. Nine-year-old Cassie, who narrates the dramatic events in their lives, has a hot temper and a habit of speaking her mind that can be dangerous in her world. Cassie's valiant mother, who risks her job by teaching black history, and her grandmother Big Ma, who still works the fields, try to prepare Cassie and her brothers for an unjust world without stifling their spirits. Readers will be moved to anger and tears by the evils of racial prejudice that endanger the Logan family. A powerful novel, beautifully written. Winner of the Newbery Medal. Other books include *Song of the Trees*, *Let the Circle Be Unbroken*, and more.

Tomlinson, Theresa. *The Forestwife*. 1995. Hard: Orchard. Ages 11–14.

In this wonderful reworking of the Robin Hood legend, Maid Marian precedes Robin into Sherwood Forest. She is fleeing from an arranged marriage with the help of her old nurse Agnes. Wise Agnes leads her to the Forestwife, a woman who lives in the forest and helps all who ask. There Marian learns about herbs and healing and how to survive in the forest. Poor folk, broken by the greedy lords, come seeking cures, food, shelter, and understanding. Marian grows more indignant as she sees the results of injustice. She and her friends attract a group of strong women and a few men, including Agnes's son Robert, who joins in the useful work when he isn't off fighting. Although he and Marian find romance together, Marian's first loyalty is to her work and those who need her help. In this superb revision of an old legend, independent women take fate into their own hands and change it. Highly recommended.

Fantasy and Science Fiction

Alexander, Lloyd. *The Arkadians*. 1995. Hard: Dutton. Ages 11–14.

This frolic through Arkadia, a country much like mytho-logical Greece, follows the fortunes of Lucian, a palace bean counter. After he discovers embezzlement by powerful offi-cials, Lucian has to flee the palace of the fierce King Bromios with the help of the poet Fronto, who has been changed into a donkey. The two meet up with Joy-in-the-Dance, a young woman who leads and protects them as they travel to the land of the Lady of Wild Things to cure Fronto. Although Lucian is the central character, Joy-in-the-Dance is a close second, and is clearly the wiser and stronger of the two. On their way they meet different people and hear wondrous tales, including ver-sions of Greek myths in which women look wise and men look foolish. Women once ruled in Arkadia and still hold impor-tant powers. The inevitable happy ending points to a future in which women will regain their power. This charming adven-ture combines storytelling and fights, calamities and romance, with a large dose of humor and an unusual tribute to women.

Dickinson, Peter. *Eva*. 1989. Hard: Delacorte, o.p. Pbk: Dell. Ages 12–14.

When Eva wakes in a hospital bed after a car accident, she is in for a shock that few human beings could face: Her brain has been transplanted to the body of a chimp. Only a mas-terful writer like Dickinson could handle such a strange plot, but he makes it believable and fascinating. Because Eva was raised interacting with chimpanzees, as part of her father's work, she survives the blow. As she adjusts to her new life, she finds her loyalty divided between humans and chimps, and begins to question how humans treat chimpanzees. Eva grows into a thoughtful, powerful leader who must make difficult choices. Set years in the future, the story raises issues about the environment and the nature of progress, but the issues never get in the way of the gripping story. An utterly original, thought-provoking novel.

Engdahl, Sylvia Louise. *Enchantress from the Stars*. 1970. Hard: Peter Smith. Pbk: Aladdin. Ages 12–14.

Elana, a member of an advanced civilization, appears to be an enchantress to Georyn, who is a native of the planet Andrecia. Elana, her father, and the man Elana plans to marry are trying to save Andrecia from colonization by the Imperials, people from a civilization less sophisticated than Elana's but more advanced than Georyn's. The interaction among these three groups raises intriguing questions about what it means to "help" another group of people, and when such help may actually harm them. Elana ponders these questions as, despite her inexperience, she takes on a central role in their mission. She learns rapidly because she takes risks, even when it means disobeying her father's orders. Thrusting herself into dangerous situations, she must rely on her wits to get out. In the end, success is mixed with pain in this suspenseful adventure that is also a moving love story. A challenging book in which excitement, ideas, and romance will keep the reader captivated. A Newbery Honor Book.

Fletcher, Susan. *Dragon's Milk*. 1989. Hard: Atheneum. Pbk: Aladdin. Ages 12–14.

Kaeldra knows she is different from the people of Elythia, where she lives with her foster family, but she doesn't realize that she is a dragon-sayer, one of those who can speak with dragons. While trying to save her younger sister from death, Kaeldra becomes attached to three young dragons and finds herself responsible for them. The four set off on a perilous journey, pursued by men intent on killing the dragons. Only through Kaeldra's courage and ingenuity do they reach their final destination. Kaeldra has undertaken her mission at great danger to herself and in the process learned to cherish her unique strengths. A fast-moving fantasy adventure.

Hamilton, Virginia. *The Magical Adventures of Pretty Pearl*. 1983. Hard: Harper. Pbk: Harper Trophy. Ages 12–14.

This unusual fantasy incorporates folklore from Africans and African-Americans into a magical story. It opens on a mountaintop in Africa, where the god child Pretty Pearl lives with other gods, including John the Conqueror. The two of them travel to America during the time after the Civil War, where Pretty Pearl gets involved with a group of blacks who live hidden in a forest. The god child, who splits into a young self and an older self called Mother Pearl, joins the community of independent blacks, which is threatened by the coming of a railroad that will disrupt their home. Pretty Pearl, although powerful, has a lot of growing up to do and makes some serious mistakes along the way, but the community supports her through her hard times. The strength of this original work lies in the beautiful language and the magical realism that merges folklore with historic reality. A unique contribution to fantasy writing from an award-winning author.

Hughes, Monica. *The Promise*. 1989. Hard: Simon & Schuster, o.p. Pbk: Aladdin. Ages 11–14.

Unknown to many of its inhabitants, the planet of Rokam is sustained by one aging woman, the Sandwriter. It is time to train her ten-year-old successor, Princess Rania, who reluctantly leaves her luxurious urban life for an ascetic life in the desert. Rania gradually learns the old woman's magic, but as she grows older, she realizes what she has lost and struggles with her desire for a more normal life. She must choose between great power, which entails solitude, and her growing interest in a young man of the desert. The old woman sends Rania away to work as an ordinary maid in an inn, where her final choice becomes clear. This is a moving, sometimes mesmerizing story of romance, adventure, and fantasy. An earlier book, now out of print, is *Sandwriter*.

Lee, Tanith. *Black Unicorn*. Illustrated by Heather Cooper. 1991. Hard: Atheneum. Pbk: Tor. Ages 11–14.

Tanaquil has spent all of her nearly sixteen years in the desert castle of her mother Jaive, a sorceress. The castle drips with magic gone astray, with flowers coming out of the water faucet and birds flying out of oranges. Tanaquil, whose strongest talent is for mending anything broken, is bored. One day she follows a peeve, a desert animal who speaks, and they dig up bones together in the desert. After Tanaquil arranges the bones, a blast of magic brings them to life as a unicorn. Tanaquil follows it to a seaside city, where she becomes friends with a princess, another strong young woman. Tanaquil learns that her fate is to aid the unicorn through a test of her strength and mechanical skills. A suspenseful fantasy about a heroine with unusual talents.

Mahy, Margaret. *The Changeover: A Supernatural Romance*. 1984. Hard: McElderry. Pbk: Puffin. Ages 13–14.

Fourteen-year-old Laura Chant has known for some time that she has extrasensory powers, and she gets warnings about the future. When her three-year-old brother is imperiled by an evil male witch, she draws upon her powers in order to save him. With the help of three witches—an older boy named Sorenson, his mother, and his grandmother—Laura goes through a perilous rite of passage in hopes of becoming a witch herself. An engaging supernatural story in which a girl mines her inner strength to overcome evil.

McKinley, Robin. *Beauty: A Retelling of the Story of Beauty and the Beast*. **1978. Hard: Harper. Pbk: Harper Trophy. Ages 11–14.**

Beauty, whose real name is Honour, is an intelligent, courageous teenager in this retelling of the familiar fairy tale. While her family is rich, she studies intensely in hopes of attending the university, a rare dream for a woman. She enjoys translating Sophocles, but also loves horses. When the family falls on hard times, Beauty takes on tasks a boy would ordinarily do—chopping wood, gardening, and helping her brother-in-law, a blacksmith—and learns to fish and snare small animals. Known for her temper and stubborn will, she can't be talked out of her choice to go to the Beast in her father's place. At the Beast's magical castle, Beauty deals with her loneliness by horseback riding every day. Her relationship with the Beast develops through their love of literature and proceeds in an understated manner. Unlike the envious fairy-tale sisters, Beauty's are loving and respectful. The happy ending results less from magic than from Beauty's integrity and strong sense of self. A masterful retelling about an unconventional girl coming of age.

McKinley, Robin. *The Blue Sword*. **1982. Hard: Greenwillow. Pbk: Ace. Ages 10–14.**

In this outstanding fantasy, Harry, a girl restless with her life in what seems to be a British colony, is kidnapped by the desert king Corlath. She discovers that she has magical powers when she trains with one of Corlath's soldiers and becomes an extraordinary swordswoman and rider. Corlath, who senses Harry will play a key role in his kingdom, gives her the blue sword of Aerin, a sword that only a woman can bear. Visions of Aerin, the female dragon-killer who is the main character in *The Hero and the Crown* (see below), appear to Harry and bolster her spirit. In a culture where women had once been warriors, Harry is welcomed as the damalur-sol, a lady hero. She plays a major role in a battle against a formidable enemy, leading an extraordinary group of women and men, including some experienced soldiers willing to follow a woman into battle, a rare scenario in fiction or reality. One of the best books with strong heroines for this age group, this is definitely not to be missed. A Newbery Honor Book.

McKinley, Robin. *The Hero and the Crown*. 1984. Hard: Greenwillow. Pbk: Ace. Ages 10–14.

In this prequel to *The Blue Sword*, another extraordinary heroine makes a place for herself in an unfriendly world through her courage and strength. Aerin is the daughter of the king of Damar, but the Damarians fear her because they believe her mother was a witch. Her only real friend is her cousin Tor, heir to the throne, who teaches her the skills of hunting, fishing, riding, and swordplay. After Aerin rehabilitates her father's injured warhorse Talat and learns to ride him without stirrups and reins, Talat and Aerin start to fight small dragons that plague the kingdom. But when they meet a fearsomely large dragon, Aerin the Dragon-Killer barely survives. Her hero's welcome back to the city honors her as no woman in recent history had been honored. In her next challenge, which looks even more hopeless, she faces an evil sorcerer with the help of the Blue Sword, a weapon of great magic. A magnificent story, this Newbery Medal winner well deserves its many fans.

O'Brien, Robert C. *The Silver Crown*. 1968. Hard: Atheneum. Pbk: Aladdin. Ages 10–13.

When Ellen wakes up on her tenth birthday, she finds a silver crown on the bed next to her. Out of nowhere, tragedy strikes and she is suddenly alone in the world, with only her aunt in Kentucky to rely on. Hitchhiking to Kentucky, Ellen escapes one pursuer and gets help from a boy and a wise old woman in the hills. When she leaves their home, the boy, Otto, goes with her and they head through the woods toward Ellen's aunt. Danger soon strikes—Otto is lured into a school run by the evil pursuers, and Ellen must rescue him. Only when she enters the fortified school does she realize that her mission is even greater: She must destroy the machine that is producing the evil. With the help of another girl, Ellen calls on the power of the silver crown and the power within herself to fight off a threat to the whole country. Violent in places, this is an exciting fantasy with a stalwart heroine.

Park, Ruth. *Playing Beatie Bow*. 1982. Hard: Atheneum, o.p. Pbk: Puffin. Ages 11–13.

When she follows a strange girl named Beatie Bow out of a playground one day, fourteen-year-old Abigail Kirk travels back in time from modern Sydney, Australia, to the same city in 1873. Abigail immediately sprains her ankle and must rely on the kindness of Beatie's family. Beatie's grandmother, who has telepathic powers known as the Gift, recognizes Abby as the Stranger, someone sent to preserve the Gift for their family, so Abigail must stay in the past until she accomplishes her unknown task. In the household dominated by women, Granny is the wise, determined head. The trip to the working-class past shows Abigail how few rights and options women had. In two suspenseful scenes involving a kidnapping and a fire, Abigail's courage and ingenuity are pushed to their limits. Her time in the past teaches Abigail that life is full of hard choices and unexpected joys. An entrancing historical fantasy.

Peck, Richard. *Ghosts I Have Been*. 1977. Hard: Viking. Pbk: Dell. Ages 11–13.

Nothing fazes Blossom Culp, as she'll tell you herself. She is used to making her own way in the world and doesn't let living on the wrong side of the tracks stop her. It's 1914, so folks place a big premium on gentility, but Blossom can't afford it: "To turn me ladylike might have rendered me useless and possibly ornamental. Then I would not be able to fend for myself." Blossom thrives on excitement and creates it herself when necessary, such as the time she dresses as a ghost and scares a gang of boys. Ghosts play a bigger role when she discovers that she has inherited her mother's gift of second sight and finds herself in a trance aboard the *Titanic*—while it is sinking. Blossom, who tells the story in her wonderfully original voice, is wry and shrewd. She gets the most out of life and sometimes gets the good fortune she deserves.

Blossom first appears in *The Ghost Belonged to Me*, which focuses on another character. She continues her adventures in *The Dreadful Future of Blossom Culp* and *Blossom Culp and the Sleep of Death*.

Pierce, Tamora. *Alanna: The First Adventure*. 1983. Hard: Atheneum. Pbk: Random House. Ages 11–13.

Eleven-year-old Alanna follows the time-honored tradition

of disguising herself as a boy to seek adventure. She goes to the king's castle to train as a knight, a task made harder because she is smaller than the boys she learns with. As her first challenge, she fights a bully who has chosen her as his favorite target; to prepare she practices fighting techniques for hours on end. The bout is a nasty one, described in detail, but Alanna triumphs and goes on to her next challenge, drawing on her inner strength and her magical powers of healing to try to save a dying friend. Her final test of strength comes in a sword fight with an evil magical opponent. No fictional boy has ever been more determined than Alanna to master the fighting arts and become an outstanding knight. The other three engaging books in the Song of the Lioness series about this heroic fighter are *In the Hand of the Goddess*, *The Woman Who Rides Like a Man*, and *The Lioness Rampant*.

Pierce, Tamora. *Wild Magic*. 1992. Hard: Atheneum. Ages 11–14.

Few novels offer such strong roles to females as this fantasy series does. Daine, the main character, is an unsurpassed archer and outdoorswoman who can communicate with animals through magic. She works for a woman who is in charge of horses for a group of male and female fighters led by the country's queen. Alanna, a female knight from Pierce's Song of the Lioness series, also figures in the story. Encouraged by these strong women and a male mage, Daine expands her magical powers and learns to believe in herself. After playing a key role in thwarting an invasion of evil creatures, Daine finds a place where she belongs among people who believe in her and in the equality of men and women. Original and exciting. Daine tests her increasingly strong magical abilities in *Wolf-Speaker*, *The Emperor Mage*, and *The Realms of the Gods*.

Pullman, Philip. *The Golden Compass.* **1996. Hard: Knopf. Ages 11–14.**

This complex 400-page fantasy follows the quest of Lyra Belacqua and her daemon Pantalaimon, the animal companion who is as close to her as her own soul. Lyra has grown up in a college in Oxford, in a world only partly similar to ours. She has run wild under the lenient care of the professors, playing with servants' children, wandering the streets of Oxford, and climbing around the college roofs. Her bold-spirited escapades have prepared her for her quest to free her imprisoned father and find her friend, who has been kidnapped along with many other children. From the very start, Lyra enjoys taking risks and mastering her fears. She uses her keen intelligence to plan strategies against the many enemies she meets and finds help along the way from Gypsies, witches, other children, and a fierce armored bear. Her quest takes her to the brutally cold North and a surprising, inconclusive climax. Lyra is a daring heroine on a journey more important than even she understands.

Singer, Marilyn. *Charmed.* **1990. Hard: Atheneum. Ages 11–14.**

The Correct Combination, a group of six creatures from different worlds, must come together to defeat the Charmer, an evil man who takes different forms in the different worlds. Twelve-year-old Miranda finds herself a part of the combination with her sometimes invisible catlike friend Bastable. Three of the six allies, including the two most powerful, are female: a snake goddess with second sight, an immortal bird, and Miranda, whose imagination is vital to the quest. Their male companions are Bastable, king of his own world; Rattus, a rat with a dry wit; and Iron Dog, a young man from a world already run by the Charmer. Together the six face multiple dangers, ending up on Earth in 2030, where they take their final stand against evil. An exciting fantasy featuring strong females and nonstop action.

Biographies

Leaders and Activists

Beals, Melba Pattillo. *Warriors Don't Cry.* **1995 abridged edition. Pbk: Pocket. Ages 13–14.**

This painful autobiography introduces a girl and her family who rank among the bravest of Americans. In 1957, fifteen-year-old Melba Pattillo was one of the nine African-American students to integrate Central High School in Little Rock, Arkansas. In a voice remarkably lacking in self-pity, Beals tells of the horrors that awaited the nine inside and outside the doors of Central High: viciously screaming adults, endless physical and verbal attacks by other students, cruel telephone calls, and threats. Beals relied on her mother and grandmother for the emotional and spiritual support they provided even as they themselves suffered. Worried about threats of violence, Beals's grandmother, an expert shot, sat up nights with a rifle across her lap. She convinced her granddaughter to view herself as a warrior: "You're a warrior on the battlefield for your Lord. . . . The women of this family don't break down in the face of trouble." Beals's mother, one of the first blacks to integrate the University of Alabama, almost lost her teaching job in another district because the school board was against integration. Truly a modern hero, Melba Beals faced a battlefield that called for more courage than any teenager should have to summon. She tells her story without bitterness, in well-crafted prose. The book will hook readers with its suspense, stir their anger and shame, and probably make them cry. Don't miss it.

Bober, Natalie S. *Abigail Adams: Witness to a Revolution.* **1995. Hard: Atheneum. Ages 11–14.**

Abigail Adams's wit and intelligence come through clearly in this biography, thanks to extensive use of her letters. Quotations from her correspondence are woven into the text almost as if they are dialogue. As the wife of John Adams, who was often gone for months and sometimes years, Abigail Adams had to run their farm and a large household. She made financial decisions, including stock investments she kept secret from her husband that were crucial for their retirement. She believed in the intelligence of women and the need to educate them; she was outspoken and politically shrewd. She urged her husband to institute legal rights for women, to no avail. Although this lively biography seems to gloss over her faults, it skillfully conveys an exciting time in history and the spirit of an important American woman.

Brooks, Polly Schoyer. *Queen Eleanor: Independent Spirit of the Medieval World.* **1983. Hard: Lippincott. Ages 11–14.**

This detailed biography of an illustrious woman reads almost like a novel, adorned with black-and-white prints and paintings. It follows Eleanor of Aquitaine through her entire life, recording both personal and political aspects. She enjoyed privileges more often accorded to a man of her time; she rode, hunted, wrote and read, and traveled. She is well remembered for introducing the idea of courtly love to France and England, a tradition that gave women more influence than they had previously experienced. Eleanor sought a divorce from her first husband, the king of France, and obtained it, an unprecedented act for a woman. Married a second time, to the king of England, Eleanor enjoyed many opportunities to govern, something she did very well, while her husband and later her son were absent. She also ruled Aquitaine for some time, an area then larger than France itself. Her life was full of excitement and intrigue, and results in an absorbing story.

Fireside, Bryna J. *Is There a Woman in the House . . . or Senate?* 1994. Hard: Albert Whitman. Ages 11–14.

This is a valuable book that brings to life a neglected area of American history: women who are or have been in the U.S. Congress. First of these remarkable women is Jeannette Rankin, the first woman elected to Congress in 1917, before women could even vote in some states. Six Democrats and four Republicans are discussed, with details about their childhoods and their political careers, illustrated with black-and-white photographs. All have made an impact and served as advocates for women, while dealing with obstacles men in office do not face. The inspiring stories demonstrate that a woman can succeed in politics. As Barbara Mikulski said when she was elected senator from Maryland, she had proved it was possible for "someone who is not male, wealthy, or possessed of good looks, who is fiercely outspoken, to take a place among the wealthy white males who traditionally dominate the Senate." That sums up the spirit of this fascinating volume.

Freedman, Russell. *Eleanor Roosevelt: A Life of Discovery.* 1993. Hard: Clarion. Ages 11–14.

This compelling biography covers Eleanor Roosevelt's life from childhood through old age. Written in an inviting manner and beautifully illustrated with photographs, it emphasizes her many accomplishments, including her advocacy for women's rights. Roosevelt made her mark as an outstanding

woman in many ways: her writing and speaking, her influence
on the nation through her husband, her service to the United
Nations, and her abiding concern for social justice and world
peace. As the biography shows, she came into her own in
middle age, blossoming from a shy woman into a self-confident one. "You must do the thing you think you cannot do,"
she once said, and she lived her life according to those words.
In 1943 she traveled twenty-three thousand miles in cramped
military vehicles to visit American service-men in the Pacific.
Later in life she traveled around the world many times in her
quest to learn more and advance world peace. Eleanor Roosevelt ranks among the great women of all time, and this
exemplary biography makes it a pleasure to read about her.
The photographs that illustrate the text are supplemented by
an additional fifteen pages of photos at the end of the book,
followed by information on visiting sites related to her life; a
bibliographic essay; and an extensive index. Highly recommended. A Newbery Honor Book.

**Fritz, Jean. *Harriet Beecher Stowe and the Beecher
Preachers*. 1994. Hard: Putnam. Ages 12–14.**
Harriet Beecher Stowe's novel *Uncle Tom's Cabin* electri-
fied the United States and helped bring about the Civil War.
This excellent biography, illustrated with black-and-white
photographs, puts Stowe in the context of her family, a group
of powerful New England preachers. Her father, a famous minister, raised his sons to follow in his footsteps and cultivated
the same spirit in his daughters, even though he believed
women belonged in the home. Harriet Beecher Stowe raised
six children, writing at the same time and providing much of
the family income. Thanks to her influential novels, she met
Abraham Lincoln and was friends with important abolitionists.

Hers is the story of an intelligent, hardworking woman who used two of the few paths open to women, writing and public speaking, to make a vital difference in her country.

McKissack, Patricia C., and Fredrick McKissack. *Sojourner Truth: Ain't I a Woman?* 1992. Hard: Scholastic. Pbk: Scholastic. Ages 10–13.

This well-written biography draws on Sojourner Truth's writings and speeches, combining them with facts about her life and apt illustrations. She was an extraordinary woman who was determined to get her rights and to help others obtain theirs. She was one of the first black women in the country to win a court case, suing when her son was sold illegally out of state. The authors acknowledge her mistakes, such as trusting some fraudulent religious schemers, but dwell on her strengths. Sojourner Truth was best known as a superlative speaker who advocated abolition and women's rights. Famous in her lifetime, she addressed senators and met with presidents. The story of how she rose out of slavery to become an influential activist is fascinating and inspiring.

Parks, Rosa, with Jim Haskins. *Rosa Parks: My Story.* 1992. Hard: Dial. Ages 11–14.

Rosa Parks sets the record straight in her own account of her role in the Montgomery bus boycott, an event distorted by history. Legend has it that she was an old woman who was simply too tired to give up her seat near the front of the bus. In fact, she was forty-two, sitting in the black section, and she wasn't especially tired: "No, the only tired I was, was tired of giving in." She was already active in the civil rights movement, secretary of the local NAACP, and well informed about the legal implications of her actions. Rosa Parks's own words show her to be an intelligent, thoughtful, calm, private woman with a subtle sense of humor. She describes her childhood in segregated Alabama, her education and jobs, and her role in the civil rights movement. It is a pleasure to read her clear, straightforward account of what she has done and seen, and what she thinks about it. A graceful autobiography.

Professionals and Educators

Ayer, Eleanor H. *Margaret Bourke-White: Photographing the World.* **1992. Hard: Dillon. Ages 11–14.**
Margaret Bourke-White was a pioneer in the areas of industrial photography and the photo-essay. She photographed factories and steel mills, and World War II and other tragedies. This biography traces her fearlessness and hardworking nature to her childhood. By college she was enterprising enough to start a small business selling photographs of campus buildings. She loved a challenge and rarely let danger stop her from reaching her goal. Her own black-and-white photographs illustrate different stages in her career. Her life reads like an adventure story set all over the world during key moments in modern history.

Briggs, Carole S. *At the Controls: Women in Aviation.* **1991. Hard: Lerner. Ages 10–14.**
A group of courageous women is honored in this history of American women and planes. Generously illustrated with photographs, it begins in the 1920s with the barnstormers, women who did stunt flying in air shows, such a dangerous occupation that many died. Women flyers in the 1930s sought to break aviation records, a goal most closely identified with Amelia Earhart, who died trying to set a record. Less well

known but fascinating is the role female pilots played in World War II. In the face of severe bias, these women risked their lives ferrying planes to where they were needed, freeing more male pilots for the combat missions denied to females. Later chapters concentrate on four important women in aviation, starting with Jackie Cochran, the first woman to break the sound barrier. Jerrie Cobb, who flew dangerous international flights, passed all the necessary tests to be an astronaut, but had her dreams shattered by prejudice against having women in the space program. The stories go on, each about a brave woman who risked danger and resisted bias to fly.

Brown, Jordan. *Elizabeth Blackwell*. 1989. Hard: Chelsea House. Ages 11–14.

Elizabeth Blackwell was not only the first woman in the United States to become a doctor, but also opened the first hospital run by and for women, and the first medical college for women. Words from her diary describe the widespread, sometimes vicious opposition she faced as she applied to medical colleges and for jobs. Blackwell used humor, religious faith, and the support of friends and family to keep going. She had a talent for inspiring other women to follow in her footsteps and join in her work. She provoked even more controversy with her groundbreaking books about females and health; "I think my writings belong to the year 1998," she joked once about her progressive ideas. This entry in the fine American Women of Achievement series presents Blackwell as an unparalled pioneer of women in medicine.

Bundles, A'Lelia Perry. *Madam C. J. Walker*. 1991. Hard: Chelsea House, o.p. Pbk: Chelsea House. Ages 12–14.

This attractive biography, illustrated with many photographs, tells the memorable story of Madam C. J. Walker,

America's first black female millionaire. Born Sarah Breed-love, the daughter of former slaves, she was a self-made busi-nesswoman who invented and sold her own hair products door-to-door and through mail order. She excelled at mar-keting her products, shrewdly analyzing what customers wanted and training her workers to provide it. Known for her popular speeches urging black women to get into business for themselves, Madam C. J. Walker, as she came to be called, successfully extended her business around the country, ignoring the doubts of her husband and male advisers. Written by her great-great-granddaughter, this biography paints a glowing picture of Walker's impressive rags-to-riches story.

Burchard, Peter. *Charlotte Forten: A Black Teacher in the Civil War*. 1995. Hard: Crown. Ages 10–13.
Forten's own voice comes through in this biography about her early adult life. Entries from her diaries are woven into the descriptions of her life as a well-educated black woman in the mid-nineteenth century. Forten graduated from college and taught school afterward, first in Massachu-setts. Then she taught freed slaves during the Civil War on islands off the coast of South Carolina that were held by the North. Since she risked being forced into slavery if the islands fell to the South, Forten's courage is unmistakable. She wrote with justifiable, intense anger about the condi-tions for blacks in the North and South, and at times despaired at how she and other blacks were treated. The biography places her words in a historical context with useful information about the abolitionist movement, other prominent black Americans of the time, and the Civil War. A readable, eye-opening biography of an intelligent, sensi-tive, and brave woman.

Colman, Penny. *A Woman Unafraid: The Achievements of Frances Perkins*. 1993. Hard: Atheneum. Ages 11–14.

Frances Perkins was the first woman in the United States cabinet. She served for twelve years as the secretary of labor under Franklin Delano Roosevelt, and helped establish some of the most important reforms in federal government, including Social Security. She was a powerful woman who ventured into policy areas restricted to men and succeeded at achieving her goals there. Educated at Mount Holyoke, Perkins was a social reformer in New York City, working to improve conditions for the poor. When she married in 1913, she kept her own name, an unusual choice at the time. She was smart, canny, hard-working, and influential. Excerpts from Perkins's oral history and writings give this impressive biography a sense of her own strong voice.

Rosen, Dorothy Schack. *A Fire in Her Bones: The Story of Mary Lyon*. 1995. Hard: Carolrhoda. Ages 11–14.

Mary Lyon, who founded Mount Holyoke Seminary for women in 1837, was a brilliant student and an educational pioneer. She made education her highest priority, leaving home as a child to attend school. Enrolled at Sanderson Academy at eighteen, Lyon stunned her teachers and fellow students by memorizing an entire Latin grammar over one weekend. She resolved to establish an affordable school for training female teachers, although many criticized her goal as inappropriate for women. She didn't live to see her goal of making Mount Holyoke a college, but her work has lived on after her. This chronological retelling of her life incorporates information about the history of education. Another strong woman whose story deserves to be heard.

Scientists and Inventors

Kronstadt, Janet. *Florence Sabin: Medical Researcher.* **1990. Hard: Chelsea House. Ages 12–14.**

Because Florence Sabin believed that hard work was the key to a good life, she was still working and making a significant impact in her seventies. This well-written biography emphasizes her contributions to science and public health. After graduating from Smith College in 1893 and teaching for a few years, Sabin became one of the first women to attend Johns Hopkins Medical School, where she also became the first woman to be made full professor. Even as a student, she made notable discoveries in the laboratory and went on to have a brilliant career as a researcher, receiving many honors. In her late sixties, Sabin retired from research only to start a second career in Colorado as a public health commissioner. An advocate of women's rights, Sabin inspired and helped many younger women doctors and researchers in her long, illustrious career.

Pflaum, Rosalynd. *Marie Curie and Her Daughter Irene.* **1993. Hard: Lerner. Ages 11–14.**

Everyone should know the story of Marie Curie, an extraordinary woman far ahead of her time. This thorough biography discusses her life and work in detail, as well as her daughter's career as a scientist. Marie Curie was the first woman to get a degree at the Sorbonne in physical science, where she was first in her class. She was also the first woman to get her doctorate in France, the first to be a professor at the Sorbonne, and the first scientist of either sex to be awarded two Nobel Prizes. Irene, who worked with her, benefited from her mother's growing reputation and resources. Irene and her husband Fred were awarded a Nobel Prize for their work on radioelements. Both lives illustrate how much more women could have contributed to science in the past had they been given appropriate education, proper facilities, and encouragement. A fascinating joint biography.

Stille, Darlene R. *Extraordinary Women Scientists*. 1995. Hard: Children's Press. Ages 11–14.

This is an inspiring array of fifty women scientists from the nineteenth and twentieth centuries. Arranged alphabetically, the biographical sketches describe a wide range of work from anthropology to astronomy to medicine. The women are from all parts of the world, although most are from Europe and the United States. The sketches, which are two to six pages, speak briefly of their childhoods and personal lives, and include at least one black-and-white photograph. Strikingly, many of them were helped by, or themselves helped, other women in their fields; many were products of women's colleges. During their extraordinary careers, many won Nobel Prizes and other major honors, overcoming strong biases against women. Well written, with an attractive design, this is an exemplary introduction to fifty eminent scientists.

Vare, Ethlie Ann, and Greg Ptacek. *Women Inventors and Their Discoveries*. 1993. Hard: Oliver Press. Ages 11–14.

Ten American women inventors are profiled in this readable volume, arranged chronologically. It opens with Elizabeth Lucas Pinckney, an eighteenth-century southerner who developed the commercial crop of indigo that sustained the South Carolina economy for thirty years. The final entry is Stephanie Kwolek, a DuPont chemist who patented Kevlar, a synthetic fiber five times stronger than steel. Other women described invented signal flares for military use, the first modern-day cookbook, Liquid Paper, and more. The women were scientists, a public health doctor, a secretary, and a naval officer. One inventor, Ruth Handler, was responsible for both the Barbie doll and a well-designed artificial breast called Nearly Me. All faced obstacles, often sexism, but they persisted, put in long hours, and reaped the rewards of their efforts.

Wadsworth, Ginger. *Rachel Carson: Voice for the Earth.* 1992. Hard: Lerner. Ages 11–14.

This well-written biography traces the origins of Rachel Carson's ability to write in a powerful, beautiful way about nature. Her books helped prompt the government to start preserving the environment, specifically through the Environmental Protection Agency. She studied biology in college and had a successful career with the U.S. Bureau of Fisheries. When she wasn't at work, she wrote bestselling books about the ocean, which garnered her many honors, some never previously given to women. Her most influential book, *Silent Spring*, published in 1962, took unusual courage to write because the subject of dangerous pesticides drew hostile reactions from large corporations. A quiet, modest woman who loved nature and her extended family, Carson combined talent, hard work, and integrity to make a lasting difference.

Yount, Lisa. *Contemporary Women Scientists.* 1994. Hard: Facts on File. Ages 12–14.

This collective biography discusses ten twentieth-century scientists, seven of whom are still living and working. A biographical sketch describes each woman's work and career, with some words about how her professional life affected her personal life. A chronology and list of further reading follows each sketch, while photographs and diagrams in the text add more information. The women's fields vary from medicine to physics to astronomy; their successes include more than one Nobel Prize and a host of other prestigious awards. Readers may recognize some of them, such as shark expert Eugenie Clark and Navy Rear Admiral Grace Murray Hopper, but most are not well known. Regardless of their fields or fame, they all convey the message that, in one woman's words, science is "incredibly great fun."

Women in the Arts

Century, Douglas. *Toni Morrison*. 1994. Hard: Chelsea House. Ages 12–14.

This thoughtful biography about writer Toni Morrison traces her roots in Ohio, where a small-town upbringing and a strong tradition of black folklore influenced her future work. After college and graduate school, Morrison worked in publishing while raising her two sons alone. During this period she began writing her acclaimed novels, which focus on black women and their experiences. Each novel is discussed in some detail: its plot, what influenced it, and how it was received by critics and the public. Morrison's enormous success has brought her many honors; she was the first black woman to receive the Nobel Prize in Literature. Quotations from interviews with Morrison add a personal note to this biography of a great American writer.

Jones, Hettie. *Big Star Fallin' Mama: Five Women in Black Music*. 1995 revised edition. Hard: Viking. Ages 12–14.

Ma Rainey, Bessie Smith, Mahalia Jackson, Billie Holiday, and Aretha Franklin all made their mark in the music known as the blues. This conversational volume explores African-American musical history as it tells the stories of these significant singers. It delves into the traditions of gospel music, blues, and soul, tracing their roots to Africa and recognizing their unique place as American art forms. With their outstanding voices and musical skill, these five women made the music their own. The author places them in context, reviews their careers, and in the final chapter, reflects on how they transformed the music scene. Back matter lists available recordings, other important black women singers, and other books about the five. A highly readable, fascinating account.

Levine, Ellen. *Anna Pavlova: Genius of the Dance*. 1995. Hard: Scholastic. Ages 10–13.

When Anna Pavlova saw her first ballet at age eight, she knew she wanted to be a dancer. Two years later she entered the Ballet School in St. Petersburg, and spent the rest of her life dancing. Once she finished school, she rose quickly in the world of ballet and gained a following. But Pavlova wanted to see the world and to bring ballet to countries where it was unknown. Her organizational skills and her persistence helped her in this mission, and she and her dancers performed on nearly every continent. She was widely recognized as the greatest dancer in the world, and appeared before more audiences than any other performer of her time. Pavlova married late in life but chose not to have children, dedicating herself to her art and to her company of dancers. Sixteen pages of black-and-white photographs give the flavor of her costumes.

Lyons, Mary E. *Sorrow's Kitchen: The Life and Folklore of Zora Neale Hurston*. 1990. Hard: Scribner. Ages 12–14.

The author combines a lively, biographical narrative with Hurston's own writings to portray this trailblazing black woman.

Hurston wrote seven books as well as short stories, plays, and essays. She was the first black southerner to collect folklore from her own subculture, providing an invaluable resource for the future. Samples are given from the folktales she collected and from the voodoo traditions she studied. Hurston's life was both exciting and fraught with problems. She was poor as a child and again as an adult; she died in poverty and was buried in an unmarked grave. In 1989, writer Alice Walker erected a stone marker at Hurston's grave in Florida, with the epitaph "A Genius of the South." In recent years, Hurston's works have been reprinted and gained recognition. Hers was a truly original life, well worth reading about.

Malone, Mary. *Maya Lin: Architect and Artist.* 1995. Hard: Enslow. Ages 10–13.

Maya Lin is a remarkable woman. While an undergraduate at Yale, she won the contest for the best design for the Vietnam War Memorial. Since then she has also designed the civil rights memorial in Montgomery, Alabama. This biography covers her impressive accomplishments as an architect and sculptor, and highlights her strength as a woman in a male-dominated profession, where she has to fight to prove that "women can get things built." It is particularly appropriate that she was chosen to design a memorial honoring the presence of women at Yale University. Although the writing is choppy and the photographs disappointing, this biography is worth reading because Maya Lin provides an important contemporary role model.

Meltzer, Milton. *Dorothea Lange: Life Through the Camera.* Illustrated by Donna Diamond. 1985. Hard: Viking, o.p. Pbk: Puffin. Ages 10–14.

This biography gives a balanced portrait of one of the great

American photographers, showing both her genius and her difficulties. Born in 1895, Dorothea Lange knew early on that she wanted to be a photographer and persisted despite her mother's disapproval. She apprenticed herself to various photographers, choosing carefully to learn all aspects of the work. In 1919, she opened her own portrait studio in San Francisco, but switched to documentary photography during the Depression. Some of her best-known photographs come from that era, when she was employed on various government projects. She was among those who pioneered documentary photography, and she put her own sympathetic mark on her pictures, focusing more on capturing emotion than her fellow photographers did. Her work, which influenced government decisions at the time, continues to be shown in museums. Her personal life was less smooth, although in her second marriage she shared important work with her husband. A few of her more famous photographs are included along with some black-and-white sketches. This is a well-written introduction to an influential, dedicated woman.

Meyer, Susan E. *Mary Cassatt*. 1990. Hard: Harry A. Abrams. Ages 11–14.

This lovely biography uses many full-page color reproductions to illustrate Mary Cassatt's work. The conversational text combines information about her life with commentary on her art, setting her accomplishments in the context of the late nineteenth and early twentieth centuries when few women earned their livings as artists. Cassatt had conventional manners but unconventional artistic ambition. One of her greatest contributions to the future was persuading wealthy friends and relatives to invest in paintings, many from the Impressionists, that are now a part of important museum collections. A beautifully designed book that pays tribute to an incomparable artist.

Nichols, Janet. *Women Music Makers: An Introduction to Women Composers*. 1992. Hard: Walker. Ages 11–14.

Ten impressive women from the last four centuries are introduced in this useful volume, along with eye-opening information about the history of women in music. Most readers will be surprised to learn that a woman had a book of music published in 1644; that Clara Schumann had a sixty-year career as a concert pianist; and that there were nearly thirty all-women orchestras in the United States between 1920 and 1940. The women musicians overcame relentless bias as they strove to make careers as composers, and many broke important barriers: Ethel Smyth was the first woman to have an opera performed at New York's Metropolitan Opera House in 1903, and Florence Price was the first black woman to have a symphony performed by a major orchestra. Appendixes give short sketches of other important women; a glossary; suggested listening; and a bibliography. Of particular interest to musicians and students of women's history.

O'Connor, Barbara. *Barefoot Dancer: The Story of Isadora Duncan*. 1994. Hard: Carolrhoda. Ages 11–14.

Many consider Isadora Duncan the mother of modern dance. She pioneered an expressive, naturalistic dance that entranced some viewers and shocked others. Duncan lived from 1878 to 1927, leading a remarkably unconventional life for the time. She began evolving her dance style as a child, and by age thirteen had a successful studio where she taught younger children. Her mother and siblings accompanied her from San Francisco to New York and then on to Europe, where she became enormously successful, selling out large auditoriums for her performances. Duncan, who ignored convention and spoke out against marriage, which she thought stifled women, failed to establish a permanent dancing school to carry on her work, but she succeeded in changing the world of dance. Illustrated with many small black-and-white photographs.

Sills, Leslie. *Inspirations: Stories about Women Artists.* **1989. Hard: Albert Whitman. Ages 10–14.**

This elegantly designed book discusses the lives and art of four women: the widely acclaimed Georgia O'Keeffe and Frida Kahlo and the lesser-known Alice Neel and Faith Ringgold. Full-color reproductions illustrate each chapter, along with a few black-and-white photographs. Sills gives salient details from each artist's childhood and work and comments on the factors that made art a difficult pursuit for them. An extensive bibliography and full notes about the reproductions appear at the back of this exemplary volume.

Sills, Leslie. *Visions: Stories about Women Artists.* **1993. Hard: Albert Whitman. Ages 10–14.**

This companion volume to *Inspirations* is equally elegant and engaging. It discusses Mary Cassatt, Leonora Carrington, Betye Saar, and Mary Frank. Each biographical sketch discusses the artist's childhood and influences, then goes on to describe her work. Mary Cassatt, the best known of the four, sets the tone with her decision to break from tradition and pursue her own vision of art. Leonora Carrington, born in England in 1917, rebelled against her proper upbringing and joined the Surrealists. Californian Betye Saar, who has experienced the dual discrimination of racism and sexism, uses objects from flea markets, nature, and everyday life to create sculptures. Last in the group, Mary Frank is a successful sculptor who has recently worked in printmaking. Beautiful reproductions show the artists' work discussed in the text. Notes at the back list each piece of art, its size, and its location, and give bibliographies on each artist. Highly recommended.

Wolf, Sylvia. *Focus: Five Women Photographers.* **1994. Hard: Albert Whitman. Ages 11–14.**

Wolf presents thoughtful essays about five women photographers, illustrated with examples of their work. The first, Julia Margaret Cameron, changed the course of portrait photography when she rejected traditional stiff poses for lively, emotional expressions. This extraordinary artist took her first photograph when she was forty-eight and needed extra income for her family of twelve children. Margaret Bourke-White, by contrast, learned photography as a child from her father; she pioneered the photo-essay with her work on industry, war, and historical events. The final three women are contemporary photographers. Flor Garduno works in Latin America; Sandy Skoglund combines sculpture and photography; and Lorna Simpson uses her camera to make statements about African-American culture. All five photographers combine technical skills with innovative ideas and have found success in a male-dominated arena. Very readable text with excellent reproduction of the photographs.

Sports Biographies

Blais, Madeleine. *In These Girls, Hope Is a Muscle.* **1995. Hard: Atlantic Monthly Press. Pbk: Warner. Ages 13–14.**

Written for adults but accessible to teenagers, this conversational book honors a championship girls' high school basketball team. The members of the Amherst, Massachusetts, Regional High School team come to life through descriptions of their personalities and families, and through excerpts from their diaries and conversations. They forge strong bonds as teammates and friends, learning from their male coach and from each other. These strong-minded girls make the most of an experience previously reserved for boys. As one girl analyzes it, "The court is where you can be all those things we're not supposed to be: aggressive, cocky, strong." Dedicated to their team, they take the sport and themselves seriously, a spirit rarely captured in a book about girls and athletics.

Connolly, Pat. *Coaching Evelyn: Fast, Faster, Fastest Woman in the World.* **1991. Hard: Harper. Ages 12–14.**
    Coach Pat Connolly describes her work with runner Evelyn Ashford from their first encounter at UCLA in 1976 to the 1984 Olympics, where Ashford won two gold medals. As the new UCLA women's track coach in 1976, three-time Olympian Connolly took women's athletics very seriously indeed. She pushed the team by increasing practice time and devising new training techniques better suited to women. Connolly left UCLA but continued to coach Ashford and a few other Olympic-level athletes. She gives details about training and races, upsets and triumphs, and describes her relationship with Ashford as a coach and friend. She discusses conflicts over racial issues that arose because Connolly is white and Ashford black; she also reveals herself to be a controlling person, the source of other conflicts. Connolly is outspoken about the importance of women athletes and about her anger that they are undervalued. An interesting look into the inherently difficult coach-athlete relationship.

Cushman, Kathleen, and Montana Miller. *Circus Dreams: The Making of a Circus Artist.* **Photographs by Michael Carroll. 1990. Hard: Little, Brown. Ages 10–14.**

In 1988, an American teenager named Montana Miller became the first American to study at the world-acclaimed National Center for Circus Arts in France. One of only twenty people in her class, she received instruction in all aspects of being a circus performer: juggling, clowning, bareback riding, tightrope, and more. The diary format, illustrated with many black-and-white photographs, records her first year, during which she decides to become a trapeze artist. She confronts homesickness as well as the physical fear inherent in her field. "Learning to fly," she writes about the trapeze, "means facing the fear, not just the first time but again and again." The terrific photographs supply an immediate sense of the danger and excitement. The other three girls in her class also appear in the photographs, looking impressively strong as they practice bareback acrobatics on horses. An inside look at a young woman pursuing a rare dream.

Krone, Julie, with Nancy Ann Richardson. *Riding for My Life.* **1995. Hard: Little, Brown. Ages 12–14.**

Jockey Julie Krone has excelled in a world dominated by men and become the "winningest" female jockey ever. She has won races that no woman had previously competed in and received numerous honors in recent years. As this readable autobiography reveals, she earned her success with relentless hard work and perseverance. Injuries and a drug problem have set her back, but she has always recovered and returned to riding. She has had some physical fights with other jockeys and learned to hold her own during rough races. She describes herself as "a steaming locomotive, barreling down the tracks, at times derailing, but always learning how to correct my errors." This entertaining book about an out-standing athlete was written for adults but will appeal to adolescents, too.

Macy, Sue. *A Whole New Ball Game: The Story of the All-American Girls Professional Baseball League*. 1993. Hard: Holt. Pbk: Puffin. Ages 11–14.

From 1943 to 1954, women played professional baseball in this country. Yet for the following thirty years, little was heard about these remarkable women. Finally in 1988 the National Baseball Hall of Fame in Cooperstown, New York, paid tribute to the All-American Girls Professional Baseball League with a collection called "Women in Baseball." This gracefully written history of the league sets women's baseball in the context of World War II and its aftermath. It brings the games and the players to life with intriguing details and anecdotes, conveying their intense love for the game and capturing their unique experience as women who worked and traveled together as a team. More than 550 women played in the league over twelve years and, during 1948 alone, drew more than 910,000 fans to their games. Photographs and memorabilia illustrate this readable account, which will fascinate sports lovers and anyone interested in women's history.

Macy, Sue. *Winning Ways: A Photohistory of American Women in Sports*. 1996. Hard: Holt. Ages 11–14.

Fascinating photographs have been gleaned from many sources to illustrate this essay about the history of women in sports. The graceful writing delves into the biases and controversies that thwarted women as they tried to enjoy athletics, with anecdotes that will open the eyes of anyone who takes girls' sports teams for granted. Interviews and newspaper stories add another dimension to this intriguing exploration. The priceless photographs, which convey a sense of the past and capture amazing moments in women's sports, will mesmerize readers and reshape their view of history. There are tennis players in 1886 in long skirts and petticoats; women boxers from 1912; a rodeo rider from the first half of this century; and a weight lifter from the 1930s. These women, who faced disdain and sometimes virulent opposition, paved the way for the women athletes of today. A fascinating social history, this unique photo-essay is a pleasure to look at and read. Highly recommended.

Plowden, Martha Ward. *Olympic Black Women.* **Illustrated by Ronald Jones. 1995. Hard: Pelican. Ages 11–14.**

This collective biography packs a lot of information onto each page. It describes the ancient Olympics and the history of the modern Olympics, then gives short sketches of twenty-five athletes. Many of the twenty-five black women made their mark in track and field, with astonishing and often record-setting performances. Brief information about their personal lives reveals that many grew up in poverty and succeeded against strong odds. Unfortunately, the writing is choppy, sometimes no more than a list of facts, and the black-and-white drawings of each woman add little. However, this is unique in its focus and powerful in its impact as the reader learns about one amazing athlete after another. The appendixes include a list of other black Olympic women, a glossary, a bibliography, and more.

Women in History

Ashby, Ruth, and Deborah Gore Ohrn, editors. *Herstory: Women Who Changed the World*. 1995. Hard: Viking. Ages 11–14.

This inspiring volume tells the stories of 120 important women throughout history. The material is broken into three sections: prehistory to 1750, 1750 to 1850, and 1890 to the present. Written by nine contributors, biographical sketches of two or three pages highlight each woman's accomplishments, explain the obstacles she faced as a woman, and set her story briefly in context. Photographs or other portraits accompany many of the sketches, and sidebars add information on related topics. Some of the 120 women are famous, others more obscure. Even readers conversant with Western European history may not be familiar with such strong women as Vietnam's Trung sisters and India's Lakshmi Bai. *Herstory* is both a reference book and a volume for browsing through. It will transform many readers' understanding of history and the role women have played in creating it.

Atkinson, Linda. *In Kindling Flame: The Story of Hannah Senesh 1921–1944*. 1985. Hard: Lothrop. Pbk: Beech Tree. Ages 13–14.

Hannah Senesh was a Hungarian Jew who escaped to safety in Palestine during World War II but then returned to her country as a parachutist to help rescue Allied prisoners and Jews. A young woman of strong convictions, she showed her characteristic strength and enthusiasm when she joined an Allied rescue mission to Hungary, amazing her colleagues with her fearlessness at parachuting. Once behind enemy lines, she proved to be a strong-willed, impatient leader and an inspiration to others. This beautifully crafted biography relies heavily on Hannah Senesh's own writing and the words of those who knew her. The suspenseful story seamlessly incorporates information about the war and the history of the Jewish people, highlighting the story of the Jewish Resistance fought against impossible odds. A heartbreaking, important book.

Chang, Ina. *A Separate Battle: Women and the Civil War*. 1991. Hard: Lodestar. Pbk: Puffin. Ages 10–14.

This exemplary book fills in a gap in American history with its stories about women's roles in the Civil War. With photographs or drawings on every other page, it explains their work as abolitionists, nurses, soldiers in disguise, and spies. It also describes the massive efforts by women—particularly in the North—to provide supplies for the army. Chang quotes from diaries and letters to give voices to the women of the time and uses well-chosen anecdotes and stories to make her points. Her writing is lively and full of intriguing details. Sidebars add information about certain important women and other topics such as wives who followed their soldier husbands from camp to camp. A top-notch book likely to interest not only history buffs but a wide audience of readers.

Colman, Penny. *Rosie the Riveter: Women Working on the Home Front in World War II*. 1995. Hard: Crown. Ages 11–14.

Many of the women who worked during World War II lost their jobs as soon as men returned home. But "they never forgot that once there was a time in America when women were told that they could do anything. And they did." So concludes this outstanding history book about the six million brave, competent women whose work was vital to the war effort and kept the nation going. Excellent photographs portray women at their jobs from shipyards to farmyards, jobs previously closed to women, who were considered too weak or delicate for them. It is inspiring to read about the individual women who took on difficult work and succeeded at it, and infuriating to see them suddenly out of work when the war ended. The book's back matter includes an index, a bibliography, a chronology, and additional facts and figures. A well-crafted, exciting book about women's history.

Dash, Joan. *We Shall Not Be Moved: The Women's Factory Strike of 1909.* **1996. Hard: Scholastic. Ages 10–14.**
In 1909, women workers in the garment district in New York united to strike for better working conditions and recognition of their union. One out of every five factory workers was female and got paid a much lower wage than male workers did. Organized and run by women, with little support from the big union officials, the strike peaked when thirty thousand workers walked out. Poor immigrant women, many of them Jewish, worked with college students and even some wealthy socialites to reach their goals. Young women unexpectedly found themselves leaders and public speakers. The strike, which was both exhilarating and difficult, lasted longer than expected and in the end achieved only some of its goals. But it got many women involved in union work and increased union membership enormously. Illustrated with photographs, this is an inspiring book about the power of women united in a cause.

De Pauw, Linda Grant. *Founding Mothers: Women of America in the Revolutionary Era.* **Wood engravings by Michael McCurdy. 1975. Hard. Houghton, o.p. Pbk: Houghton. Ages 12–14.**
Many books about American women's history start with

the women's movement that began in 1848. This exceptional book concentrates instead on the women of Revolutionary War times, an era in which women had more freedom than they did in the next century. With fascinating details from newspapers, civic records, letters, and journals, De Pauw paints a picture of a rougher, more informal time in which widows took over their late husband's businesses and ran them successfully. One-third of the taverns were owned by women; women ran farms, plantations, stores, and even a few black-smith and gunsmith shops. Although laws gave women little power, the times made it possible for women to leave bad marriages and still make a living. Chapters on black and Indian women highlight their accomplishments; other chapters detail women's roles on both sides of the war. A top-notch history book that will reward the reader again and again with fascinating information.

Faber, Doris. *Calamity Jane: Her Life and Her Legend.* 1992. Hard: Houghton. Ages 10–13.

Although Calamity Jane was a real person, her life's story has been greatly exaggerated thanks to her own wild imagination and some dime novels based only vaguely on the real woman. The first few chapters of this well-illustrated biography carefully record the known facts about Martha Jane Cannary, her real name. She was on her own in the West by age sixteen, sometimes dressing as a boy to get better jobs than a girl could. She worked as a bullwhacker, driving teams of oxen yoked to strings of supply wagons, a job that required her to use a twenty-foot whip. But the facts begin to get clouded early, and there is little to back her later claim that she was a scout for General Custer. In truth, Calamity Jane often drank too much and, to the disapproval of more sedate citizens, hooked up with quite a few men she claimed to have married. Her reputation as a legend grew through the writing of Ned Wheeler, who published wild sensational stories of her deeds. A final chapter examines Calamity Jane's more recent inclusion in novels and movies as a symbol of a brave woman who ignored stifling social conventions. An intriguing combination of American history and legend.

Frank, Anne. Translated by B. M. Mooyaart-Doubleday. *Anne Frank: The Diary of a Young Girl*. 1967. Hard: Doubleday. Pbk: Bantam. Ages 11–14.

Anne Frank wrote with courage in the face of evil and fear. Hiding from the Nazis in Amsterdam, she and her family heard repeatedly of the tragic fates of their friends, and they knew they might face the same. Nevertheless, this adolescent girl kept up her spirits and coped stalwartly with her problems. After almost two years in hiding, she admonished herself to quit grumbling and "Be brave!" She tried to view her family's confinement as a "dangerous adventure" and maintained her sense of humor. A talented writer with an ear for language, she chose apt anecdotes and snips of conversation to draw her pictures of her surroundings. She conveyed the personalities of those around her and made the details of their limited, everyday existence interesting. Her ability to draw the reader into her world is so extraordinary that the final note about her death in a Nazi concentration camp feels like a personal loss. A stunningly powerful work that everyone should read.

Miller, Brandon Marie. *Buffalo Gals: Women of the Old West*. 1995. Hard: Lerner. Ages 10–14.

The plentiful photographs are the highlight of this book about women in the Old West. Although small, the pictures capture fascinating subjects: a female rodeo rider; newspaper-women setting type in the 1880s; Wyoming pioneer women with their guns and animal skins; and two women dressed in long skirts, capering on a Yosemite peak. The history covers the trip west by covered wagon, frontier homes, women's work, entertainment, and the lives of Native American women. The dense text, with its many quotations from letters and diaries, is packed with surprising details. For example, in 1910, 10 percent of the homesteaders on the Great Plains were single women, an amazing statistic. The writing is not as effective as the photographs, but will reward persistent readers with an unusual view of history.

Reit, Seymour. *Behind Rebel Lines: The Incredible Story of Emma Edmonds, Civil War Spy.* 1988. Hard: Harcourt. Pbk: Harcourt. Ages 10–13.

Emma Edmonds was a truly unusual woman. She dressed as a man, calling herself Frank Thompson, and served in the Union army for two years. During that time, she acted as a spy for the North and went on eleven spying missions to gather information behind enemy lines about Confederate troops and plans. She successfully disguised herself as an old black man, a handsome Confederate sympathizer, and a matronly Irish peddler. During each venture into Confederate territory Edmonds risked her life, coming close to dying more than once. The only person who shared her secret was a chaplain's wife, who helped Edmonds in her disguises. Many years after the war, she secured a veteran's pension by a special act of Congress. Historians believe that Edmonds was one of more than four hundred women who disguised themselves as men to fight in the Civil War. An exciting fictionalized biography.

St. George, Judith. *Dear Dr. Bell . . . Your Friend, Helen Keller.* **1992. Hard: Putnam. Pbk: Beech Tree. Ages 11–14.**

Although the childhood of Helen Keller is well known, her accomplishments as an adult are not. This elegant biography tells of both, with a focus on Keller's friendship with Alexander Graham Bell. Bell, who was deeply involved in issues concerning the deaf, was indirectly responsible for Annie Sullivan's role as Keller's teacher. With Sullivan's help, Keller, who was deaf and blind, succeeded at the seemingly insurmountable task of learning to understand language, to read and to write. Bell attributed their success to the "genius" of Sullivan and the "brilliant mind" of Keller. Keller went on to graduate from Radcliffe College and become a writer and activist whose impressive achievements broke stereotypes about what the disabled can do. Many quotations from their letters bring the personalities of Keller and Bell to life in this outstanding biography.

Stanley, Jerry. *Big Annie of Calumet: A True Story of the Industrial Revolution.* **1996. Hard: Crown. Ages 11–14.**

This is the story of an ordinary woman who became a hero. In 1913, increasingly dangerous working conditions and eleven-hour workdays drove nine thousand copper miners on the upper peninsula of Michigan to strike. Every day workers and their families marched down the streets of Calumet, led by Annie Clemenc, a miner's wife who carried an American flag on a ten-foot staff. Six feet two inches tall, the powerful woman inspired the miners with her courage and strength. When the company hired three thousand thugs to break the strike with violence, Clemenc and others, many of them women, were jailed while the men who attacked them went free. The violence escalated, and a tragic incident took the heart out of the strike, which finally ended on unsatisfactory terms. But Clemenc remains a symbol of courage in Michigan, where she was the first woman nominated to the Women's Hall of Fame. Illustrated with well-chosen photographs, this is an exemplary blend of history and biography.

Stefoff, Rebecca. *Women of the World: Women Travelers and Explorers*. **1992. Hard: Oxford University Press. Pbk: Oxford University Press. Ages 11–14.**

This collective biography describes nine extraordinary women who traveled to destinations visited by no other woman from the West, proving that women could rival men at surviving harsh conditions and appreciating new places. Isabella Bird Bishop, born in 1831, found that travel transformed her from a sickly, frail woman to a robust explorer who visited parts of Japan unknown to the West. Fanny Bullock Workman from Massachusetts set many climbing records for women, and even posted a sign reading "Votes for Women" on a peak in Pakistan. The other women described ventured to Tibet, the Arctic, and the Arabian peninsula, canoed through Africa and spied in the Soviet Union. Photographs and maps add to the pleasure of reading about these explorers. A high-quality volume, certain to entrance would-be travelers.

Watkins, Yoko Kawashima. *So Far from the Bamboo Grove*. **1986. Hard: Lothrop. Pbk: Beech Tree. Ages 11–14.**

In 1945, an eleven-year-old Japanese girl named Yoko Kawashima, her sixteen-year-old sister Ko, and their mother made an arduous journey from northern Korea, where they lived and Yoko's father worked, to their homeland of Japan. Separated from Yoko's father and older brother, they tramped through harsh countryside, disguised themselves as Korean soldiers, and finally arrived by boat in Japan, only to find their relatives had died in the war. They lived for months on end in train stations and warehouses, scavenging for food in garbage cans. Ko stayed disguised as a male to protect herself, and their mother relied on a small concealed sword. At first the bewildered Yoko complains about their hardships, but she gains courage and endurance as their trials continue. A remarkable portrait of strong females who survived in a terrible time, this true story is hard to put down.

6

Resources
for Parents

Locating Books

Libraries

Public libraries are a great resource for parents. They are free, and typically offer a broader and deeper range of books than bookstores do. Libraries are the best place to find books that are out of print, an important service because many children's books go out of print quickly. Libraries are also more likely than bookstores to carry books from smaller presses.

Good libraries are increasingly easy to use. Some public library catalogs can be accessed from home, using a computer and a modem. Many libraries are part of a branch system or a large cooperative system, so you can use your card at more than one library. In such cases you can usually return books to the library closest to you, even if you checked them out elsewhere. Most libraries have book drops so that you can return books when the library is closed.

Computerized catalogs may intimidate some library users, but most people get accustomed to them quickly. Like the traditional card catalog, the computerized catalog shows you whether your library owns a book, with the added feature of indicating if it is on the shelf or checked out. Often computerized catalogs also show whether a nearby library has the book, which you could then borrow through interlibrary loan.

Interlibrary loan (ILL) is a convenient way to get access to many more books than your local library has in its collection. In many libraries, it is free to borrow a book through ILL, although some public libraries charge a small fee per book. Some computerized catalogs allow you to input your library card number if you want to request a book from another library. Your local library will call you or send a notice when it arrives, often in a few days.

While you are signing out books, find out what other programs and services your local library offers. You may discover storytimes for younger children, summer reading programs for a wide range of ages, junior critic clubs for older children, programs on parenting, and more. Many libraries carry books on tape and videos, too.

School libraries come in all sizes, and the large ones will probably have many of the books in this guide. Some school libraries are open during the summer, although most are not. Whether parents can sign out books depends on the school.

Bookstores and Catalogs

Bookstores vary enormously in their selections of children's books. Some offer a wide array of books, usually with an emphasis on paperbacks. Others have only a small selection or carry mostly books in popular series. Some cities have bookstores devoted just to children's books, a treat for children's book lovers.

It is important to realize that most bookstores will order a book for you for no charge, if the bookstore doesn't carry it but can get it easily from another source. If you don't see the book you want, ask about placing such a special order.

Bookstores are increasing the services they offer for families, adding storytimes, author book signings, and other programs. Several large bookstores now offer children's books by mail through the World Wide Web, and some give recommendations of children's books at their web sites.

Most catalogs and book clubs offer such a small selection that they carry only a few books about strong girls and women. One exception is *Chinaberry Books*, an outstanding catalog of more than five hundred children's books, with thoughtful descriptions of each title. It covers toddlers through adolescents, with a section on parenting books and a small selection of novels for adults. Chinaberry Books, 2780 Via Orange Way, Suite B, Spring Valley, CA 91978. 1-800-776-2242.

Keeping Up with Children's Book Publishing

If you are interested in keeping up with what's new in children's books, here are some recommended magazines and review journals. Also keep an eye on your local newspaper, which may have regular or occasional articles on new children's books. Libraries often provide booklists that highlight recent recommended books. For example, each year the American Library Association publishes an annotated list of approximately seventy-five Notable Children's Books, a useful resource available in most libraries.

Children's Book Review Magazine, P.O. Box 5082, Brentwood, TN 37024-9767. 1-800-543-7220.

Children's Book Review Magazine is a glossy quarterly magazine aimed at the general public that highlights recently published children's books. An accessible, attractive source of information, available at bookstores and libraries and by subscription.

The Horn Book Magazine, 11 Beacon Street, Boston, MA 02108. 1-617-227-1555.

The Horn Book Magazine is a well-established bimonthly journal about children's books. It prints insightful reviews of recommended books and well-written articles about children's literature. Available at bookstores and libraries and by subscription.

School Library Journal, P.O. Box 57559, Boulder, CO 80322-7559. 1-800-456-9409.

School Library Journal is a professional journal that librarians rely on for purchasing children's books. It reviews most of the children's books published each year as well as videos and computer software. It carries articles of interest to librarians and educators. Available by subscription and in many libraries.

Book Links, 434 W. Downer, Aurora, IL 60506. 1-708-892-7465.

Book Links is an attractive, useful magazine of great interest to children's librarians and educators, published by the American Library Association. It highlights books on selected topics, geared toward curriculum needs. Available by subscription and in many libraries.

Tips on Reading Aloud

Reading aloud well does not come naturally to everyone. Here are techniques you can practice until they come easily. *The Read-Aloud Handbook* by Jim Trelease (Penguin, 1995, 4th edition) offers more ideas about how to go about it.

- If you haven't read the book already, scan it to get a sense of its contents before you start reading aloud.
- Choose books you are excited about or your child is excited about. It is hard to read a book you don't enjoy, especially a long one.
- Read with expression. A monotone is hard to listen to. Children need to hear changes in your voice to indicate when you are reading dialogue. Vary your pace, too. Slow down to build up suspense, and speed up during exciting scenes.
- Create voices for different characters if you enjoy it, but it isn't necessary for a good reading. A story can be read effectively in a straightforward manner as long as you have expression and enthusiasm.
- Read at a moderate pace, not too fast. Listening is a challenge for many children, and you don't want to leave them behind as you speed ahead. Picture-story books require time for enjoying the illustrations.
- Feel free to stop and discuss the book if you and your listener want to. Answer questions as they come up. How much you want to stop and explain new words is up to you. If they can be understood in context, you may want just to keep reading. Stopping too often to explain can undermine the story's impact.

- Keep in mind that children can look bored or restless and still be listening. Some children need to be moving around or fidgeting with something. The real question is, Are they following the story? If so, let them squirm or even draw pictures as they listen.
- Sometimes a book will lead to conversations afterward, sometimes not. Play it by ear. Either way is fine.
- If your child wants to read to you sometimes, great. Beginning readers especially enjoy their new skills. You can trade off pages or chapters, or just sit back and listen.
- If your child is not enjoying a book, you are not obliged to finish it. This is most likely to come up with chapter books. You don't want to abandon a book quickly, but if a book has not sparked interest after several sessions, try another one. If this is a pattern, you may want to switch to shorter books and build up to longer ones.

Reading aloud has a host of educational benefits, but it works best if it isn't approached as an educational exercise. Parents have been known to have children repeat each word after them, as a device to teach reading. Such a tedious approach is more likely to dampen enthusiasm for books than to promote learning. Just enjoy the books together; the increased vocabulary, understanding of story structure, exposure to correct grammar, and other benefits will follow naturally.

Activities with Books

Books stand on their own as art and entertainment, and sometimes the best approach is simply to read a book and savor it. In other cases, discussing the book enriches the experience. But it can also be fun to pair books with activities such as crafts, trips, cooking, and more. Most of the following ideas are geared toward picture-story books and biographies, but reading a novel together can also lead to shared activities. Brainstorm with your child about other possibilities, with the goal, as always, to make reading a wonderful experience.

- Take a low-key field trip in conjunction with a picture-story book. Read *Pond Year* and then take a walk at a pond. Read *Lottie's Circus* before going to a circus or *If Anything Goes Wrong at the Zoo* before a trip to the zoo.
- Add props to your reading of a picture-story book. Get a squirt gun or set of Groucho Marx glasses for reading *Chester's Way*. Find a metal Band-Aid box and fill it with coins before reading *The Purse*.
- Read *Mermaid Janine* before going swimming or starting swimming lessons.
- Plan to go to a library story hour, and first read *Red Light, Green Light, Mama and Me*.
- Read *How to Make an Apple Pie and See the World*, then bake together. Cooking is surprisingly eductional, combining math, such as fractions and measuring, and reading.
- Read *Zin! Zin! Zin! A Violin* before going to hear instrumental music.

- Read *Owl Moon* and go out on an evening hike to look for birds.
- Read *June 29, 1999* and try a science experiment. Libraries have many science experiment books for children.
- After reading a book illustrated with collage, try making a collage. Or paint with watercolors after looking at watercolor illustrations in a book.
- Encourage your child to write and illustrate her own books. She can dictate the words to you if she doesn't know how to print yet. Remind her to add an About the Author paragraph.
- Read a biography about a woman artist. Take a trip to a museum and point out art by women. Paint a picture or make a sculpture together.
- Since children's books have a limited number of reproductions of paintings, find a book for adults with even more pictures to look at.
- Read a folktale from another country and then locate the country on a map. Find a book with photographs of that country.
- Read a folktale, then a parody of the tale, such as *Cinderella* and *Cinder Edna*. Talk about the similarities and differences.
- Read about a female athlete. Go to a local girls' sports event, such as a high school or college game or track meet.
- Read a novel together that has been made into a video. Watch the video and compare the two.
- Read about a marine biologist, such as Eugenie Clark or Sylvia Earle, in conjunction with a visit to an aquarium.
- Listen to a book on tape together on a long trip. A number of the novels in this guide have been recorded and are available at your library or for rental through the mail.

- With a child who can read independently, start a mother-daughter book group, or help your daughter start a book group with her friends.
- Before a space shuttle launch, follow the stories in the newspaper together and read about a female astronaut.
- Read *Sarah, Plain and Tall* together. Then each write a letter such as Sarah wrote describing yourself to someone who has never met you.
- Read a novel in conjunction with a trip to a geographic region: *Caddie Woodlawn* for Wisconsin; *Eight Mules from Monterey* for California; *The Missing 'Gator of Gumbo Grove* for Florida; and many more.
- Visit a place on vacation connected with important women. For example, read about the history of women's rights before going to the Women's Hall of Fame in Seneca Falls. Or visit the National Museum of Women in the Arts in Washington, D.C.
- Donate a book about a strong female that you both like to your daughter's school or your public library.
- Alert teachers and librarians to books about strong females that you and your daughter especially enjoyed.
- Read about an important woman in conjunction with Take Our Daughters to Work Day.

Further Reading for Parents

Here are some recommended books about raising daughters, gender issues, and related topics.

Bingham, Mindy, and Sandy Stryker with Susan Allstetter Neufeldt. *Things Will Be Different for My Daughter: A Practical Guide to Building Her Self-Esteem and Self-Reliance from Infancy through the Teen Years.* 1995. Pbk: Penguin.

Packed with information and ideas, this nearly 500-page volume addresses many aspects of girls' development and needs, and what parents can do to support them. Practical exercises and step-by-step plans included.

Brown, Lyn Mikel, and Carol Gilligan. *Meeting at the Crossroads: Women's Psychology and Girls' Development.* 1992. Hard: Harvard University Press. Pbk: Ballantine.

Based on interviews with a hundred girls, this important book provides insights into the problems girls face at adolescence. By well-known experts in education and human development.

Eagle, Carol J., and Carol Colman. *All That She Can Be: Helping Your Daughter Achieve Her Full Potential and Maintain Her Self-Esteem During the Critical Years of Adolescence.* 1993. Hard: Simon & Schuster. Pbk: Simon & Schuster/Fireside.

Detailed, useful information on girls' social and psychological development. Full of examples and specific suggestions from a psychologist whose practice is geared toward adolescent girls.

Elium, Jeanne, and Don Elium. *Raising a Daughter: Parents and the Awakening of a Healthy Woman.* **1994. Hard: Celestial Arts. Pbk: Celestial Arts.**

The authors reflect on the special challenges facing parents of girls in today's world, offer parenting advice, and take the reader through each stage of a girl's development. Also authors of *Raising a Son: Parents and the Making of a Healthy Man.*

Gilligan, Carol. *In a Different Voice: Psychological Theory and Women's Development.* **1982. Hard: Harvard University Press. Pbk: Harvard University Press.**

The groundbreaking book by a Harvard psychologist about girls' and women's psychological development. Readable and thought-provoking.

Godfrey, Joline. *No More Frogs to Kiss: 99 Ways to Give Economic Power to Girls.* **1995. Pbk: Harper.**

An exceptionally useful guide to helping girls look at the world around them in terms of business and economic opportunity. A fine combination of practical ideas and inspiring stories.

Mann, Judy. *The Difference: Growing Up Female in America.* **1994. Hard: Warner. Pbk: Warner.**

Reporter Mann takes a sociological look at the forces that hold girls back. Based on interviews with experts in different fields and on the experience of her daughter and her daughter's friends, this accessible volume is full of interesting insights and observations, with some thoughts about how to change society.

Pipher, Mary. *Reviving Ophelia: Saving the Selves of Adolescent Girls*. 1994. Hard: Putnam. Pbk: Ballantine.

This compassionate bestseller addresses parents' fears and concerns about raising an adolescent daughter in a threatening world. Using examples from her practice as a clinical psychologist, Pipher examines the problems and offers guidance to parents and their daughters.

Sadker, Myra and David. *Failing at Fairness: How America's Schools Cheat Girls*. 1994. Hard: Scribner. Pbk: Simon & Schuster/Touchstone.

A landmark study of sexism in our schools and what can be done about it. Readable and inspiring.

Stenmark, Jean Kerr, Virginia Thompson, and Ruth Cossey. *Family Math*. Illustrated by Marilyn Hill. 1986. Pbk: Lawrence Hall of Science, University of California at Berkeley.

For children ages five to eighteen and their parents. Written with girls in mind, this wonderful collection of math exercises is meant to be shared by parents and children. Although ideally the book is used in conjunction with a Family Math class, the class isn't necessary. The book explains hands-on activities that teach problem-solving skills in all areas of mathematics. A great resource.

Books for Children on Sex and Growing Up

It is vital for children to understand the changes that will take place in their bodies when they become adolescents. They need accurate information about sex and reassurances about puberty and its effects. Here are some recommended books with age guidelines.

Andry, Andrew C., and Steven Schepp. *How Babies Are Made*. Illustrated by Blake Hampton. 1968. Hard: Time-Life Books, o.p. Pbk: Little, Brown.

For ages five to eight. Simple information for younger children about sexual reproduction in flowers, animals, and humans. Illustrated with cut-paper illustrations.

Cole, Joanna. *How You Were Born*. Photographs by Margaret Miller. 1993 revised edition. Hard: Morrow. Pbk: Morrow/Mulberry.

For ages four to seven. Color photographs and diagrams show the development of the fetus and the birth process, and the welcome arrival of newborn babies into several families.

Gravelle, Karen, and Jennifer Gravelle. *The Period Book: Everything You Don't Want to Ask (But Need to Know)*. Illustrated by Debbie Palen. 1996. Hard: Walker. Pbk: Walker.

For ages nine and up. A simple, conversational discussion of the changes puberty brings for a girl, illustrated with humorous cartoon drawings. A solid introduction.

Harris, Robie H. *It's Perfectly Normal: Changing Bodies, Growing Up, Sex & Sexual Health.* **Illustrated by Michael Emberley. 1994. Hard: Candlewick. Pbk: Candlewick.**

For ages nine and up. A well-crafted book that answers children's questions about their bodies and sexual reproduction. The straightforward text is balanced by funny, apt cartoon drawings, many of nude figures.

Jukes, Mavis. *It's a Girl Thing: How to Stay Healthy, Safe, and in Charge.* **1996. Hard: Knopf. Pbk: Knopf.**

For ages ten and up. An upbeat, honest approach to adolescence that covers sexual issues; drugs, alcohol, and smoking; and staying safe. Written in a personal, good-humored tone to make readers feel comfortable and reassured.

Madaras, Lynda, and Area Madaras. *The What's Happening to My Body? Book for Girls: A Growing Up Guide for Parents and Daughters.* **1987 revised edition. Hard: Newmarket. Pbk: Newmarket.**

For ages nine and up. A comprehensive, readable handbook filled with useful information, mainly about females, although some facts about male puberty are included. Madaras has written a companion volume for boys.

Marzollo, Jean. *Getting Your Period: A Book about Menstruation.* **Illustrated by Kent Williams. 1989. Hard: Dial. Pbk: Puffin.**

For ages nine and up. Facts and factual drawings are combined with the voices of girls talking about their reactions to puberty and specifically menstruation. A thorough, calm introduction.

Empowering Your Daughter

I have gleaned these ideas from many sources. Try some you haven't considered before, keeping in mind that no parent can expect to be doing all of them all the time. For excellent suggestions to introduce business and entrepreneurial thinking into your daughter's everyday life, see *No More Frogs to Kiss*, listed previously.

- Let your daughter get dirty. Children need to explore the world around them and be physically active. Science, nature, sports, arts and crafts—all these important parts of growing up entail getting dirty.
- Give her time to try to do a task herself rather than "rescue her" by giving advice or doing it for her. Encourage her to be persistent in working out her own solutions.
- Encourage your daughter to state her opinions and thoughts, and listen respectfully to what she says. If she has trouble speaking out in class, practice with her at home and help her plan strategies for the classroom.
- Notice how you compliment girls. Typically girls get compliments on what they wear or how they look, while boys get compliments on what they do. Try to give compliments on specific accomplishments, not general qualities. "Your speech had a powerful opening," not "You are a good speaker."
- Encourage her to participate in sports. Give her the support to join a team sport. Show her you value physical fitness and strength in girls and women.

- Watch television together and discuss the portrayal of women, how realistic it is, what messages it sends. Extend this to movies, videos, magazines, and computer games.
- Find ways to help your daughter develop math, science, and computer skills. Provide games that develop spatial skills such as puzzles, model kits, checkers and chess, etc. For older girls, look into after-school classes or summer camps on math, science, and computers.
- See that she learns some mechanical, building, and repairing skills, and becomes familiar with tools. Give young girls blocks and simple tools. Have older girls learn to repair their bicycles and encourage them to take apart old appliances, etc.
- Emphasize the importance of developing talents and interests. Such pastimes give girls pleasure and a self-image that doesn't rely on appearance, popularity, or relationships. Girls need to be good at doing things as well as at dealing with people.
- Examine your expectations for girls and boys. Do you give boys more leeway to be rowdy, physically active, outspoken? Do you expect girls to be more domestic, caring, polite, thoughtful? Do you expect boys to help with outdoor tasks and girls with indoor ones?
- Introduce her to strong female role models. Expose her to a variety of career possibilities and women who enjoy their work. Teach her to assume she will have to make her own living someday, as most women do. Participate in Take Our Daughters to Work Day in April. For more information on Take Our Daughters to Work, contact the Ms. Foundation for Women, 120 Wall Street, 33rd Floor, New York, NY 10005. 1-800-676-7780.

- Support your daughter in pursuing her interests and in taking risks. Be ready to help, but encourage her to make her own decisions and choices. Praise her for her intelligence, abilities, and initiative as well as her hard work and dedication. Most of all, believe in her.

Recommended Out-of-Print Books

Here are some books about strong girls and women that are no longer in print but are available in libraries. The list, which is by no means conclusive, is arranged in the same order as this guide.

Picture-Story Books

Aitken, Amy. *Kate and Mona in the Jungle.* Bradbury, 1981.

Aitken, Amy. *Ruby the Red Knight.* Bradbury, 1983.

Allison, Beverley. *Effie.* Illustrated by Barbara Reid. Scholastic, 1990.

Berry, Christine. *Mama Went Walking.* Illustrated by María Cristina Brusca. Holt, 1990.

Blake, Quentin. *Mrs. Armitage on Wheels.* Knopf, 1987.

Boynton, Sandra. *Hester in the Wild.* Harper, 1979.

Engel, Diana. *Josephina the Great Collector.* Morrow, 1988.

Galdone, Joanna. *The Little Girl and the Big Bear.* Houghton, 1980.

Gantschev, Ivan. Translated by Karen M. Klockner. *The Christmas Train.* Little, Brown, 1982.

Garland, Michael. *My Cousin Katie.* Crowell, 1989.

Hilton, Nette. *A Proper Little Lady.* Illustrated by Cathy Wilcox. Orchard, 1989.

Isadora, Rachel. *"No, Agatha"*. Greenwillow, 1980.

Major, Beverly. *Over Back*. Harper, 1993.

Mayer, Marianna. *The Little Jewel Box*. Illustrated by Margot Tomes. Dial, 1986.

Mendoza, George. *Need a House? Call Ms. Mouse!* Illustrated by Doris Susan Smith. Grosset & Dunlap, 1981.

Murphy, Shirley Rousseau. *Tattie's River Journey*. Illustrated by Tomie de Paola. Dial, 1983.

Pfanner, Louise. *Louise Builds a House*. Orchard, 1987.

Root, Phyllis. *Soup for Supper*. Illustrated by Sue Truesdell. Harper, 1986.

Sleator, William. *Once, Said Darlene*. Illustrated by Steven Kellogg. Dutton, 1979.

Van Woerkom, Dorothy. *Alexandra the Rock-Eater*. Illustrated by Rosekrans Hoffman. Knopf, 1978.

Williams, Barbara. *Kevin's Grandma*. Illustrated by Kay Chorao. Dutton, 1975.

Woodruff, Elvira. *Tubtime*. Illustrated by Sucie Stevenson. Holiday, 1990.

Young, Ruth. *Daisy's Taxi*. Illustrated by Marcia Sewall. Orchard, 1991.

Zimelman, Nathan. *Mean Murgatroyd and the Ten Cats*. Illustrated by Tony Auth. Dutton, 1984.

Folktales

de la Mare, Walter. *Molly Whuppie*. Illustrated by Errol Le Cain. FSG, 1983.

Lobel, Anita. *The Straw Maid*. Greenwillow, 1983.

Maestro, Betsy and Giulio. *A Wise Monkey Tale*. Crown, 1975.

Matsutani, Miyoko. *The Witch's Magic Cloth*. Illustrated by Yasuo Segawa. Parents' Magazine Press, 1969.

Mayer, Marianna. *Noble-Hearted Kate*. Illustrated by Winslow Pels. Bantam, 1990.

McClenathan, Louise. *My Mother Sends Her Wisdom*. Illustrated by Rosekrans Hoffman. Morrow, 1979.

Riordan, James. *The Woman in the Moon and Other Tales of Forgotten Heroines*. Illustrated by Angela Barrett. Dial, 1985.

Va, Leong. Translated by James Anderson. *A Letter to the King*. Harper, 1991.

Van Woerkom, Dorothy. *The Queen Who Couldn't Bake Gingerbread*. Illustrated by Paul Galdone. Knopf, 1975.

Wahl, Jan. *The Cucumber Princess*. Illustrated by Caren Caraway. Stemmer House, 1981.

Williams, Jay. *Petronella*. Parents' Magazine Press, 1973.

Williams, Jay. *The Practical Princess*. Parents' Magazine Press, 1969.

Williams, Jay. *The Silver Princess*. Parents' Magazine Press, 1971.

Books for Beginning Readers

Alexander, Sue. *World Famous Muriel*. Little, Brown, 1984.

Baker, Betty. *All-by-Herself*. Illustrated by Catherine Stock. Greenwillow, 1980.

Baker, Betty. *The Turkey Girl*. Illustrated by Harold Berson. Macmillan, 1983.

Boegehold, Betty. *Here's Pippa Again!* Illustrated by Cindy Szekeres. Knopf, 1975.

Boutis, Victoria. *Katy Did It*. Illustrated by Gail Owens. Greenwillow, 1982.

Paton Walsh, Jill. *Birdy and the Ghosties*. Illustrated by Alan Marks. FSG, 1989.

Schulman, Janet. *Jenny and the Tennis Nut*. Illustrated by Marylin Hafner. Greenwillow, 1978.

Smith, Lucia B. *My Mom Got a Job*. Illustrated by C. Christina Johanson. Holt, Rinehart, 1979.

Tompert, Ann. *Sue Patch and the Crazy Clocks*. Illustrated by Rosekrans Hoffman. Dial, 1989.

Van Woerkom, Dorothy. *Becky and the Bear*. Illustrated by Margot Tomes. Putnam, 1975.

Books for Middle
Readers

Aiken, Joan. *Black Hearts in Battersea*. Doubleday, 1964.

Aiken, Joan. *The Stolen Lake*. Delacorte, 1981.

Bloch, Marie Halun. *Aunt America*. Illustrated by Joan Berg. Atheneum, 1964.

Cebulash, Mel. *Ruth Marini of the Dodgers*. Lerner, 1983.

Corbett, Scott. *The Hockey Girls*. Dutton, 1976.

Duder, Tessa. *Jellybean*. Viking, 1985.

Ellis, Anne Leo. *The Dragon of Middlethorpe*. Holt, 1991.

Flory, Jane. *Golden Venture*. Houghton, 1976.

Knudson, R. R. *Julie Brown: Racing Against the World*. Illustrated by J. Brian Pinkney. Viking, 1988.

Knudson, R. R. *Zanballer*. Delacorte, 1972.

Pelta, Kathy. *The Blue Empress*. Illustrated by Leslie Morrill. Holt, 1988.

Proboz, Kathilyn Solomon. *The Girls Strike Back: The Making of the Pink Parrots.* Warner, 1990.

Rappaport, Doreen. *Trouble at the Mines.* Illustrated by Joan Sandin. Crowell, 1986.

Selfridge, Oliver G. *Trouble with Dragons.* Illustrated by Shirley Hughes. Addison-Wesley, 1978.

Smith, Alison. *Billy Boone.* Scribner, 1989.

Springstubb, Tricia. *With a Name Like Lulu, Who Needs More Trouble?* Illustrated by Jill Kastner. Delacorte, 1989.

Stevenson, Drew. *One Ghost Too Many.* Cobblehill, 1991.

Streatfield, Noel. *Thursday's Child.* Random House, 1970.

Books for Older Readers

Altman, Millys N. *Racing in Her Blood*. Lippincott, 1980.

Austin, Jennifer. *Ticket to Danger*. Illustrated by Ann Meisel. Grosset & Dunlap, 1990.

Bach, Alice, and J. Cheryl Exum. *Miriam's Well: Stories about Women in the Bible*. Illustrated by Leo and Diane Dillon. Delacorte, 1991.

Bober, Natalie S. *Breaking Tradition: The Story of Louise Nevelson*. Atheneum, 1984.

Colman, Penny. *Breaking the Chains: The Crusade of Dorothea Lynde Dix*. Shoe Tree Press, 1991.

De Pauw, Linda. *Seafaring Women*. Houghton, 1982.

Farley, Walter. *The Black Stallion and the Girl*. Random House, 1971.

Hall, Lynn. *Tin Can Tucker*. Scribner, 1982.

Hilgartner, Beth. *Colors in the Dreamweaver's Loom*. Houghton, 1989.

Hilgartner, Beth. *A Necklace of Fallen Stars*. Illustrated by Michael R. Hague. Little, Brown, 1979.

Hoover, H. M. *Orvis*. Viking, 1987.

Howard, Elizabeth. *Mystery of the Magician*. Illustrated by Michael Wm. Kaluta. Random House, 1987.

Mathieson, David. *Trial by Wilderness*. Houghton, 1985.

Meltzer, Milton. *Betty Friedan*. Viking, 1985.

Murphy, Claire Rudolf. *To the Summit*. Lodestar, 1992.

O'Dell, Scott. *Alexandra*. Houghton, 1984.

Park, Ruth. *My Sister Sif*. Viking, 1991.

Roper, Robert. *In Caverns of Blue Ice*. Sierra Club Books, 1991.

Sanders, Scott Russell. *The Engineer of Beasts*. Orchard, 1988.

Author Index

AUTHOR INDEX

Henkes, Kevin, 55, 56
Herzig, Alison Cragin, 212
Hesse, Karen, 156, 225
Higginsen, Vy, 296
Hoban, Russell, 56
Hoffman, Mary, 56
Honeycutt, Natalie, 57
Hong, Lily Toy, 116
Hooks, William H., 116, 143, 157
Hoover, H. M., 236
Hopkinson, Deborah, 57
Horenstein, Henry, 178
Houston, Gloria, 318
Hughes, Monica, 326
Hughes, Shirley, 58
Hurwitz, Johanna, 264
Hyatt, Patricia Rusch, 225

Igus, Toyomi, 275
Isaacs, Anne, 117

Jackson, Alison, 213
Jackson, Ellen, 117
Jacques, Brian, 236
James, Betsy, 58
Jeram, Anita, 59
Johnson, Angela, 60, 297
Johnston, Johanna, 276
Johnston, Norma, 277
Jonas, Ann, 60
Jones, Hettie, 347
Jordan, June, 157
Jukes, Mavis, 60, 381

Kamen, Gloria, 265
Karnes, Frances A., 248, 259
Karr, Kathleen, 226, 318
Katz, William Loren, 277
Kaye, Marilyn, 297
Kate, M. M., 237
Keams, Geri, 118
Keats, Ezra Jack, 61
Keene, Carolyn, 219
Kehret, Peg, 219
Keller, Beverly, 237
Keller, Holly, 61
Kellogg, Steven, 118
Kent, Deborah, 178
Kidd, Nina, 62
Kimmel, Eric A., 62, 63, 119
King-Smith, Dick, 238
Kiser, SuAnn, 63
Klause, Annette Curtis, 238
Kline, Suzy, 64
Knudson, R. R., 271
Knutson, Barbara, 120

Konigsburg, E. L., 206, 319
Krause, Ute, 64
Krone, Julie, 355
Kronstadt, Janet, 344
Krull, Kathleen, 179
Kunstadter, Maria A., 65

Lamborn, Florence, 240
Landon, Lucinda, 158
Langton, Jane, 198
Lansky, Bruce, 134
Larche, Douglas W., 47
Larson, Jennifer, 270
Lasker, Joe, 65
Lasky, Kathryn, 65
Lattimore, Deborah Nourse, 66
Lauber, Patricia, 253
Lazo, Caroline, 249
Le Guin, Ursula K., 120
Lee, Jeanne M., 66
Lee, Tanith, 327
L'Engle, Madeleine, 239
Levin, Pamela, 250
Levine, Caroline, 158
Levine, Ellen, 348
Levinson, Nancy Smiler, 144
Levy, Elizabeth, 214
Levy, Marilyn, 305
Lewis, Thomas P., 144
Lindgren, Astrid, 199, 206, 240
Lionni, Leo, 67
Lisle, Janet Taylor, 207, 240
Little, Jean, 67
Livingston, Myra Cohn, 179
Lord, Bette Bao, 214
Lotz, Karen E., 68
Lovejoy, Bahija, 196
Lowry, Lois, 227
Luenn, Nancy, 68, 69
Lunn, Janet, 227
Lurie, Alison, 135
Lyon, George Ella, 69, 70
Lyons, Mary E., 265, 348

Maccarone, Grace, 145
MacLachlan, Patricia, 159
Macy, Sue, 356
Madaras, Area, 381
Madaras, Lynda, 381
Mahy, Margaret, 70, 241, 327
Malone, Mary, 349
Mann, Judy, 378
Mark, Jan, 298
Markham, Marion M., 159
Marshall, Edward, 145
Marshall, James, 71

AUTHOR INDEX

AUTHOR INDEX

Title Index

TITLE INDEX

TITLE INDEX

TITLE INDEX

TITLE INDEX

TITLE INDEX

Category Index

CATEGORY INDEX

CATEGORY INDEX

CATEGORY INDEX

CATEGORY INDEX

CATEGORY INDEX

CATEGORY INDEX

CATEGORY INDEX

ABOUT THE AUTHOR

KATHLEEN ODEAN is a librarian, reviewer for *School Library Journal*, and a nationally recognized expert on children's books. She served on the Caldecott and Newbery Award committees and lives in Barrington, Rhode Island.